MICK JONES

STAYIN' IN TUNE

The Unofficial Biography
by **Mick O'Shea**

Published by
Eleusinian Press Ltd
www.eleusinianpress.co.uk

First Edition published 2015
© Mick O'Shea

Printed and bound in Great Britain
by Copytech (UK) Ltd

A catalogue record for this book is available from The British Library

ISBN 978-1-909494-06-0

CONTENTS

AUTHOR'S NOTE

It was Confucius who sagaciously observed that the longest journey starts with the first step, and if we borrow from this age-old aphorism to say the weightiest volume begins with the opening phrase, then when penning a biography about one of your foremost musical heroes one must take extra-special care where one treads. True, I'd touched on The Clash's early career in *Only Anarchists Are Pretty* (Helter Skelter, 2004), and again in more detail in *The Anarchy Tour* (Omnibus Press, 2012), but as with any iconic group, it's infinitely less daunting writing about the collective sum rather than singling out one of its individual parts.

Having just turned sixteen I was the archetypal impressionable teenager when The Clash played Blackburn's King George's Hall on the Out On Parole Tour in July 1978. Like countless others I'd had my head turned by the Sex Pistols the previous summer in the wake of the furore surrounding the release of 'God Save The Queen' in the year of Queen Elizabeth II's Silver Jubilee, but I'd yet to embrace punk rock per se. Indeed, I'd gone along to the King George's Hall that balmy Thursday evening naively believing the Pistols would get back together to put The Clash, as well as any other usurpers, in their proper place, but came away again – in spite of Steve Jones joining the group on stage for the encore – with my allegiance forever realigned.

I saw The Clash on every ensuing tour – including the Out Of Control Tour of February '84 (sorry, Mick) – and while I still believe Joe to be the quintessential frontman, Topper the best drummer of his generation, and regard Paul to be one of the coolest fuckers to walk the earth, my eyes were always invariably focused stage right. In

5

hindsight I like to think it was because we're both Cancerian, or that we unknowingly shared a passion for the film *Zulu*. But in reality, it's because if there was ever a guy born to play guitar, it was Mick Jones.

True, Joe, Paul, and especially Topper, each played their part in the Clash breaking free from punk's self-imposed restraints and expanding their repertoire by embracing a multitude of musical genres, be it reggae, rockabilly, jazz, soul, funk, and even gospel, but it was the effortless ease which Mick encapsulated The Clash's essence within a simple yet infectious melody that proved fundamental in their achieving greatness.

Flaubert warned us against touching our idols, lest the gilt rub off on our hands. Yet whilst this has undoubtedly proved true on occasion, Mick was geniality personified when I inadvertently happened upon him at a Glen Matlock solo show at The Borderline in Soho in August 2000. I was working on *Anarchists* at the time, and though Mick had the Transvision Vamp-ish Wendy James on his arm at the time, I threw caution to the wind and cheekily asked if I might have five minutes of his time.

To my astonishment, he abandoned Wendy at the bar and guided me away to a quiet alcove where he not only patiently answered every one of my questions, but threw in a few choice anecdotes of his own.

Over the years, The Clash's career has been expertly and painstakingly documented by the likes of Kris Needs, Marcus Gray, Pat Gilbert, and their devoted master-at-arms, Johnny Green, while Chris Salewitz penned Joe's posthumous biography, *Redemption Song* (Harper Collins, 2006). Yet despite his having gone on to achieve notable success with Big Audio Dynamite, as well as enjoying a third bite at the cherry with Carbon/Silicon, it seems no one thought a tome dedicated to Mick's near four decade-long career worthy of inclusion into the Clash literary canon?

I first began touting the idea for *Stayin' In Tune* back in February 2011, but despite receiving nods of encouragement from several commissioning editors, it felt as though I was destined to plough a furrow in ever-decreasing circles until Alastair at Eleusinian Press stepped up to the plate.

Books: Needs, Kris *The Clash, Joe Strummer and the Legend of the Clash* (Plexus, 2004), Coon, Caroline *1988: The New Wave Punk Rock Explosion* Omnibus Press, 1982), Gilbert, Pat *Passion Is A Fashion* (Aurum, 2004), Gray, Marcus *Last Gang In Town* Fourth Estate, 1995), Tobler, John *The Clash: A Visual Documentary* (Omnibus Press, 1983), Robb, John *Punk: An Oral History* (Ebury Press, 2006), Broad, John *A Riot Of Our Own: Night and Day with The Clash* (Orion, 1999), Gray, Marcus *Route 19 Revisited* (Vintage, 2011), Letts, Don *Culture Clash* (SAF Publishing, 2001), Doane, Randal *Stealing All Transmissions* (Custos 2012), Albertine, Viv *Clothes Clothes Clothes Music Music Music Boys Boys Boys* (Faber and Faber 2014).

Magazines, Periodicals and TV Documentaries: *That Was Then... This Is Now, Westway To The World, Viva Joe, Melody Maker, New Musical Express, Time Out, Blitz* magazine, *Mojo, ZigZag, The Sun, Record Mirror, Q* magazine, *LA Times, Trouser Press, The Armagideon Times, Austin Chronicle, Rolling Stone, Creem, Pulse Magazine, Chicago Tribune, Vox* magazine, *All Music, News Of The World, Guitar World, Pulse* magazine, *The Guardian, The Independent, Daily Mirror, CNN, The Telegraph, New York Times.*

Websites: *www.blackmarketclash.com*
www.clashblog.com
ultimateguitar.com
www.gibson.com
www.sabotagetimes.com
www.blogs.citypages.com
www.deangoodman.com
www.thequietus.com
www.philly.news.com
www.carbonsilicon.com
www.teletext.co.uk
www.louderthanwar.com
www2.gibson.com
www.musicfilmweb.com.

Professional thanks to Bernard Rhodes, Gary Stonadge, Steve Dior, and Nick Reynolds. Front cover design by Pistol and Rottenpunk Productions (check out their website *www.pistolart.com*).

Special thanks to Tasha 'Bush' Cowen and Shannon 'Mini-B' Stanley for keeping the kettle on semi standby, the sweet bowl filled, and for putting up with my moods when things weren't quite going according to script.

Thanks also to Lisa 'T-Bag' Bird, Paul Young (not the singer), Becky Boo Johnson, Alex 'Chef Boy' Jones, James Willment, Amun James, Zoe Johnson, and Joel & Aggie at The Old House At Dorking.

Also, a special mention to my mum and dad (Pat and Frank) who suffered through 'That Time!!!' as mum refers to my teenage punk rock phase. Well, mum, considering my first tome was based on the Sex Pistols, and this is my fifteenth book to date, you have to admit 'that time' wasn't without its merits...

On a more serious note I'd like to dedicate the book to Graham Jackson who was tragically taken from us way before his time at just 54.

Rest In Peace, brother

Mick O'Shea
Still Living The Dream
August 2014

– INTRODUCTION –

'I came into rehearsal just like any other day and, funnily enough, Topper had turned up to see how we were'

– Mick Jones

As Mick Jones arrived at Lucky Eight, The Clash's new rehearsal facility – with a state-of-the-art sixteen-track studio, and an upstairs recreation area replete with a fridge stacked with cans of Red Stripe – sometime during the afternoon of Monday 22 August 1983, he might well have been pondering the injustices of the Rolling Stones having just signed to CBS UK for a whopping $28 million while The Clash's own six-years-and-counting £100k contract hung about their collective necks like the proverbial millstone, or perhaps pondering whether the weather might hold out until the coming weekend and the annual Notting Hill Carnival. However, it's far more likely that his mind was focused on the tricky middle eight on a new tune for a song he'd written called 'Trans Cash Free Pay One'*, which was tentatively earmarked for the group's follow-up album to the previous year's million-selling *Combat Rock*.

The Clash had recently returned to the soot-encrusted shadow of Rehearsal Rehearsals, the Camden Lock compound where they'd started their odyssey some seven years earlier, but they were no longer the same 'Garageland' group that had thrown three chords together during the heady summer of 1976; more tellingly, nor were they the same people. Whereas Mick had his eye on the future, and wanted to

---

* The song would subsequently be re-titled 'The Bottom Line' and appeared on BAD's 1985 debut album, *This Is Big Audio Dynamite*.

store away his Gibson Les Paul in favour of a Bond Electraglide, or the 'Dalek's Handbag' as Paul uncharitably referred to the carbon fibre guitar, ever since Bernard Rhodes' reintroduction to the managerial reins Joe and Paul were insisting The Clash return to their punk roots.

This, of course, was anathema as far as Mick was concerned, because while he'd been happy to copy the Ramones' blitzkrieg-bop backbeat for The Clash's own eponymous debut album, punk was a sepia-toned memory. Indeed, his refusal to play 'White Riot' during the final encore at the Top Rank in Sheffield back in January 1980 during the Sixteen Tons Tour had seen him and Joe come to blows backstage. True, he'd gone back out for the encore, but midway through the song he'd made his position clear by unslinging his guitar and walking off stage, and they didn't play 'White Riot' again until the tour hit London some two weeks later.

While he still believed *The Clash* to be a great album, with the possible exception of 'Police And Thieves', which wasn't even theirs anyway, the songs were of their time – both musically and ideologically. And wasn't that the reason they'd dropped '1977' from the set-list as soon as the calendar rendered the song obsolete?

Combat Rock had given The Clash their first Billboard Top 10 album, so how could Joe and Paul possibly think the way forward was to take a backward step in ploughing punk's clichéd furrow. In doing so they ran the danger of becoming as anachronistic as the bin-liner and safety-pin.

Had Mick been of a superstitious nature then his being first to arrive may have seemed a telling portent that something out of the ordinary was in the offing. After all, his tardiness when it came to rehearsals was legendary within The Clash camp, and never before had he been called upon to switch on the lights. Further evidence that the fates were conspiring came with Topper Headon's unexpected arrival.

Though Topper had been sacked the previous May owing to his spiralling heroin addiction, he was still on speaking terms with his erstwhile colleagues and finding himself in Camden and with a couple of hours to kill Topper thought he'd drop in for a chat. Finding Mick was the only one there Topper leapt behind the kit and the two were soon jamming away as in days gone by. However, rather than risk embarrassing his replacement, Pete Howard, or even worse, receiving a reprimand from the irascible Bernard, Topper put down his sticks and with a glance at the clock suggested he should perhaps make a move. Mick agreed, remarking that he didn't know what could be keeping the others.

Once Topper had departed, rather than sit around twiddling his thumbs Mick took a stroll to a nearby bookshop. He returned an hour or so later to find Pete sat behind his kit giving the cymbals a cursory wipe blissfully unaware as to who'd been crashing them but a short while earlier. Mick picked up his guitar, but Joe and Paul, made no move for their own instruments. They hadn't come to rehearse, but rather to inform Mick that he was out of the group.

At that moment, Mick's new guitar tech, Digby Cleaver, came in carrying a pot of freshly-brewed tea. He'd been in another part of the building so was blithely unaware as to the seismic events unfolding around him, but knew seeing Mick packing up his guitar that something serious was going down. Though relatively new to the role, Digby had quickly come to regard The Clash as Mick's group. Up until the moment of Joe and Paul's pronouncement Mick had thought the same, despite his being outvoted over Bernard's retaking the managerial reins.

Had Joe and Paul delivered their bombshell during the heat of the moment, then Mick might well have gone away and allowed time for tempers to cool before showing his face at the rehearsal door. But there had been no crossing of swords, or even a heated exchange. This was a coolly calculated coup d'etat, with Bernard waiting in the wings with Mick's severance cheque.

– CHAPTER ONE –

MY GRANDPA CAME FROM RUSSIA...

'We all come from a pretty large extended family of Jewish immigrants that escaped Russia and settled in London at the turn of the century, so there's quite a lot of us.'

– Mick Jones

THE SLEEVE FOR THE CLASH'S debut single 'White Riot b/w 1977'* – which was released on March 18 1977, would serve as the group's clarion call to arms for the remainder of their career and beyond. It depicts Mick, Joe, and Paul dressed in their urban battle fatigues, facing a nondescript wall with their hands raised above their heads as though they have just fought a losing battle with the law and are awaiting the consequences of their actions. Joe and Paul, standing on either side of Mick, have the two song titles daubed upon the back of their respective boiler suit, whilst Mick's shirt bears the spray-painted aphorism: 'Sten-guns in Knightsbridge'.

They'd written the song in response to the violence that had flared up between heavy-handed police and certain sections of London's West Indian community at the Notting Hill Carnival over the previous August Bank Holiday weekend. At the time, The Clash came in for much criticism for their perceived agitprop posturing, for whilst the trendy upmarket central London thoroughfare was once renowned as being the haunt of highwaymen, robbers, and cut-

---

* The photo was taken by music journalist Caroline Coon at Rehearsal Rehearsals.

throats targeting travellers on the western route out of London, the likelihood of automatic weapons being discharged in anger appeared remote in the extreme.

However, what had initially appeared an ill-conceived cliché would prove eerily prescient in the coming decade with the SAS storming of the Iranian Embassy, the IRA's car-bomb attack on Harrods, and the £60 million Knightsbridge Security Deposit heist.

Somewhat appropriately, Sten-guns were fired in anger on the afternoon of Sunday, 26 June 1955 – the day Michael Geoffrey Jones made his inauspicious entry into the world at the South London Hospital for Women in Clapham – when South African police were called in to break up a 3,000-strong protest rally against Johannes Strijdom's National Party's newly-implemented laws on apartheid in a non-white suburb of Johannesburg.

♪♪♪

It is perhaps rather fitting that Mick spent his formative years growing up in the multicultural melting pot that was mid-Fifties Brixton. The south London borough was already home to thousands of dispossessed souls from every corner of war-ravaged Europe when the majority of those now celebrated 492 West Indian émigrés – having been the first to take up the British government's offer to work in England under the newly-ratified British Nationality Act – disembarked from the *MV Empire Windrush* at Tilbury Docks on 21 June 1948.

One of those who would have undoubtedly felt empathy with the newly-arrived émigrés was Mick's maternal grandfather Morris Zegansky, who'd fled his native Russia in the wake of the revolution that had brought down the Romanovs to start life anew within the bustling heart of the British Empire.

Mick would subsequently romanticise his multicultural ancestry in the song 'Beyond The Pale', which appeared on Big Audio Dynamite's second album *10 Upping Street* in 1986. In the lyric, Morris, a furrier by trade, had arrived in London after stowing away in some bails, and had taken his Jewish bride-to-be, Esther Stella Class – who at 27, was five years older than himself – dancing down to where the air-raid sirens hailed. Mick is surely stretching poetic license here somewhat, because while Morris and Stella had pledged their love at Holborn Register Office on 30 May 1927, Stella having given birth to Mick's mother, Renee, late the following year, they were no longer speaking to each other – let alone dancing cheek to jowl whilst jitterbugging the night away in defiance of the Doodlebugs – by the time Hitler's tanks rolled into Poland.

What is indisputable about Stella's activities during the war years and beyond, however, is that aside from continuing working as a milliner, she, along with the teenage Renee, departed the marital home in Kensington and moved into flat 61 in the newly-built Christchurch House on Christchurch Road in Streatham, south London. And that a week before Christmas in 1952, at Wandsworth Register Office, she got married for a second time, to forty-nine-year-old divorcee Hyman Markis. Like many Jewish émigrés trying to make his way in his adopted home, Hyman, who was employed as a wireless salesman, had thought to alter his name to the more Anglican-sounding 'Harry Marcus'.

Within a year, Stella found herself back at Wandsworth Registrar Office when Renee tied the nuptial knot with Mick's father, twenty-three-year-old Thomas Gilmour Jones.

Though too young to serve in the armed forces during the war, like every other healthy male between the ages of eighteen and twenty-one, Thomas, or 'Tommy' as he preferred to be known, had been called up for National Service on his eighteenth birthday. When the National Service Act 1948 first came into effect (1 January 1949), the period of enlistment was eighteen months, but was subsequently extended to two years owing to Britain's involvement in the Korean War.

Whereas the majority of those press-ganged to serve queen and country either never left England, or were sent to serve in the army of occupation in Germany, Tommy was instead posted to the Middle East, which was in turmoil owing to the United Nations' intention to partition Palestine to create an independent Jewish state.

Whatever his views on the United Nations' intent on giving the Jews their own homeland prior to his posting, he ultimately returned to London a changed man owing to the horrors he witnessed with his own eyes. Mick has always maintained that it was no coincidence that his father subsequently married a Jewish woman.

♪♪♪

By the time Mick was born, Tommy and Renee had set up home at 20 Fair Green Court in Mitcham, which, though some of its more snobbish residents would have us believe comes under the Surrey fringe, actually lies within the boundary of the South London borough of Merton. When appearing on BBC2's 1988 retrospective series *That Was Then… This Is Now*, Mick would say that his first musical memory was of the Life Guards Band marching down Mitcham High Street, but this is obviously nothing more than a drum and pipe dream as Tommy and Renee were already back living with Stella and Harry at 61 Christchurch House by the time of Mick's second birthday.

It was at Christchurch House; a nondescript late-thirties council tenement that stood like a stark sentinel on the north-west corner of the crossroads where Brixton and Streatham Hills collide, where Mick was to spend the next eight years. He and his parents remained with Stella and Harry for several months before finally getting the keys to their own flat at number 109. However, when Harry suffered a fatal heart attack in May 1961, the ever-conscientious Renee – who by this time was working as a cosmetic jewellery saleswoman – elected to move her family back in with Stella at number 61.

Having her nearest and dearest living under her roof again might have brought succour to the grieving Stella, but Mick's memories from that period are somewhat less than harmonious. Finding himself under Stella's matriarchal yoke once again certainly didn't sit well with Tommy, and served to put extra strain on an already crumbling marriage. Mick would struggle to get to sleep owing to his parents' near-constant arguing, and the hostilities often became so intense that Stella would take Mick down into the building's disused bomb shelter where she would regale him with fanciful tales about her own upbringing in Whitechapel until the latest flare-up had subsided.

Sadly, however, with Mick out of hearing Renee and Tommy's arguments merely increased in intensity until their differences became irreconcilable.

Tommy promptly moved out, and following a period of estrangement he and Renee were divorced in 1963. 'Because of my parents' separation I was often on my own and I'd do lots of things on my own,' Mick later said. 'I filled my time with doing stuff that interested me, like collecting things and thinking about stuff. I guess I must have inhabited my own world really. It was like; I guess I was trying to fill a gap – though I wasn't aware of it. That's how I ended up like I am, I guess. It was definitely a kind of built-in self-preservation thing that I've got. It's inherent. To survive, I created my own private world.'[1]

Mick's private world would soon be rocked to its core when his mum announced she was moving to America. Having had her head turned by the pelvic-thrusting Elvis Presley, the newly-independent Renee had no desire to waste her life on either Streatham or cosmetic jewellery, and instead set her ambitious sights on making a better life for herself in the home of rock 'n' roll and Coca-Cola. However, while one has to admire her desire to start life anew, it beggars belief that she would do so leaving her only offspring behind. Divorce may have been more commonplace in the early Sixties than when Stella and Morris went their separate ways, but the abandonment of one's children was virtually unheard of.

The happy-go-lucky Tommy had no aspirations to seek greener pastures, however; and was content to continue working as a London cabbie. According to Mick, his father also looked after a South London betting shop, as well as having connections with the local boxing fraternity. Indeed, seeing his father on television loitering in the background of Billy Walker's dressing room on fight night on the telly is one of the outstanding memories from his childhood.

His father rubbing shoulders with the 'Golden Boy' of British boxing was no doubt thrilling for Mick, but the irregularity of Tommy's working hours meant Mick remained at Christchurch House under his Stella's doting tutelage, which to all intents and purposes saw her step in to become his surrogate mother.

Mick doesn't seem all that aggrieved at Renee's migration: 'My mother had been a wild person. She fell in love with an American soldier in World War II and he took her on a boat to America with him. She was a stowaway – and she got as far as Texas before the authorities found out and called my grandparents. My grandfather had to go and bring her back.'[2]

Once again, however, Mick appears to be romanticising the past somewhat, because while the nineteen-year-old Renee did indeed stowaway on a cargo ship bound for America – only to have her dreams of making a new life in America thwarted by a diligent crew member – it is stretching the bounds of credibility that the GI Joe to which Mick alludes would only book himself passage on the ship and leave his English Rose to fend for herself hiding out in one of the lifeboats.

If Renee succeeded in stepping off the boat as Mick claims, then surely all that was required for her to be allowed to stay in America was for the guy to marry her – and wasn't that the whole idea of them going to America in the first place?

Rather than head for the bright lights of Manhattan, or Hollywood and Vine, Renee instead opted for the leafier confines of Armwood, Michigan, where she subsequently married a mining engineer called George Tiitu, and opened a second-hand clothes store.

Mick may have been deprived of a cosseted nuclear family upbringing, but spending his seminal years living with a lone grandparent didn't prove much of a hindrance, or hardship. Indeed, the bond first forged by his parents' separation grew ever stronger over the years until Stella's death in 1989. Mick would dedicate Big Audio Dynamite's third album *Megatop Phoenix* to her memory.

♫♫♫

The withdrawal of food rationing in Britain in July 1954 is generally regarded by historians as bringing closure to the Second World War, but for Londoners, myriad bomb sites peppering the capital still served as stark reminders of those dark days. To Mick, however, the weed-strewn vacant lots could be utilised for football kick-abouts, the staging of mock battles, and erecting bonfires, and in winter, the sloping ground was perfect for sledging.

Saturday mornings were usually taken up with forays to the local flea-pit cinema, and then in the afternoon more often than not Mick would buy himself a 'rover' bus pass and while away the hours observing London landmarks such as Tower Bridge, St. Paul's Cathedral, and the Houses of Parliament through the nicotine-stained windows on the upstairs deck. On other occasions he would take to the streets on foot, particularly to Carnaby Street where he and his chums embarked on petty nicking sprees whilst humming along to the music blaring out from the boutiques.

'It was a pretty exciting time to grow up,' he later recalled. 'There was music everywhere it seemed; coming out of shops, on the radio. It was like we had a soundtrack to our lives.'[3]

In September 1966, Mick's personal soundtrack was augmented somewhat with his enrolment at The Strand School in Elm Park Hill, a relatively short walk from his home on nearby Christchurch Road. It's ironic that while Joe would find his credibility threatened over his having attended the City of London Freeman's School (CLFS), Mick escaped a similar pillorying by the punk police. The Strand may not have been a fee-paying establishment like the CLFS, but it was nevertheless a cut above your average secondary modern.

Founded in 1890 as a subsidiary of King's College in the Strand in central London – hence its name – the boys-only grammar had relocated to the Elm Park site in 1910, which at the time was a very upmarket area. 'It was a grammar school, but it was originally the school that everyone who went there used to go straight into the civil service, in like the 1900s. It was really old-fashioned. All the teachers had mortar boards, and they all seemed to have been tortured by the Japs in World War II. They had deep psychological scars which they took out on the pupils!'[4]

While the main topic of conversation amongst London's adult population would have been the recent insensible slaying of three plain-clothes police officers in broad daylight in East Acton, in what the tabloid press dubbed the 'Braybrook Street Massacre', Mick, like the vast majority of eleven-year-old kids up and down the country, no doubt arrived for the first day of school with the memory of England's victory over West Germany in the World Cup Final at Wembley several weeks earlier still fresh in his mind.

He would have also no doubt been hoping his passable footballing skills would catch the eye of the Strand's PE teacher, and put him in contention of a place in the school's football team. Alas for Mick, however; though he could hold his own in the playground kick-abouts, he was overlooked when it came to serious competition as his small stature meant he was easy to nudge off the ball.

Playing football was only one facet of Mick's fascination with the national game, as aside from pledging life-long allegiance to Queen's Park Rangers (who would win the old League Division Three in the 1966/67 season), at weekends he could often be found – a dog-eared copy of the *Topical Times Football Book* in hand – laying in wait either outside the players' entrance at QPR's Loftus Road, or within the portals of the West End hotels frequented by visiting teams to secure the autographs of the top players of the day.

During his thirty minutes under the *That Was Then... This Is Now* spotlight, Mick would readily assert that as far as he'd been concerned there were really only two legitimate means open to those from a working-class background to escape a life of mundane nine-to-five drudgery: achievement in either sport or – since the mid-Fifties, at least – popular music. 'I'll always remember going into the office of the careers advice people at school and saying 'I wanna be in a band', and they said, 'Well, you can't be, if you're too useless you go into the Army or the services. Or there's the Civil Service.' There were no real choices; there wasn't a vegetarian option on the menu.'

Realising sport would never feature on the menu; Mick hung up his footie boots and began focusing his full attention on rock 'n' roll. Mick appropriated his nan's radiogram so that he could tune in to the pirate radio stations of the day such as Radio London where future Radio One stalwart John Peel would spin the latest hits from the UK, as well as America's West Coast, on his now-legendary late-night show, the *Perfumed Garden*. In addition he began setting his paper round money aside so that he could start assembling his own record collection.

His first choice was *Disraeli Gears*, the second album from the so-called supergroup Cream, and as soon as he'd amassed another 33s 3d in his piggy bank he returned to his local record shop and grabbed a copy of the Jimi Hendrix Experience's singles compilation album, *Smash Hits*. 'I used to listen to them over and over again – Hendrix especially. I knew from an early age that I wanted to do music.'[5]

With music now his sole obsession 'Rock 'n' Roll Mick', as he was soon to be known – both in and out of school – was a walking musical encyclopaedia, and would regularly walk to school with an album clutched tightly under his arm to show which group was currently meriting his allegiance. While his classmates followed the ongoing triangular top-of-the-table battle between Manchester United, Nottingham Forest and Tottenham Hotspur, Mick was more interested in seeing The Beatles and the Rolling Stones battling it out for the top spot on the hit parade. He also devoured the features and articles in *Melody Maker* and *New Musical Express;* little knowing that his image would one day adorn the front pages of both magazines.

Mick's first live music experience came on Saturday, 27 July 1968, when Traffic, the psychedelic rock outfit fronted by the former Spencer Davis Group frontman, Steve Winwood, performed an open-air free concert in Hyde Park. 'They used to put on free gigs in [Hyde] Park back then, not like today where they charge an arm and a leg for any old rubbish. That gig was put on by Blackhill Enterprises who later managed us (The Clash) for a time.'[6]

Also on the Hyde Park bill that day were the Pretty Things, whom the British media rather unkindly dubbed 'the uglier cousins of the Rolling Stones'. A little under a year later on 5 July 1969, Mick was in Hyde Park to see their Satanic Majesties release hundreds of white butterflies from the stage as a tribute to the Stones' founding member Brian Jones who'd drowned in the swimming pool at his home Cotchford Farm several days earlier.

'I wormed my way the whole day through the crowd to get to the barrier just before they came on. It was like a great trek or odyssey. I was like "Excuse me, coming through… Oh, sorry…" treading on people all the way through Hyde Park. I wormed my way through and then the Hells Angels came through the crowd on their motorbikes! Everyone was going "Oh my god!" It was a wonderful moment.'[7]

♫♫♫

Joe would subsequently opine that 1968 was a 'great year to come of age'. The on-going war in Vietnam was raging out of control and in March a protest against the war staged outside the US Embassy in Grosvenor Square resulted in ninety-one people being injured, and some two hundred demonstrators being arrested. In May, student protests in Paris almost brought down the French government (future Sex Pistols' manager Malcolm McLaren would subsequently falsely claim that he and Bernard Rhodes had been manning the barricades in the French Quarter at the time), and the whole world had been rocked the following month with the assassinations of both Senator Robert Kennedy, and Civil Rights leader Martin Luther King Jr.

1968 would also bring upheaval for Mick and Stella as they moved from Christchurch House to another council high-rise on the Edgware Road in west London, where Stella's older sister, Cissie, and her sister-in-law, Celia Green, were already living. 'My Nan and I were on the [council] housing list for years and occasionally went to see flats, but it just never seemed to happen. I was living with three old ladies, which was pretty strange. 'They were really Jewish, too. I remember I once got a Snoopy and the Red Baron T-shirt and they freaked because it had an iron cross on it, so they confiscated it.'[8]

While the Class sisters objected to unsavoury reminders of Hitler's atrocities, their adherence to their faith wasn't all encompassing, especially seeing as Renee was allowed to marry a non Jew. This in turn, meant little or no pressure was applied towards Mick becoming a Bar Mitzvah when he turned thirteen.

The Clash, of course, would get plenty of mileage from Mick's tower block teenage existence, but unlike Christchurch House – and the ultra-depressing Wilmcote House where Mick would be living when first putting The Clash together – 90 Park West was a decidedly upmarket nine-storey late-Deco-period private mansion block with porterage, and its own underground car park. It was also rumoured to have an underground swimming pool.

The relocation also meant several miles being added to the daily round trip to school, but whereas this would have undoubtedly proved too daunting a prospect for most thirteen-year-olds, Mick elected to remain at the Strand. This, however, would prove something of a double-edged sword, for while remaining at the Strand allowed him to befriend the fourteen-year-old Robin Crocker* – who would go on to become a life-long friend and confidante – their sharing a desk would ultimately see Mick's grades take a dramatic downturn.

Robin was one of those kids who frustrate teachers, because while being above average intelligence, he found schooling intolerably dull. He would do just about anything to alleviate the boredom, which often resulted in a visit to the headmaster's office for a caning. This became such a regular occurrence that he took to wearing a pair of Lederhosen under his school trousers to absorb the sting, while his total disregard for school discipline was the reason for his being held back a year.

Rock 'n' roll was as important to Robin as it was to Mick; so much so, that their first interaction came in a stand-up argument over whether Bo Diddley was a better guitarist than Chuck Berry. Robin was for Chuck, who was best known for his 1958 hit 'Johnny B. Goode', whilst Mick championed Berry's Chess Records' label-mate Bo who was hailed as 'The Originator' by his peers owing to his role in the transition of blues to rock 'n' roll. The ensuing roll-about on the classroom floor might not have endeared them to maths teacher, but it served to create a brotherly bond that has lasted to the present day. Having agreed to disagree on Chuck and Bo, Mick and Robin cemented their friendship with a shared passion for the Rolling Stones.

Another favourite was the Stones-esque Faces, who at the time were fronted by Rod Stewart, and of course, featured future Rolling Stone Ronnie Wood in the line-up.

'He [Robin] was the class joker, and [was] always making me laugh,' Mick reflected. 'We were in detention once, and he said something which made me laugh out loud. I can't remember what it was, but I couldn't stop laughing and the headmaster went berserk because we weren't taking our punishment seriously.

'We used to be in detention every week. Robin used to run a protection racket at school and when it got found it was on the *Tonight* programme or something, and all the pupils were like

---

* Robin's involvement with The Clash would lead to his getting a job with ZigZag magazine where he adopted the punning nom de plume, Robin Banks.

blacked out like professionals because they didn't want to be seen. When it all came out Robin had to take this walk of shame. We were caned and everything.'[9]

Robin's waywardness would lead to his being expelled which meant Mick saw less and less of his friend – especially as his evenings were now being taken up trying to learn the guitar by playing along to his burgeoning album collection. Though it had been Robin who'd taught Mick the rudiments of guitar – most notably the simple yet effective stop-start riff to Willie Dixon's one chord blues classic, 'Spoonful', made famous by Howlin' Wolf – he himself had no real ambition to be a rock 'n' roll star. Instead he got a job selling advertisement space and writing copy at the *West London Weekly* newspaper, and it was only when he was laid off that he began hanging out with several n'er do well's with a penchant for robbing off licenses and betting shops.

Sometime in late 1973, the gang decided to expand their horizons by attempting what Robin describes as a 'stick-up' in Streatham, south London. He and the rest of the gang were caught and convicted of armed robbery.

However, with Brixton being a remand prison, unlike the couplet in 'Stay Free', Robin actually began his three-year sentence in Wormwood Scrubs before subsequently being transferred to Albany; the maximum security facility on the Isle of Wight, where he had the dubious distinction of being the prison's youngest inmate.

– CHAPTER TWO –

MARK ME ABSENT

'I wanted to play the guitar because I always imagined it was the coolest spot to be in. No one was cooler than the guitar player. Provided you stay in tune you could just cruise.'

– Mick Jones

Bo Diddley, Cream, Jimi Hendrix, and the Rolling Stones had each played their respective roles in Mick's musical education, but it would be the glam-rocking Mott The Hoople who that were to truly fired his imagination.

Mott The Hoople had first been set on their trajectory by the mercurial, musical Svengali Guy Stevens who would, of course, not only serve as a significant fork in the road on Mick's own career path, but would also work with The Clash. However, while Guy was responsible for giving Mott The Hoople the all-important makeover by having them change their name (to the title of a Willard Manus novel he'd read whilst serving a nine-month prison sentence for being caught in possession of cannabis), replacing their hapless singer Stan Tippens for the perennially-shaded Ian Hunter, as well as securing them a recording contract with Island Records, they ultimately owed their subsequent success to David Bowie.

Unlike today, bands were given time to develop and hone their craft, but with four albums having failed to make any impression on the charts in either the UK or America, the disillusion within the Mott

The Hoople camp was such that they were considering calling it a day when Bowie – who unbeknown to anyone was a huge fan – stepped in and offered them 'Suffragette City', which was earmarked for the soon-to-be-released *The Rise And Fall Of Ziggy Stardust And The Spiders From Mars*.

Somewhat surprisingly, the group declined the offer, but Bowie was unruffled by the rejection and instead presented them with a new song he'd penned.

The anthemic 'All The Young Dudes' would give Mott the Hoople a UK Top Three hit in July 1972, and as a further testament to his belief in the group, Bowie offered to produce their next album. And as everything the self-styled 'Starman' touched turned to gold, it was goodbye to Guy, and hello CBS.

Mott The Hoople's new brand of aggressive rock coupled with Hunter's Dylan-esque vocals was soon enthralling audiences on both sides of the Atlantic. It also brought them to the attention of several Strand School sixth-formers. Amongst this small, yet dedicated, clique of Mott obsessives were John Brown and Kelvin Blacklock: both of whom would subsequently play in pre-Clash bands with Mick.

♪♪♪

John, Kelvin, and the rest of the Strand gang naturally viewed themselves within the school's hierarchy, and usually wouldn't be seen mixing with kids from the lower years. Mick was still only fourteen but with his appreciation for Mott The Hoople matching their own he was readily accepted into their circle. His acceptance came with a caveat, however, as his new-found friends delighted in calling him 'Little Mick'.

Despite Kelvin and John's subsequent insistence that this was devised as a means of differentiating him from another Mick in the gang, it nonetheless served a dual purpose in reminding Mick of his size and lowly status.

The Strand gang were naturally keen to see their heroes play live, but with the vast majority of the venues on the London circuit being licensed premises, this was far easier said than done. Thankfully however, the bouncers working the doors at the clubs where Mott The Hoople were wont to play on a regular basis, such as the Roundhouse on Chalk Farm Road, weren't overzealous in their under age restrictions. And on recognising several familiar faces in the crowd, Stan Tippens, who'd benignly accepted the role of manager following his dismissal, began letting the gang in for free; a gesture which encouraged them to attend as many 'Saturday Gigs' as logistically possible.

The group members were highly appreciative of their unwavering dedication to the Mott cause and began making themselves available both before and after shows. Mick, for one, found this unnerving at first and following a show in Dagenham he was so overawed at finding himself standing next to Mott's guitarist Mick Ralphs at the bar, that he missed his mouth and spilt his drink down the front of his shirt. Now that they regarded themselves as friends as well as fans, it wasn't long before the gang began plotting forays to see their heroes play further afield, and the easy going Stella's lax attitude towards her grandson's out-of-school activities meant Mick could usually tag along.

'I followed Mott the Hoople up and down the country,' Mick revealed. 'I'd go to Liverpool or Newcastle or somewhere, sleep on the Town Hall steps, and bunk the fares on the trains, hide in the toilet when the ticket inspector came around. I'd jump off just before the train got to the station and climb over the fence. It was great times, and I always knew I wanted to be in a band and play guitar. That was it for me.'[1]

During the summer of 1970, having been welcomed into Mott's inner sanctum to breathe the heady backstage air, it was perhaps only natural that the Strand boys decided to take things to the next level by forming their own group in the hope that reach a point where they'd be able to play as a support act at future Mott shows.

Kelvin, being something of an extrovert, and buoyed by the thrill of having Ian Hunter occasionally invite him up on stage to share vocal duties on 'Walkin' With A Mountain' (from Mott The Hoople's second album, *Mad Shadows*), duly elected himself as the singer/guitarist, while John played second guitar and provided backing vocals. The as yet unnamed fledgling outfit's rhythm section comprised of Bob Goffman on bass, and the unassuming Jim Hyatt on drums.

With Kelvin the designated leader calling the shots, the others would have to schlep over to Thessaly Road in Battersea where he was living at the time in order to rehearse. These ad hoc rehearsals, where friends – including Robin Crocker – could come along and sit in, usually took place in a local youth club. On other occasions they would set up in the disused church hall* situated a little further along the road.

Mick wouldn't get involved with Schoolgirl – the cringe-worthy name the embryonic group had decided on once they resumed group duty after sitting their A-Levels – until March 1972; even then, it was only in an unofficial capacity as Hyatt's drum roadie. There had, however, already been several changes to the line-up by this juncture. Kelvin had abandoned the guitar in favour of concentrating on his vocals, while John had switched to bass to replace Goffman who'd chosen academia over a cappella and headed off to university.

John's replacement as the group's second guitarist was a guy called Glen, while both the line-up and sound had been augmented by a saxophonist/guitarist by the name of Pete.

'There was a band at school and I was a year lower than them. I was kind of the little one, but always curious about making music and I started off roadying for them,' Mick later recalled. 'I was happy enough to lug the gear for a bit. Then I gradually built myself up to playing the guitar, though I played drums too, and the bass. The guitar came after that.'[2]

Mick wouldn't emulate his friends by staying on for A-Levels, but he'd yet to bid farewell to his Alma Mater as he'd opted to stay on at the Strand School and re-sit the three O-Levels he'd failed the previous spring. He'd already retaken his Art O Level in the January, and was set to re-sit History and English Language. This time round, he would also be sitting English Literature and Sociology.

Not only would Mick pass all five exams with flying colours, he even attended the Strand's graduation ceremony sporting a specially-hired top hat and tails. Whilst there's no shame in striving to gain some

---

* In 1972, The Who would take possession of the church hall and convert it into Ramport Studios where they recorded Quadrophenia.

creditable qualifications, it nevertheless strains the poetic license in the couplet, 'When we got thrown out, I left without much fuss' from 'Stay Free'...

♪♪♪

Schoolgirl made their live debut sometime around March 1972, and followed this inauspicious entrée with a dozen or so equally lacklustre appearances at various low-rent pubs and clubs. Indeed, the only noteworthy incident to occur during their brief career came with Ian Hunter showing up to cast an eye over their worth. Kelvin had invited Hunter along in the hope he might be persuaded to offer Schoolgirl a support slot at one or other of Mott The Hoople's forthcoming London dates. Hunter was so underwhelmed by what he saw on stage that he suggested Kelvin sack everyone except John because they were 'utter shit'.

Whether Kelvin would have acted on Hunter's damning verdict is open to speculation, as guitarist Glen jumped before he could be pushed. Having replaced Glen with another old Strand boy Paul Wayman on guitar, Schoolgirl would make four further live appearances during 1973. But with the impetus gone they decided on hanging up their pinafores.

Schoolgirl might not have made much of an impression on Ian Hunter, but they did at least alert Mick to the fact that he could do as well – if not better. Whilst serving his time as Jim Hyatt's roadie Mick had familiarised himself with the drums, but as the drummer was usually the least recognised member of any group, his ego led him to abandon the idea and he bought himself a second-hand Hofner guitar using some of the earnings he'd accrued from a summer job working in a local warehouse.

Mick would later bemoan the Hofner's asking price of £16 to a bemused Caroline Coon, before gleefully adding that he subsequently sold it for £30 to a Sex Pistol.

'I never had any lessons. Robin [used to tune] the guitar for me before I knew how to,' he recalled. 'I almost took my first guitar back to the shop because it wasn't in tune. I thought there was something wrong with it. I learned playing along to records and spent a year in the bedroom just playing along, learning the solos and all the little nuances on Stones records. Music was definitely the main thing for me, from the age of twelve or so.'[3]

It was no doubt his remembering having to rely on Robin to tune the Hofner's strings before he could go off and practice Keith Richards' 'little nuances' that he uncomplainingly did the same for Paul during the early days of The Clash.

♪♪♪

In the spring of 1973, Mick and Stella were on the move again to the aforementioned Wilmcote House. One might have thought that the bureaucratic powers-that-be at the GLC (Greater London Council) would have seen to it to offer the now seventy-three-year-old Stella a ground-floor flat. But no, their new home stood on the eighteenth floor of a Sixties high-rise situated on the Warwick Estate, just off the Harrow Road.

Kris Needs, who would go on to be the editor at *ZigZag* magazine during punk's '77 heyday, formed his lasting friendship with Mick around this time and spent occasional evenings at Wilmcote House listening to Mick's impressive array of rare American import albums. According to Kris' recollections, while Stella did her best to keep the flat spotless – with the obvious exception of Mick's bedroom – the building itself was every inch the stereotypical tower block which The Clash would celebrate in song – 'rotting from the inside with piss-stained, graffiti-sprayed lifts that were terminally out of order.'[4] Like Robin Crocker, John Brown, and just about everyone else who visited the flat, Kris also bore witness to Mick's occasional demeaning attitude towards Stella where he might demand his dinner upon walking through the door, or order Stella to make him and his friends a cup of tea with nary a please or thank you. Of course, like everyone else, Kris was never in any doubt that Mick was utterly devoted to his Nan.

Wilmcote House sits a stone's throw from the A40 (M) flyover – more colloquially known as 'The Westway', and though at the time, the eighteen-year-old Mick would have undoubtedly lambasted the council's logic in placing a widowed septuagenarian up in the gods, the late-night twinkling panoramic vista of Bayswater and Knightsbridge afforded from their lofty concrete eerie would at least inspire a visiting Joe Strummer to pen the lyric to 'London's Burning'.

Mick's decision to add English Literature and Sociology to the three re-sit exams had more to do with the number of qualifications, rather than the qualifications themselves as five O-Levels was the minimum requirement needed to gain acceptance to art school. Yet though he now had the required grades, he was still only seventeen, and therefore twelve months below the minimum age requirement for college. Most students would have used the time to build up a portfolio, but Mick's only reason for going to art school was to meet like-minded musicians and form a group, while using the annual grant to fund his further educational escapades.

He would have probably liked nothing better than to take a sabbatical and wile away the days improving his slinky guitar skills, but as liberal-minded as Stella was towards his musical proclivities, he thought it best to plot a strategy of sorts. Although he was more or less assured a place at art school once he turned eighteen, he didn't want to leave anything to chance, and as a contingency plan he signed on at night school to study for his A-Levels. As he would also have to wait twelve months before he could get his hands on a grant, he decided to put his hard-earned qualifications to good use and got himself gainful employment with the Department of Health and Social Security.

Mick became a Clerical Assistant in the Benefit Office, which at the time was at number 5 Praed Street in Paddington, a short walk from his home at Park Way. Judging from his recollections, his time at the Benefit Office wasn't particularly rewarding. 'It was on the first floor of a modern building across the road from [the] station, and there were these old fashioned benches around the wall for people to sit on,' he revealed. 'One day I saw this guy who'd been there all day, being given the run around. They used to employ the most unsympathetic people at the counters – to give short shrift to anyone making bogus claims.'[5]

Mick may have been counting down the days till his eighteenth birthday, but his time working in the service of the state would subsequently prove beneficial to The Clash in providing the inspiration for the telling couplet 'I hate the civil service rules, I won't open letter bombs for you,' in the second verse on 'Career Opportunities'. Five years later, during an *NME* interview, part of which was conducted deep beneath the streets of the metropolis by Tony Parsons, and subsequently appeared as the 'Clash on the Circle Line' interview on the Capital Radio *NME* freebie EP, Mick would help propagate the escalating Clash myth by informing Parsons how his supervisor at the DHSS had him opening the incoming mail at the height of the IRA's letter-bomb campaign on mainland Britain because of his long hair and unruly appearance.

It's a good yarn, and one aimed at setting The Clash up as anti-establishment rebels with applause. In hindsight, however, it's easy to see that Mick had been prepped by Bernard before the group's meeting with Parsons. Bureaucracy undoubtedly has many faults, but the notion that someone in authority would have a seventeen-year-old trainee opening potentially-lethal packages simply because his hair wasn't regulation short back and sides is stretching credibility.

♪♪♪

In September 1973, Mick began his Art Foundation course at the Hammersmith School of Art at Lime Grove in Shepherd's Bush. As he passed through the school's hallowed portal that autumnal Monday morning, he was no doubt hoping this was where the seeds of his musical dreams would bear fruit. After all, John Lennon had befriended Stuart Sutcliffe at the Liverpool College of Art; Keith Richards had encountered his old primary school acquaintance Mick Jagger on a platform at Dartford railway station whilst en route to Sidcup Art College, and Pete Townshend had formed his first group, the Confederates, with his childhood friend Jon Entwistle whilst the pair were enrolled at Ealing Art College.

Mick was so convinced that he would find his own three-chord collaborator amongst Hammersmith's student throng that at the midmorning break he'd made a beeline for the toilets expecting to find like-minded souls huddled together showing each other their licks.

Mick's disappointment at discovering he was the only student at Hammersmith who knew his da Vinci's from his 'diminished seventh', was compounded by his having to sit through his first year adhering to the school's curriculum before finally being allowed to express himself on canvas. During this time he'd come to realise that he wasn't expressing himself on guitar as he would have liked and thought the answer lay in switching to bass; his reasoning being there were only four strings to master instead of six.

Borrowing a Vox Precision from John Brown, he set about familiarising himself with the instrument. He even got as far as purchasing his own bass – a second-hand Shaftsbury Ned Callan Cody – before deciding the bass was too cumbersome to be sexy. Though he would persevere with the bass for several months after this date, it's fair to say the catalyst for his reverting back to the guitar came on Wednesday, 28 November 1973, after seeing the New York Dolls in all their sling-back and feather-boa glory on *The Old Grey Whistle Test*.

BBC2's late-night 'serious' alternative to the teen-oriented *Top Of The Pops*, had been running for two years by the time the New York Dolls – who were in London on the UK leg of a European jaunt to promote their recently-released eponymous debut album – tottered onto the studio's soundstage. Unlike *Top Of The Pops*, groups invited onto the '*Whistle Test*' as it was colloquially known amongst its predominantly bearded, Afghan coat-wearing, university graduate TV audience, were expected to play live – if only to show they were a cut above the manufactured pop acts of the day whose very existence relied on their being Radio One friendly.

Just why the Dolls were allowed to mime their way through 'Looking For a Kiss' and 'Jet Boy' – both of which appear on their eponymous debut album – has never been properly explained, but their being given carte blanche to prance and preen without the need to worry about keeping the beat made for a truly spellbinding performance.

The show's presenter, the DJ and journalist 'Whispering Bob' Harris, whose staid, laid back delivery could have served as a sleep cure for insomniacs, dismissed the Dolls as 'mock rock', but those eight high-octane infused minutes caught the imagination of those who preferred their rock 'n' roll heroes to have attitude rather than aptitude.

Despite being labelled 'faggots' and 'freaks' by the New York press, the Dolls had built up a fanatical following on their home turf owing to their penchant for taking to the stage dressed like Harlem hookers, and playing catchy, high-energy rock 'n' roll. However, it really would prove to be a case of 'Too Much Too Soon' for the Dolls, because by the time their second album went on sale the group were on a terminal downward slide.

Billy Murcia, their original drummer had overdosed on Mandrex in a London hotel the previous summer whilst the group had been on the verge of signing a £100,000 deal with the newly-incorporated Track Records. And with guitarist Johnny Thunders and Murcia's replacement Jerry 'Niggs' Nolan both dabbling in heroin, they were hardly likely to shake their 'junkies' tag.

The Dolls' management team had also recognised the writing on the wall, and began devoting their time, money, and energies to the other act on their books, Aerosmith. It was therefore left to self-professed Dolls junkie Malcolm McLaren to try and rejuvenate their ailing career. Instead of settling for giving the Dolls' a makeover by decking them out in tight-fitting patent red leather ensembles, Malcolm also had them perform in front of a hammer and sickle backdrop. This, of course, was at the height of the Vietnam War, and his ill-advised 'better red than dead' stance was never going to sit well down on the Bowery while American troops were returning home from south-east Asia in body-bags draped in the stars and stripes.

It's become something of Clash folklore that it was his seeing the Dolls' careening about the *Whistle Test* stage that blew Mick's mind to the point where he fired off a missive to Robin Crocker at Albany raving about the New York Dolls. And yet during a 2006 *www. gibson.com* interview he claimed he was already hip to the brash New Yorkers by the time of their UK TV debut: 'I saw them on *The Old Grey Whistle Test*, but I saw them live too. They were supporting the Faces at Wembley Stadium. I must have been thirteen or fourteen, that perfect influential age, when you're really gonna be changed. And I was! I pretended to be Johnny Thunders for a bit.

'At that time, I was living with my grandmother, her sister, and her sister-in-law,' he continued. 'That was very strange, growing up with three old ladies. When I started dressing like Johnny Thunders, they were a bit worried, to be quite honest. But I assured them that everything was okay.'

Many of Mick's future punk contemporaries would cite seeing the Dolls' incendiary *Whistle Test* shenanigans as being their wake-up call, but thanks to his mum Renee having the wherewithal to include copies of cutting-edge US underground magazines *Rock Scene* and *Creem* in her monthly care packages, Mick was already alert to what was happening musically stateside.

As such, his record collection already boasted albums by Detroit's seminal punk pioneers, the MC5 and the Stooges. 'I was lucky she was living in America,' Mick explained. 'When I saw that stuff I was like, "Wow!" There weren't many people over here who were into that sort of music in those days; only a handful.'[6]

– CHAPTER THREE –

TEENAGE DELINQUENT

'Songwriting came to me at the same time I was learning so it all came together at that point. I was sixteen when I started on guitar but before then I was always asking, "How do you do this?" "How do you do that?"'
– Mick Jones

DESPITE HAVING LIVED OUT of each other's pockets for the best part of twelve months, it wasn't until May 1974 that Mick tentatively suggested to John Brown that they should perhaps start a group of their own. He did so after espying a notice for a forthcoming science-fiction convention being held at a hotel on Russell Square on the notice board at the National Film Theatre which happened to be screening a season of his favoured science-fiction films. Taking a stall at the convention he then sold some of the more collectable American sci-fi comics that Renee had sent over from America so as to raise the £80 asking price for a second-hand black Fender Telecaster he'd set his heart on.

It's ironic that Mick should choose a guitar that would forever be associated with his future songwriting partner, because whilst the Fender Telecaster perfectly suited Joe's 'six strings or none' approach to guitar-playing, the instrument's thin tone was never going to compliment Mick's style.

Paul Wayman was brought in on lead guitar, while drummer Mike Dowling arrived via the time-honoured *Melody Maker* classifieds.

Although Dowling was married, and wasn't all that much better than Jim Hyatt behind the kit, his father-in-law's owning a garment factory where the group could rehearse of an evening free of charge saw Mick and John overlook his shortcomings.

With the line-up complete, Mick and John set about racking their brains for a cool-sounding name. They briefly toyed with the idea of calling themselves 'Coca Cola Douche' after the song of the same name by the New York psychedelic rock outfit, The Fugs, before settling on The Delinquents.

They may have been Delinquents by name, but no one could accuse them of loitering without intent as within less than a month they made their live debut in the Students' Union bar at the Queen Elizabeth College in Kensington on 19 June 1974. John and Paul, of course, had already played together with Schoolgirl, and Mike also had previous experience of playing live, but for Mick this was his first time in the spotlight and no amount of practising in his room or rehearsing at the factory would have prepared him for the adrenaline surge as he stepped up onto the stage.

The college crowd were largely appreciative of their efforts, yet it would be another six months before The Delinquents appeared in public again. The reason for the lengthy lay-off had nothing to do with Mick having suffered first night nerves, but rather because he was unhappy with playing a set consisting of covers.

Playing off-the-beaten-tracks such as MC5's 'Sister Anne', the Flamin' Groovies' 'Second Cousin', and 'Sometimes Good Guys Don't Wear White' by the Standells, had undoubtedly set the group apart from the run-of-the-mill covers acts, yet Mick was desperate to avoid their being dismissed as just another human jukebox.

♪♪♪

The Delinquents had gone into self-imposed exile primarily to work up a half-hour set of original material, but thanks to John having spotted an ad in the *Melody Maker*'s classifieds offering cheap and above average recording facilities at £3.50 per hour, they'd headed across London to Budget Studios in High Holborn and put together a highly polished promotional package, which included promo leaflets, publicity photos, and a demo acetate seven-inch single featuring two of their new compositions: 'You Know It Ain't Easy' b/w 'Hurry'.

Given that Mick, John, and Paul were all Mott The Hoople maniacs, it was perhaps to be expected that The Delinquents' sound wasn't all that far removed from that of their heroes. Another home-grown influence – as stated on the promo leaflet – were The Sharks, which featured a pre 'Motorbikin'' Chris Spedding in its line-up. Aside from being an accomplished guitarist, Chris was an aspiring producer, and his hand would be at the helm when the Sex Pistols made their first foray into the recording studio in May 1976.

Prior to their second live outing at the Thomas à Beckett on the Old Kent Road on 25 November, Mick placed two ads in the 26 October 1974 issue of *Melody Maker*; the first touting for further gigs, while the second let it be known the group was seeking professional management.

The Delinquents may have only chalked up one solitary show, but such was the *Melody Maker*'s circulation at that time that both ads generated a modicum of interest in the 'Raunch Rock 'n' Roll' they were promising to deliver; the most attentive coming from a highly-reputable agency who invited them to a meeting at their offices on Oxford Street.

According to Mick's recollections, the meeting was akin to the Kit Kat TV ad from the 1980s, where the music exec tells the Flock of Seagulls-esque hopefuls that they 'can't sing, can't play, and look awful'. However, instead of sitting back, snapping his chocolate wafer snack and telling The Delinquents they ought to go far, the agent nonchalantly wandered over to the fire doors, whipped out his dick, and proceeded to urinate over the fire escape. Having succeeded in exposing himself, the voyeuristic agent's interest in The Delinquents was at an end.

It must have seemed as though the agent had delivered the piss of death to The Delinquents' aspirations, for although the Thomas à Beckett show earned them a return to the Old Kent Road on 9 December, the impetus which had carried them thus far was on the wane. A portent of the ill-wind that would soon deflate the group's sails came three days after the second Thomas à Beckett outing when they performed at the Hammersmith School of Art.

Mick, of course, was already well known at the college, if only for his outlandish 'Keef Thunders' garb, but that wasn't enough to save The Delinquents from being given a frosty reception from his fellow students. Not everyone in the audience proved impervious to Mick's charms, however.

Recounting that evening as part of a *Blitz* magazine Clash retrospective in 1988, the future Slits guitarist, and vivacious punk siren, Viv Albertine, admitted to thinking her soon-to-be-boyfriend looked great in his leather jeans, frilled shirt, and black high-heeled slingbacks. Viv had been equally impressed with Mick's classroom ensemble the first day she encountered him in Hammersmith College's canteen: tight red-and-white checked trousers, a too tightly-fitted girl's jacket, the same black high-heeled slingbacks, '[and] all topped off with fluffy, backcombed hair.'[1]

'I see a flash of colour – a blur of dark hair, high-heeled shoes, fluttering chiffon scarves and the longest, thinnest legs I've ever seen. And then it's gone, disappeared into the men's loo. "Was that a *guy*?"'[2]

Following the festive break, The Delinquents reconvened to plan their strategy for the coming year. However, the holidays had given Dowling's Greek wife plenty of time to express her displeasure at his playing popstar and rather than endure his wife's lashings in a foreign tongue, he decided to put away childish things and concentrate on his parental responsibilities.

Given that Mick and John didn't think much of Dowling's musicianship this was as good as finding an unopened prezzie whilst packing away the Christmas decorations, but the ink was barely dry on their ad for a no-nonsense, commitment-free drummer when Wayman announced he was quitting the group.

Losing two members in as many weeks would have sounded the death-knell for many wannabe rockers, but any despondency Mick and John might have had over their old Strand School pal's unexpected departure evaporated into the ether when a Norwegian drummer by the name of Geir Waade responded to their appeal.

Realising that his rock'n'roll aspirations would wither on the bough if he remained in his homeland, Geir, together with his keyboard-playing pal Casino Steel (a.k.a Stein Groven) had arrived in London four years earlier. Whereas Casino's keyboard trickery was soon snapped up, Geir found there wasn't quite the same demand for drummers and he was forced to find regular work in order to meet the rent. By the time he saw the Delinquents' 'DRUMMER REQUIRED' ad in *Melody Maker*, he was working for Richard Branson's Virgin Records, which was on its meteoric rise up the record company rankings thanks to the phenomenal success of Mike Oldfield's debut album *Tubular Bells*.

Mick and John were suitably impressed by Geir's claims to have been invited back for a second audition for the quirky American duo Sparks who'd scored a number two on the UK Singles chart in April 1974 with 'This Town Ain't Big Enough For The Both Of Us', but they soon realised his drumming prowess was no better than that of the recently-departed Dowling. However, they were both swayed by Geir's fashion sense and agreeable nature, while an added bonus came with his Nordic looks ensuring a surfeit of female attention whenever they went out on the town.

It was Geir who also found Paul Wayman's replacement in the form of former Hollywood Brats' guitarist Eunan Brady, or 'Brady' as he'd taken to calling himself; his acquaintanceship with Brady stemming from Casino having been in the Hollywood Brats.

Despite their having never heard of the Hollywood Brats, Geir's shameless eulogising of the Dublin-born guitarist's talents was enough to arouse Mick and John's interest. Simultaneously, he'd bragged to Brady about what The Delinquents had to offer, though both parties were unaware of the Norwegian's playmaking until they were all sitting around the same table at Brady's Maida Vale flat.

♪♪♪

Brady was already painfully aware of Geir's limitations from the latter having occasionally sat in at Hollywood Brats rehearsals, but he was equally disparaging of Mick's and John's musicianship. There was, however, no denying their drive and passion, and although he still harboured misgivings about taking what he saw as a backward step following his time with the Brats, he allowed himself to be carried along on the tide of enthusiasm.

Brady's introduction undoubtedly brought The Delinquents an added dynamic, but it also brought about an irrevocable shift in the balance of power within the group. Mick and John might have been the founding members, but that counted for naught seeing as they now only held a fifty per cent share of the vote when it came to decision-making. And as Brady and Geir both preferred playing with an out and out frontman, they pressed Mick and John into placing another ad in the *Melody Maker* classifieds.

The ad – which appeared in the paper's 22 February 1975 issue – failed to unearth a 'DECADENT VOCALIST' in the Mick Jagger and David Johansen vain, but it did at least serve to bring them to the attention of Tony Gordon, whose management company, Wedge, happened to be looking to bolster its client roster.

Gordon duly attended a Delinquents rehearsal, and while he made the obligatory appreciative grunts, he shared Geir and Brady's concerns about Mick's singing voice and said they should give him a call once they'd found a frontman.

Rather than shell out for another ad, however the group decided to take a more proactive approach and began trawling the usual musical haunts on London's live circuit such as the Red Cow in Hammersmith, the Golden Lion on Fulham Broadway, or the Windsor Castle in Maida Vale, in search of someone who fit the Jagger/Johansen mould.

It was on one of their sorties that Mick and John bumped into their old Strand School buddy Kelvin Blacklock.

On hearing Kelvin say how his group, Overtown, which also included ex-Schoolgirl drummer Jim Hyatt, had secured a residency of sorts playing alternate Wednesdays at the Marquee Club on Wardour Street throughout January and February, Mick and John agreed to come long to their next show as a show of support for their friends; little realising that Brady and Geir would be totally blown away by Kelvin's vocal and onstage showmanship.

Realising where this unconcealed show of gusto for Kelvin was heading, Mick and John immediately set about dampening Brady's and Geir's enthusiasm with less-than-complimentary tales of the Kelvin of old.

Their powers of dissuasion appeared to have the desired effect – especially when a second attempt to unearth a suitably 'DECADENT MALE VOCALIST' was made courtesy of the 22 March 1975 issue of *Melody Maker*.

Once again, however, their net brought in shrimps instead of sharks, and they were deciding what their next course of action should be when fate's fickle fingers lent a hand and John received a letter from Tony Gordon enquiring how they were getting on with their search for a singer. Fearing that Gordon might lose interest should they respond in the negative, Brady and Geir recommenced with their 'we want Kelvin' campaign. Although Mick maintained his anti-Kelvin stance, John's indecision over Gordon's letter was enough to carry the vote.

They might have found their man, but cajoling Kelvin into listening to their overtures would be no easy matter seeing as Overtown had not only secured a residency at the Marquee, but were also set to go into the studio to record a single. Given that Mick, John, and Geir's collective skills couldn't have improved all that much in so short a time, Kelvin's acquiescence could only have come from Brady's talents coupled with Tony Gordon's interest.

Kelvin officially became a Delinquent following a full audition on Friday, 11 April 1975, and just as Mick and John had foreseen, their new singer wasted little time in stamping his authority. To his mind, he should be the group's principle songwriter, and from that point on rehearsals became a 'battle-of-the-bards' as the newcomer used every trick up his sleeve – including wilfully drawing from the plagiarism well in an attempt to usurp Mick.

Despite the in-house one-upmanship, the Delinquents knuckled down to knocking their new set-list – which included cover-versions of Chuck Berry's 'Little Queenie' and the Yardbirds' 'I'm Not Talking' – into shape before performing a showcase in front of Tony Gordon at a suitably dingy rehearsal space in King's Cross that the Hollywood Brats had used on occasion.

Their effort to project a deadbeat image was completely wasted on Gordon, however, as his only prerequisite before drawing up a managerial contract was that the group changed its name to 'Little Queenie' after the Chuck Berry song.

♪♪♪

On 7 May 1975, the newly-named Little Queenie performed a second showcase for Gordon at the far more upmarket Track Studios in Acton. Gordon had brought along a friend of his from Pye Records, whose pressing service The Delinquents had used for their promo demo the previous September. Having received a favourable nod from the Pye man, Gordon invited the group to Wedge's offices at 13 Duke Street. Perhaps not surprisingly, given that The Delinquents/Little Queenie were virtually unknowns, the management contract weighed heavily in Gordon's favour.

Kelvin and Brady cared little for the contractual small print, and now that they'd secured professional representation, coupled with the possibility Little Queenie might secure a recording contract with Pye, the duo decided they could no longer afford to carry what they saw as dead Norwegian wood.

Two days after signing with Gordon a meeting was convened at Gladsmuir Road, where Mick was now living having taken over one of the upstairs bed-sits. Mick viewed Kelvin and Brady's pronouncement as an act of betrayal, but with John having suffered most from Geir's wayward drumming, his was the sole voice of dissension. He thought that with Tony Gordon anxious to get the group into Pye's Bryanston Street 16-track studio at the earliest opportunity to record some new demos Geir might be granted a stay of execution, but Kelvin had already surreptitiously sounded out Jim Hyatt.

Somewhat surprisingly, given they'd enough compositions of their own to choose from, when they accompanied Gordon into the Pye studio they ended up recording Chuck Berry's 'Little Queenie', as well as the Frankie Miller Band's 'A Fool In Love', which Kelvin and

Jim were already familiar with as the song had been a staple of the Overtown live set.

Rather than pay for Pye's in-house producer, Gordon elected to produce the two tracks himself, but while Mick and John were pleased with the finished results, Brady and Kelvin were less so. They were also harbouring doubts about Gordon's managerial capabilities, and prior to going into the studio Kelvin had done the rounds visiting every other management company in London to see if he might secure a better deal. It was on one of these forays that that he bumped into Guy Stevens.

♪♪♪

Aside from pointing Mott The Hoople in the right direction, Guy, who'd first come to prominence on the London music scene during the early-Sixties while DJing at The Scene Club in Soho, had enhanced his Midas touch reputation by heading the UK division of Sue Records for Island Records' supremo Chris Blackwell. Following Mott The Hoople's decision to decamp to David Bowie's MainMan team, however, Guy's career had been in terminal free-fall; the tailspin being propelled by his proclivity for hard-drinking and drug-binging.

Guy's ever-increasing daily intake of speed and spirits had left him something of a pariah in London, but he still had important friends in America who were always willing to take his calls; the most notable being Warner Brothers' president, Mo Ostin, who was happy to keep Guy on a £100 per week retainer.

When Kelvin appeared within his drug-induced fug saying how Little Queenie were on the verge of signing a recording contract, but were unhappy with their management, Guy readily seized the opportunity to get himself a slice of the Pye.

A meeting was hastily arranged in Marylebone at one of Guy's favoured watering holes, but while the free-flowing drink coupled with an endless stream of amusing anecdotes from his time in the industry made for an enjoyable afternoon, it was going to take more than Guy's name to persuade Tony Gordon to release Little Queenie from their contract. Luckily, Kelvin had a cunning plan…

Gordon is still in the music business, and boasts a CV that includes managing Sham 69 and Culture Club, as well as overseeing Boy George's subsequent solo career. Yet despite The Clash having been one of the best known bands in the world during that particular time-frame, he claims to have no recollection of Little Queenie, or the bizarre events that occurred at his offices on the afternoon of Monday, June 2, 1975, when Kelvin leapt up onto his desk and writhed around until Gordon capitulated and signed a release form.

Mick was thrilled to have Guy as their manager, but his euphoria would prove short-lived for having sat in on the next Little Queenie rehearsal Guy deemed him surplus to requirements. Taking Kelvin and Brady to one side Guy told them he believed Little Queenie would benefit from sacrificing Mick in favour of a keyboardist.

When Kelvin and Brady delivered Guy's verdict at the next Gladsmuir Road group meeting John thought the idea insane, and in a fit of pique announced he was quitting the group. However, with Guy supposedly having Mo Ostin's ear he knew he would be cutting his nose off to spite his face and having got Mick's blessing he subsequently retracted his resignation.

When reminiscing about the decision that would ultimately prove one of the most heavily disguised blessings of all, Mick graciously said he understood Guy's reasoning. 'You see I was a pretty limited guitar player when I got fired, and that made me go back to my bedroom and practise along to all my records for a year,' he explained. 'When I came out again I was accomplished. At first I was terrible, and it was almost righteous that I should get chucked out but the only thing was – and I didn't really realise it at the time – but I was actually the main song writer in the group, so it screwed up that whole situation because they chucked me out.'[3]

Three weeks after Mick's dismissal on 27 June, and having fulfilled the second stage of Guy's master plan by changing their name to Violent Luck, the newly-truncated four-piece played a showcase for a Warner Brothers representative at PSL studios in Battersea. Just why Guy forged ahead with the showcase without having brought in the keyboardist supposedly pivotal to his plans for Violent Luck is anyone's guess, but within days of the showcase Jim Hyatt was summoned to Gladsmuir Road.

Warner Bros. may have been impressed enough to hand Guy the money to take Violent Luck into Air Studios in Oxford Circus to record some demos – with Leo Sayer's drummer, Theodore Thunder, filling in for Jim, and ex-Mott The Hoople keyboardist Verden Allen on hand to flesh out the sound – but with Mick gone the dynamic would never be the same.

While Mick was still with Little Queenie, Kelvin had introduced him to a bass player called Tony James, who was reading mathematics at Brunel University. What Mick didn't know at the time was that Kelvin had met Tony after responding to the latter's *Melody Maker* 'ad whilst with Overtown. Tony had been on the hunt for a frontman for his prog rock outfit, Random Frog, and had been piqued when Kelvin opted to be a Delinquent at the eleventh hour. The two had kept in touch, however, which was how he came to accompany Kelvin to several Little Queenie rehearsals.

Kelvin has since claimed it was he who put Mick and Tony together, but Mick remembers things differently. 'We (Little Queenie) were in this place down in South London practising,' he explained. 'I didn't know it at the time, but I was just about to be taken out for a drink, which means getting fired. Kelvin brought this guy in to soften the blow. He sort of introduced me to Tony, so it was soon after that I got fired from the group. By that time I'd become Tony's friend, so we started putting a band together the two of us.'[4]

– CHAPTER FOUR –

WHAT'S MY NAME?

'I met Bernie Rhodes in 1975, in a place in West Kensington called the Nashville Rooms. He had this cap on and he looked rock 'n' roll, sort of like Gene Vincent, so I went over to talk to him and said, 'Are you a piano player?' and he said, 'No, I'm not, but you're wearing one of my T-shirts.'

– Mick Jones

ACCORDING TO LEGEND, WITH the notable exception of the Sex Pistols, every other group that graduated from the fabled 'Class of '76' could lay claim to having had at least one former member of the fabled London SS within its line-up at one time or another. The Damned could boast two ex-SSers in Brian James (no relation to Tony), and Rat Scabies, while future Clash-gangers Paul Simonon, Terry Chimes, and Topper Headon would all try out for the group with varying degrees of success. However, the two names that will forever be indelibly linked with London SS are, of course, Mick Jones and Tony James.

Mick would subsequently claim that London SS stood for 'London Social Security', rather than an overt reference to Hitler's dreaded Schultz Staffel. Yet while his being Jewish on his mother's side adds gravitas to this explanation, it's worth remembering that his latest guitar hero Johnny Thunders had recently caused an uproar at Orly Airport during the Dolls' European tour by sporting a swastika armband.

In July 1975, Mick and Tony placed an ad in the *Melody Maker* classifieds seeking a lead guitarist and drummer whose musical influences matched their own – Stones, NY Dolls, Mott etc. Another, perhaps, more important, prerequisite for those thinking of applying was that they have 'a great rock'n'roll image'.

One of the first to respond was the aforementioned Brian James, who'd formed his own Dolls/MC5-inspired three-piece outfit, the colourfully named 'Bastard', the previous summer. On realising London wasn't yet ready for what he was offering, however, he'd suggested the trio try their luck on the continent.

Bastard settled on Belgium, but having realised that the Flemish pastures were no greener than they were in Frognal Brian had kept a watchful eye on the *Melody Maker* classifieds. On spotting Mick and Tony's ad he'd headed for Ostend and booked a seat on the next ferry home. 'It was like, Christ! Somebody in this country has actually heard of these people,' Brian explained. 'These were bands I'd been into for a couple of years, and in England there was nothing like that.'[1]

Though willing to commit himself fully to the London SS cause, Brian thought it only fair that he return to Belgium to break the news to his unsuspecting bandmates in person. In the meantime, Mick's idea for London SS gradually coalesced into a group of sorts; with Geir Waade and Casino Steel, Casino's fellow ex-Hollywood Brat, Andrew Matheson, and future Boys frontman Matt Dangerfield getting together on a regular basis at Dangerfield's squat at 47a Warrington Crescent in Maida Vale.

It was during this time that Mick would encounter the man who would play a significant role in his musical fortunes.

♪♪♪

Mick's apocryphal meeting with Bernard Rhodes (call him 'Bernie' at your peril) occurred on Saturday, 2 August, at the Nashville Rooms* on the North End Road in West Kensington where an up-and-coming Liverpool outfit called Deaf School were showcasing their talents. Despite its flash-sounding name, the Nashville was a squalid pub, with

---

* Now the Famous Three Kings pub.

even seedier décor and clientele; its only saving grace being that it hosted regular live music.

Mick and Tony had gone along to the Nashville that evening as much to be seen on the scene as they were to check out what the risqué-sounding Deaf School were offering. They naively assumed they and their circle of friends were the only souls in London – if not the entire country – who knew about the New York Dolls, The MC5, and The Stooges. Their unshakable belief that they were two of the coolest kids in school was therefore shattered on seeing some little bloke in a peaked cap sporting the same T-shirt as Mick.

Bernard was the peak-capped sporting bloke, and the T-shirt in question bore the now iconic motif: 'You're Gonna Wake Up One Morning And Know Which Side Of The Bed You've Been Lying On', beneath which was a 'Hates' list featuring those pop stars, artists, politicians and fashion houses that they deemed to have gone beyond their sell-by date, and a corresponding 'Loves' list featuring the names of those the entrepreneurial trio considered fresh and relevant.

Mick had purchased his shirt from SEX, the happening World's End emporium situated on the wrong end of the ultra-fashionable King's Road that he and Tony had discovered recently, so was somewhat taken aback that the diminutive, mole-like character standing before them could possibly know about the shop.

By the time Malcolm McLaren, and his business partner/girlfriend Vivienne Westwood, first set up shop at 430 King's Road in October 1971, Bernard – one of several profiteering ventures – was running a stall on the nearby Antiquarius Antiques Market selling second-hand leather jackets. 'Malcolm and Vivienne were jealous of me because my second-hand leather jackets were selling as fast as I set them out on the stall. They didn't like that, so they brought me in. We tossed some ideas about, and they brought me in to help them out by coming up with designs for a range of T-shirts.'

Mick remembers asking Bernard if he was a piano player, while Tony says he half-jokingly told him to 'piss off out of it' as he was cramping their style, to which Bernard angrily retorted that they should be the ones doing the pissing off as he'd designed the T-shirt.

In what can be best described as a sartorial stand-off between the three, Bernard then demanded to know what Mick and Tony had going for them. During the ensuing conversation, Mick and Tony told Bernard about London SS, while he in turn revealed he was involved with a group operating out of Tin Pan Alley, an outfit who were calling themselves the Sex Pistols.

It's Bernard's ongoing reticence to go before the camera, which allowed Malcolm to downplay his part in the Sex Pistols' nascent history, relegating him to the role of babysitter whilst he was over in New York playfully tossing lighted matches onto the few remaining bridges the ailing New York Dolls had at their backs.

As Malcolm told the same tale at every turn, said tale inevitably became set in stone. Yet, when trawling through the storage crates while preparing for a house move in August 2012, Bernard happened upon a batch of dog-eared letters that Malcolm had written to him c/o 430 Kings Road, in which – aside from discussing new ideas for clothes, and his encounters with Andy Warhol – he repeatedly urges Bernard to concentrate his energies on having Steve and Paul learn the stolen instruments which were apparently collecting dust within the SEX storeroom.

'I loved Malcolm, but he fucked me over on the T-shirts, and he fucked me over on the Pistols,' says Bernard today. 'I was the one looking after them while he was in New York with the Dolls but when he came back to London, he was like, "It's my band."

'I thought right, if that's the way you want to play it, I'm gonna fuck you over. And I did it by planting a bomb with a slow-burning fuse. I knew immediately that John [Rotten] would fuck with Malcolm. He was obnoxious and Southern Irish, so he had a huge chip on his shoulder.'

Like Mick, Bernard was of Russo-Jewish descent, and had forebears who'd fallen victim to the SS death squads following the Nazis' invasion of Russia in June 1941, but he was sufficiently intrigued by Mick and Tony to offer his services as their manager.

Having selected an appropriate artistic metaphor in telling his new charges to visualise the future of rock 'n' roll as a blank canvas – one with no room for Elvis, The Beatles, or the Rolling Stones – Bernard's first act as manager was to call his charges to a meeting at the Bull and Bush pub on Shepherd's Bush Green, where he proceeded to dump a bag full of SS paraphernalia – swastikas, Iron Crosses SS daggers etc. – on the table in full view of the other patrons.

Mick and Tony were horrified and pleaded with Bernard to put the Nazi ephemera back in the bag, but Bernard remained undaunted, telling them that if they were determined to call themselves 'London SS' then they were going to have to deal with everything it entailed.

♪♪♪

Upon recognising the contact number listed beside the postage stamp-sized ad for a WHIZZ KID GUITARIST, no older than 20, and no worse looking than Johnny Thunders, within the classified section of the 27 September issue of *Melody Maker*, Bernard thought the timing right to introduce Mick and Tony to the Sex Pistols. Accompanying them to the Pistols' Denmark Street hideaway that night were Andrew Matheson, and Casino Steel.

It would prove a revelatory eye-opener for all concerned: Mick and Tony's surprise stemming from their 'competition' having short hair, while having cited Johnny Thunders in their *Melody Maker* ad, while Glen, Steve and Paul were bemused to find Bernard had got involved with a bunch of throwbacks in platforms and bell-bottoms, with hair down to their arses. Mick may have looked like an extra from *Hair*, but the three Sex Pistols felt a kindred spirit and invited him to jam with them.

Bernard, of course, had purposely taken them to Denmark Street to show them the error of their hirsute ways, and while Mick would cling on to his bangs and curls and frilly shirts a little while longer, he returned to Warrington Crescent knowing his image was in need of a serious overhaul.

What he didn't know, however, was that Malcolm had been forced to place the 'Whiz Kid Guitarist' ad in the *Melody Maker* to quell Paul's dissatisfaction at Steve's rudimentary playing, or that Paul and Glen had been sufficiently impressed with his guitar style that Glen and Malcolm would subsequently make an abortive foray to an address on

London Street in Paddington (Andrew Matheson and Casino Steel's flat where Mick stayed on occasion) to offer him the gig.

As they were going behind Bernard's back, they'd only had a vague idea where Mick was living, and the opportunity for the future of rock 'n' roll to take a left oblique was lost as a belligerent Casino would only converse with them through the letterbox.

♫♫♫

On discovering that Malcolm had secured the Denmark Street lease for the Sex Pistols with a £1,000 deposit, Mick and Tony, together with the recently returned Brian James, set about badgering Bernard into making a similar gesture by finding them a HQ they might call their own.

Bernard duly obliged by striking a deal with the owner of a greasy spoon café called the Paddington Kitchen on Praed Street opposite the entrance to St. Mary's Hospital. With a weekly stipend covering the cost of the electricity the group used while rehearsing in the cellar, they could also use the café to hold court; an added bonus coming with the owner allowing them to stack the jukebox with their favourite records. '[It's] where we used to meet people and sort of vet them,' Mick subsequently revealed. 'If they passed the vetting process we used to take them round the back to the rehearsal room. We saw all the main players.'[2]

One of these 'main players' was a Croydon-based drummer called Chris Miller (soon to be rechristened 'Rat Scabies'), who'd been monitoring Mick and Tony's *Melody Maker* ads for several weeks before finally picking up the phone in early December. A professed liking for the MC5 had proved sufficient to get Chris through the vetting stage, but with their having already auditioned scores of drummers in recent weeks, Mick, Tony, and Brian (and indeed Bernard) appeared more interested in the old war film playing on the battered black and white TV set in the corner.

Rat was understandably irked by their insensitivity, and to draw their attention away from the film he set about pounding the kit with a ferocity that would subsequently become his trademark style with The

Damned. Mick and Tony didn't seem all that impressed and kept their gaze on the flickering screen, but Brian latched onto Rat's playing and began soundtracking an aerial dog fight in the film with a screeching guitar solo.

One thing that did grab Bernard's attention, however, was Chris' constant scratching between songs. When he confessed to having contracted the highly-infectious skin disease scabies, Bernard leapt up and hurriedly covered all the chairs with newspaper.

Chris was deemed worthy of a second audition, but whereas Mick and Tony were willing to overlook his skin ailment, they were less happy with his scruffy appearance. Brian, however, had been growing steadily suspicious of Bernard's motives, and this show of snobbery proved the last straw. He didn't give a fuck what the auditionees looked like as long as they could play.

'It was a very drifting situation regards [to] who was supposed to be getting the group together,' Mick revealed while subsequently giving his own interpretation about London SS' criteria to journalist John Tobler. 'Sometimes people fitted the bill because they looked right like, and they couldn't play – they couldn't play a note or nothing – they just didn't know nothing about instruments. At one time there was only about two of us who knew how to put a chord together. The rest of them would be just stoned people, just falling all over the drum kit...'[3]

Bernard's high-handed attitude wasn't solely reserved for potential auditionees as Tony often found himself the target of his ire. One such occasion occurred when Bernard called the bassist at his parents' home in Twickenham and began berating him for not knowing his Sartre. Armed with a list of titles provided by Bernard, Tony dutifully paid a visit to his local library and took out every book he could find on Jean Paul Sartre and Dadaism. In doing so, however, he came to realise that Bernard was simply trying to get him and Mick to look beyond what they were doing and grasp the bigger picture.

Of course, this enlightenment didn't spare Tony from further torment. With Christmas approaching, Bernard called demanding that he forego the turkey and trimmings in favour of spending the day with the hookers operating out of Praed Street. And that if he wasn't willing to do that then he might as well buy a copy of *Gay News* or *Spare Rib* from his local newsagent.

'I don't think I was too hard on Tony at all,' Bernard says, shrugging away the memory. 'Just look what he went on to achieve with Generation X and Sigue Sigue Sputnik? And anyway, he was a bit like Glen [Matlock] in forever standing around with an "anxious to please" look on his face like some girl hoping to be fucked.'

Tony chose to ignore Bernard's counsel to forego a family Christmas and engage in some festive fornication. Yet although he was happy to tag along on recces to check out suitable candidates for the group, he was no longer willing to tolerate Bernard's management style and furtively began perusing the 'Musicians Wanted' notices in the *Melody Maker*.

Shortly into the New Year, a drummer called Roland Hot – having responded to yet another of Mick and Tony's *Melody Maker* missives – had arrived at the Paddington Kitchen to try out for the vacant drum stool.

Hot's skills ultimately proved to be rather tepid, but he nevertheless stayed around long enough to feature on the only known recording of London SS material in existence – recorded while Tony was still in the line-up. The songs covered were the MC5's 1969 hit 'Ramblin' Rose', Jonathan Richman's recent transatlantic release 'Roadrunner' – which the fledgling Sex Pistols also happened to be covering at the time – and The Strangeloves' 1965 US Top 30 hit 'Night Time'.

The quality of the recording was your typical 'let's-see-what-we-sound-like' job, which in all probability would have been long since consigned to the dustbin had it not been for its subsequent significance.

Hot's brief tenure with London SS would also prove significant. Owing to his apprehension about making the journey to Praed Street alone for his initial audition he'd cajoled an art college friend into tagging along for moral support. And there was something about the gap-toothed, Rimbaud-esque ruffian that caught Bernard and Mick's eye.

Like Mick, twenty-year-old Paul Simonon came from a broken home; his parents having split up when he was eight. His mum subsequently remarried to a budding composer, and when he won a twelve-month scholarship to study music in Sienna, Tuscany, his new family went with him.

On returning to London, the family set up home in Herne Hill, where Paul rekindled his love for reggae and became something of a teenage tearaway. His relationship with his step-father had also deteriorated to the point where it was suggested he might like to live with his dad in Notting Hill.

It was whilst attending the Isaac Newton Boys Secondary School that Paul's talent for art first came to the fore, and thanks to his art teacher's diligence he applied for a scholarship at the prestigious Byam School of Art in Holland Park which accepted pupils on the quality of their portfolio rather than exam results.

Paul appeared to have all the prerequisites for a frontman: tall, lean, blond, and roguishly handsome. He'd only come along in a show of moral support for his mate, but it didn't take much persuasion from Mick to get him to step up to the mic for a run-through of 'Roadrunner', and The Standells' 'Barracuda'. The ever tactful Mick suggested Paul should perhaps stick to painting, but Bernard recognised a similar rough and ready street persona to that of the irascible John Lydon, and filed Paul's name away for possible future use.

♪♪♪

Tony was already tired of Bernard's incessant nit-picking, but after nine frustrating months of trying to get London SS out of the rehearsal room and onto a stage he decided enough was enough and informed Mick that he was going to try his luck with a proto-punk outfit called Chelsea. Mick was naturally gutted at his friend's decision, but for Bernard it was a godsend. He and Malcolm had long envisioned a new scene, and with the Sex Pistols beginning to create a bit of a buzz about town there were suddenly a clutch of kids hanging about desperate to get in on the action. 'Malcolm and Bernie would be planning some group or other and I'd be sent over to some rehearsal,' Mick laughingly told the *NME*'s Chris Salewitz when reflecting on Bernard's pre-Clash musical meddling.

One of Bernard's 'three-chord coalitions' saw Mick jamming with a sassy Ohioan called Chrissie Hynde, who would, of course, go on to achieve mainstream success with The Pretenders. 'I met Chrissie through Bernie and for a while we were going to put a band together,' Mick revealed. 'We'd go up to my nan's bedroom and play songs together as duets. That's where "Every Little Bit Hurts"* came from. We never did get the band together. She did cut my hair, though.'[4]

In the booklet accompanying the *Clash On Broadway* box set, Mick admitted to occasionally losing heart after Tony's defection, and that it had been Bernard's foresight that had seen them through. Bernard's steadfast belief that he and Mick were on the right path was to be rewarded when Mick happened upon Paul Simonon on the Portobello Road. On hearing about this fortuitous happenstance, Bernard told Mick to stop moping after Tony and to start a group with Paul.

Paul was surprisingly open to the idea of learning an instrument, and with Mick having accumulated several guitars it made sense to let Paul try his hand with one of these. One get-together, however, was enough for Mick to realise Paul's limitations and so he suggested they borrow a bass from Tony.

Paul wasn't initially thrilled with the idea. 'Mick told me there was an exhibition of paintings at Camberwell Art College by someone called Stuart Sutcliffe who used to be in the Beatles,' he revealed. '[Mick said] how he couldn't play the bass either. So after Mick's history lesson I started to learn.'[5]

The first step in Paul's musical education came with his learning where to put his fingers on the fretboard, which he inventively accomplished by sticking notes on the relevant frets. He then started playing along to his sizeable reggae collection at home, but as he had to rely on Mick to tune the bass for him it made sense to move into the Davis Road squat in Acton Vale where Mick was now living with Viv Albertine.

Another frequent visitor to the one-bedroom upstairs maisonette was Julian Keith Levene who, like Mick, had taught himself to play guitar. Mick had already encountered Keith, as he preferred to be called, whilst hanging out with the Warrington Crescent crowd, so

---

* 'Every Little Bit Hurts' was a 1964 hit for Motown singer Brenda Holloway.

was familiar with his precocious talent. 'I met Mick and got on really well with him,' says Keith. 'The main thing we had in common was we knew we really wanted to get a group together. That was it.'[6]

After the disappointment of losing Brian James to Rat Scabies and seeing Tony James lose heart, Mick now had the nucleus of a group to work with. The bonding that all bands need came one Saturday afternoon when he, Paul and Keith each purchased a gaudy ladies car coat from a second-hand stall on the Portobello Road Market.

With Paul coming on in leaps and bounds, the trio began to focus their attentions away from garish garb and onto finding a frontman. As he had with Tony, Mick took Keith and Paul on regular sorties on the pub and club circuit, gradually narrowing down their search until only one candidate remained. 'I saw Joe play with the 101ers many times,' Mick revealed. 'They were nearly at the point of being the best band in London. They were lumped in with the pub rock scene, but they were really a squat band, from the squatting communities. Joe was part of that scene, which was very big in the early Seventies. And we'd seen them many times. We just thought he was the best guy out there. We were looking for a singer and said, "Let's see if we can get Joe."'

John Graham Mellor was born in Ankara, Turkey, in August 1952, where his parents – owing to his father Ronald being a clerical officer with British Foreign Office – were living at the time. He'd also lived in Egypt, Mexico, and West Germany before the Mellors were finally able to put down some home-grown roots of sorts by setting up home in Warlingham, Surrey, during the summer of in 1960. However, when Ron Mellor received another posting to Iran shortly thereafter, it was decided that John and his older brother David* would remain behind to concentrate on their education.

Having decided to 'live, enjoy life, [and] fuck chartered accountancy!' after hearing the Rolling Stones' 'Not Fade Away' in February 1964, the rebellious teenager did just enough in the classroom to scrape the three O-Levels necessary to gain a place at art school. He was accepted into the Central School of Art and Design, only to drop out during his foundation year. He then taught himself the rudiments of

---

* David Mellor would commit suicide in August 1970.

guitar on a two-quid ukulele, adopted the name 'Woody' in homage of the American folk singer Woody Guthrie, and embarked on a series of Jack Kerouac-esque adventures. He returned to London during the summer of 1974, moving into a spare room at 101 Wallerton Road in Maida Vale where he set about putting a rock 'n' roll group together. He also underwent a second name-change to 'Joe Strummer'

These days the mere mention of Joe Strummer conjures up images of The Clash, but at that time The 101'ers, as the Wallerton Road squat group were known, were just beginning to reap the fruits of their hard-earned labour following two years of relentless gigging. They'd also recently released their debut single 'Keys To Your Heart' b/w '5 Star Rock 'N' Roll Petrol' on the independent Chiswick Records in the hope of it helping them to secure a recording deal with a major label.

In Don Letts' Grammy Award-winning 2000 Clash documentary *Westway To The World*, Joe tells the apocryphal tale of how Mick and Paul had made their clumsy approach offering him the frontman role in their group whilst they'd been waiting in line to sign on at the Lisson Grove Labour Exchange. As he'd no idea as to why they were eye-balling him, he'd naturally assumed the two were plotting to jump him once he got outside and relieve him of his giro.

Causing a ruck was the last thing on Mick and Paul's minds. 'He [Joe] had seen us out a few times, either at his gigs or in the dole queue,' Mick explained. 'We were in the dole queue looking across at him – glaring – and he thought we were gonna start a fight with him. But we were actually looking in awe because we'd seen him play the other night! So we'd seen each other before, but he had obviously noticed us as well.

'We went to see him play with the 101ers, at the Golden Lion in Fulham. Afterwards, Bernard, our manager, went round the back and talked to him and made him the offer.'[8]

Bernard did indeed give Joe a forty-eight hour ultimatum backstage at the Golden Lion, but the latter was already at a crossroads having undergone a Damascene conversion after seeing the Sex Pistols when they'd supported The 101'ers at the Nashville Rooms in early April 1976. Despite the *Melody Maker*'s dismissal of the Pistols' performance as a 'retarded spectacle' riddled with tiresome punk clichés – whilst lavishing The 101'ers with praise – his own view was that R&B was 'yesterday's papers'.

'As soon as I saw them [the Sex Pistols], I knew rhythm and blues was dead, that the future was here somehow,' Joe told Caroline Coon in November 1976. 'Every other group was riffing their way through the Black Sabbath catalogue. But hearing the Pistols I knew. I just knew. It was just something you knew without bothering to think about.'

Such was Joe's conviction that he'd glimpsed the future he didn't even hesitate when Bernard called back after just twenty-four hours demanding an answer. 'We were in the squat in Shepherd's Bush, and he (Bernard) brought Joe around a couple days later. 'Joe had already made it in our eyes,' said Mick. 'It took a lot of courage to get him to join our group, since we hadn't done anything. But luckily, Joe had seen the Sex Pistols. [He'd] seen the new thing coming in. He obviously wanted to be a part of it, and that was to our advantage because we were part of that.

'We went into the little room where we'd put egg boxes on the walls to soundproof it and began. He didn't want to do his tunes so much, but he was into changing, improving our songs. So we had a great lyric writer working with us.'[9]

The most famous reworking of one of Mick's compositions came that first session as Mick explained: 'One of the first ones we did was "I'm So Bored with the USA". We just played a couple of each other's numbers, and Joe made that famous addition from "I'm So Bored With You" to "I'm So Bored With The USA." He took the "You" and put the "S" and the "A" in there, and that changed everything!'[10]

Mick says that Bernard also played a part in the songwriting process by making them realise they should write about the things that affected them directly. 'I don't know if we were aware of punk being an outlet for our anger. There were a lot of things that needed saying and they hadn't been said in that way before. We were just picking things out of the paper to write about.'[11]

Of course, it wasn't only song ideas that came courtesy of their perusing the papers. With the songs taking an aggressive edge they were wanted a group name that was representative of how they felt and sounded.

Having noticed how many times the word tended to feature in the headlines; Paul suggested they call themselves 'The Clash'.

– CHAPTER FIVE –

CLASH CITY ROCKER

'I used to follow bands around, and Rod Stewart kind of let us down 'cos he never had any kind of relationship with the fans. I kind of felt betrayed by him, 'cos he sold out. I always thought that if you find yourself in that situation then it's not like, "I'm the greatest." Always remember what it's like to be a fan.'

– Mick Jones

ON SUNDAY, 4 JULY 1976, while The Ramones were in London marking their homeland's bicentennial year with their debut UK showing at The Roundhouse in Chalk Farm, The newly-incorporated Clash were making their own live debut at The Black Swan* in Sheffield supporting the Sex Pistols. A 'spit and sawdust' south Yorkshire pub – known by the local populace as the 'Dirty Duck' – wasn't perhaps the most prestigious of settings to mark one's debut, but having tried and failed to get the Sex Pistols onto the Roundhouse bill (and getting unceremoniously thrown down the stairs by the promoter John Curd in the process) Malcolm had no intention of being in the capital when The Ramones road-show hit town.

Mick, Joe, and Paul had all latched onto the Blitzkrieg boppers following the eponymous debut album release back in April, and would have been at the Roundhouse that night had Bernard not elected to

---

* The Black Swan subsequently changed its name to The Boardwalk, before closing its doors for the last time in November 2010.

side with Malcolm in what was the first of several misguided shows of solidarity over the coming months.

Solidarity aside, another reason for The Clash accepting Malcolm's offer was to pip The Damned in the punk pecking order. In two days time, the Croydon quartet were set to support the Sex Pistols at the 100 Club; the subterranean Oxford Street jazz club having become the nascent scene's home owing to the Pistols' ongoing Tuesday night residency.

Bernard's having re-established a working relationship with Malcolm meant the latter would allow The Clash to bask in the Pistols' reflected glory, but the few music journalists championing punk rock – notably *Melody Maker*'s Caroline Coon and Jonh Ingham from *Sounds* – were unlikely to pass up on the chance to see The Ramones in favour of schlepping up the M1 to the wilds of South Riding.

Having recruited Terry Chimes, who'd bizarrely been turned down when auditioning for the London SS drum stool a couple of months earlier, The Clash had retreated behind closed doors and rehearsed feverishly in order to knock a thirty-minute set into shape for the Sheffield date. Another priority to be addressed in the short time available was what the group might wear for their first foray on to a stage. For despite Bernard's involvement with the risqué T-shirts on sale at 430 King's Road, copying the Sex Pistols' look would have left The Clash open to ridicule.

'We were dressed in black and white,' Mick subsequently revealed. 'A couple of us had ties on, black and white shirts with suity bits. Not good suits, a bit ripped, slightly different. We were dressed fairly straight and well-behaved in a way – maybe a rip here and a little splash of colour there; a couple of pin-type things – not safety pins. The look was still formulating.'[1]

By Mick's estimation the punters gathered in the pub's back room numbered about fifty, out of which only two appeared as though they were there for the music rather than the mead. 'There were a couple of punks, it was interesting,' he said. 'Wherever you went you would see a couple of them in the early times. Then you would see them getting more all the time – they would tell their friends. It was a big thing.'[2]

Unfortunately for The Clash, however, while the 'couple of punks' in attendance might well have rushed off to tell their mates, neither thought to put pen to paper and fire off a favourable review to the *NME*'s Carnaby Street offices. As the *NME* at that juncture was curious rather than committed to the cause – which all the music industry's bigwigs thought would have imploded by Christmas – the paper was happy to run with an anonymous missive sent in by one of the Black Swan's less-than-impressed regulars.

Citing The Clash's performance as a 'cacophonous barrage of noise', and belittling Paul's rudimentary style and glaring inability to tune his own instrument, the caustic correspondent continued his attack by saying how The Clash had 'failed dismally' in their attempt to play early Sixties R&B, before signing off by dismissing them as a second-rate Dr. Feelgood.

That the Sex Pistols' own performance suffered a similar mauling suggests the reviewer's musical tastes were too pure for punk's sonic assault on the senses, but given that Joe had left The 101'ers – who, it has to be said, were more than capable of holding their own against the Feelgoods, and had trod the Black Swan stage with the 101'ers – such a stinging critique would have been hard to ignore.

The Sex Pistols' much-vaunted first visit to Manchester's Lesser Free Trade Hall the previous month has since become part of Mancunian folklore owing to it having proved the catalyst for many of those in the audience to go away and form bands, which in turn laid the foundations for the Madchester music scene of the late-eighties and early-nineties, and yet conversely the Black Swan date failed to spark a similar reaction in Sheffield. What's perhaps even more surprising is that the show also escaped acquiring urban myth status in every Yorkshireman alive swearing they'd been there to witness the birth of The Clash.

♪♪♪

It was undoubtedly Mick's dissatisfaction at things going awry in Sheffield that lay behind The Clash's decision to retreat into Rehearsal Rehearsals to iron out the glitches. They also penned several new songs such as 'Deny', 48 Hours', Janie Jones', 'What's My Name?', and the apocryphal '1977', all of which were incorporated into the set. When The Clash finally deemed themselves ready for another crack at the stage, rather than cajole Malcolm into giving them another support slot Bernard opted for an invite-only show within the familiar settings of their rehearsal room.

The majority of the booking agents Bernard had invited dutifully came along, if only to gauge whether The Clash were indeed worthy of having their name added to the poster.

Only three of the music journalists on his list appeared willing to give up their Friday night, but Bernard was far from displeased as the three in question – Caroline Coon, Jonh Ingham and John's colleague, Giovanni Dadomo – were already proving sympathetic to the cause.

Being something of a perfectionist, Bernard made sure everything was just right – including the décor – and in doing so, he inadvertently gave The Clash an identity. 'By the second gig we had skinny ties and semi-smart jackets,' Mick recalled. 'We'd gone through the painting thing. Paul made the connection between Jackson Pollock, and our spritzing the paint on ourselves while giving the rehearsal room a lick of paint.'[3]

Glen Matlock has always contested that The Clash nicked the paint-spritzing idea from him as he'd purposely given a pair of SEX trousers the Jackson Pollock effect by flecking them with white gloss. And given that Glen had been enrolled at St. Martin's before swapping his brushes for a bass, his claim isn't without merit.

Comfortable within their paint-spritzed surroundings, and free from the nerves of playing to a paying crowd, The Clash put on a display that left those in the room in little doubt that here was a group to be reckoned with. Indeed, while penning his critique of their Rehearsals roustabout, Giovanni Dadomo described watching The Clash as akin to being repeatedly hit by a runaway fire engine, and declared them the first band to come along 'who'll really frighten the Sex Pistols shitless.'

Dadomo had signed off his review by saying he how couldn't wait to see them play in a real hall, in front of a real audience. He wouldn't have long to wait because Malcolm – as part of his ongoing determination to land the Sex Pistols a recording contract – invited The Clash (along with Buzzcocks) on to the bill for the Pistols' 'Midnight

Special' showcase at the Screen On The Green cinema in Islington on Saturday, 29 August.

Malcolm, of course, wasn't known for his altruism, and the offer came at a price. Aside from being given the task of posting the flyers, The Clash were also charged with providing the material needed for a stage, as well as erecting it on the night. Another sleight came with Buzzcocks and The Clash both being beset with sound problems throughout their respective sets; problems which were curiously rectified in time for the headliners.

Sabotaging your competitors' sound is one of the oldest tricks in the book, but one has to wonder why – especially when the general consensus within the Sex Pistols camp in regard to The Clash was that they 'weren't very good'[4] – Malcolm felt threatened enough that he had to resort to such underhand measures?

Dadomo, who was in the audience that night, rightly suspected underhand play, and when writing his review, cited the sound problems as having 'pole-axed The Clash's nuclear potential'.

One journalist unwilling to look beyond the malfunctioning PA, however, was the *NME*'s Charles Shaar Murray who uncharitably opined that The Clash were 'the kind of garage band who should be speedily returned to their garage, preferably with the motor running, which would undoubtedly be more of a loss to their friends and family than rock 'n' roll.'

The Clash were understandably hurt by Murray's put-down, for while *Melody Maker*'s Allan Jones had opined that the Sex Pistols 'do as much for music as World War II did for the cause of peace', he hadn't suggested a bomb be dropped on their Denmark Street domicile.

The Midnight Special may have proved an illusory dawn, but little could Mick, Joe, and Paul have known as they trudged away from the Screen On The Green that the events of the coming Bank Holiday Monday would provide one of the keystones to The Clash legend.

♪♪♪

London's inaugural Caribbean Carnival was staged at St. Pancras Town Hall in January 1959; the idea being to improve the morale of the West Indian Community of Notting Hill following the race riots of the previous year. With the carnival proving a resounding success, it was decided to make it an annual event and it alternated between the Seymour Hall at Marble Arch and the Lyceum on the Strand before relocating to Notting Hill in 1966.

As the carnival's starting point was the Emslie Horniman's Pleasance Park in Ladbroke Grove; Joe, Paul, Bernard, together with Joe's squat mate Pat Nother*, decided to partake in the festivities. As usual, there was a heavy police presence at the carnival, and with the black community having long since tired of what they considered unfair discrimination and harassment by the boys in blue, it wasn't long before tensions began to climb with the soaring temperature (the summer of 1976 was the hottest of the twentieth century).

The spark that lit the riotous flame of rebellion that balmy Bank Holiday afternoon came when a black youth was arrested near Portobello Road on suspicion of pick-pocketing. The youth's friends tried to intervene by pelting the arresting officers with bricks, and the ensuing scuffle quickly escalated to the point where riot police – armed with shields and batons – mounted a charge and within a matter of seconds the peaceful carnival descended into carnage.

Amid the melee, which Joe would later liken to a scene from *Zulu*, he and Paul forlornly – and rather foolishly, it has to be said – tried to set an upturned car alight with a box of matches.

As dusk fell, some 350 police officers had been injured, 68 over-zealous revellers had been arrested, and scores of buildings and cars had been looted or destroyed. Paul and Joe somehow managed to survive the melee with nary a scratch between them. Indeed, the only anxious moment came when they found themselves surrounded by a gang of black youths who demanded they turn out their pockets. Neither of them had any money, but Joe had a recently purchased second-hand transistor radio which he was refusing to give up and they could have ended up in hospital or worse had a dread whom Paul subsequently described as a 'Rasta General' not intervened.

On returning to the Davis Road squat the duo regaled Mick, Keith, and their other friends with what they'd witnessed – no doubt

---

* Pat's brother, Richard 'Snakehips Dudanski' Nother was the drummer with the 101'ers.

embellishing their involvement with each telling. With football hooliganism endemic in mid-Seventies Britain, London had seen its fair share of gang-related street brawls, but this was the first time a section of the community had risen up against the Establishment, and the experience taught them that while the blacks were prepared to stand on the barricades and shake a fist in the face of oppression, their more docile white counterparts had seemingly been schooled to accept their lot in life.

Unable to shake the thought of the Englishman's subservience to the state, Joe committed his musings to paper. The following afternoon at Rehearsals, Mick came up with an incendiary riff to match the lyric, and 'White Riot' received its first public airing on Tuesday, 31 August when The Clash supported the Sex Pistols at the 100 Club.

♪♪♪

Six days later, Mick fulfilled one of his ambitions when The Clash played the Roundhouse where he'd regularly seen Mott The Hoople. Headlining that particular weekend's 'Sundae Outing' were pub-rock stalwarts Kursaal Flyers, with rockabilly revivalists Crazy Cavan 'N' The Rhythm Rockers (featuring a pre-lip quivering Shakin' Stevens) second on the bill. This show would prove another footnote in The Clash's history as it was the last to feature Keith Levene in the line-up.

'Keith left the band because he couldn't be bothered to come to rehearsals,' Mick explained. 'As I recall, he actually said, "I can't be bothered to come to rehearsals," so Joe said, "Well, don't bloody bother to come again!"'[5]

Keith may well have voiced his disinterest in rehearsing, but Terry remembers how it was Mick's playing devil's advocate which set Keith up for the fall. 'Mick was putting forward the idea in a very roundabout way that they didn't need three guitar players in the band,' he revealed. 'I wasn't listening very much, but Joe said, "Shall we get rid of him then?" I jumped then, and thought, "You can't get rid of someone just on a whim." I thought it was Joe and his crazy behaviour, but Paul, who didn't really say very much, said, "I think you're right."'[6]

Terry may have been shocked, but in hindsight it's easy to understand why the others had all been secretly imagining a Keith-less Clash. With Keith out of the way Mick could take the lead on guitar, Paul could make the left-hand side of the stage his own, while serving notice on Keith provided Joe with an opportunity to put the Stalinistic ruthlessness Bernard had instilled into him into practice.

Bernard, however, was left somewhat piqued, if only because the decision to get rid of Keith had been made behind his back. He also feared that Mick wasn't yet up to the job of leading the line, and in an attempt to reaffirm his authority he briefly contemplated bringing Eunan Brady in as Keith's replacement until discovering the former Hollywood Brat was twenty-seven years old.

On Monday, 20 September 1976, The Clash returned to Oxford Street to play the opening night of the '100 Club Punk Festival'; the two-day event, which, though billed as a festival, was in fact simply another grandstanding vehicle for Malcolm to showcase the Sex Pistols' talents.

Another reason for Malcolm's decision to stage a punk festival in London came in response to the Sex Pistols having been excluded from the recent 'First European Punk Festival' – staged within a bullring in Mont de Marsan in southern France – owing to their reputation. The Clash and The Damned had been invited to appear at the French festival, but while The Clash promptly withdrew in another show of solidarity to the Pistols, The Damned had no such compunction and readily accompanied Nick Lowe, The Pink Fairies, Roogalator, and Eddie and the Hot Rods to Dover.

The problem facing Malcolm, of course, was that whilst the London scene was gathering a-pace, there weren't enough bona fide punk bands to merit the term 'festival'. However, unlike the Goldsmiths Free Festival debacle of several years earlier when Malcolm had incurred the wrath of the college's faculty and his fellow students when King Crimson, The Pretty Things, and none of the other named acts he'd supposedly booked showed up, he could at least guarantee the Sex Pistols' and The Clash's participation.

With The Damned headlining the Tuesday night bill, which also featured Buzzcocks, and The Vibrators (with Chris Spedding guesting),

Malcolm shored up Monday night's fare by inviting Parisian punk outfit, Stinky Toys, as well as giving Susan 'Siouxsie Sioux' Ballion's Banshees, and the equally untested Subway Sect their respective stage débuts.

'It [the Punk Festival] was quite important because it brought everyone together in one room for the first time,' Joe later recalled. 'And it was historically important because of Siouxsie and the Banshees playing, with Future Sex Pistol bassist Sid Vicious on the drums. We could see for the first time that we had something; that we weren't on our own.'[7]

The festival may have brought everyone on the scene under the one umbrella so to speak, but there was precious little evidence of the solidarity to which Joe alludes. Aside from the inter-group back-biting, a row erupted when Bernard – having taken umbrage to Siouxsie sporting a swastika armband – refused to allow the Banshees the use of The Clash's PA – now painted a distinctive bubblegum pink to thwart any opportunistic 'borrowing'.

Sid, who was sporting a ripped-up T-shirt festooned with crudely-drawn swastikas, escalated the situation by calling Bernard a 'fucking mean old Jew', which might well have curtailed the Banshees' career before it had even started had it not been for Malcolm stepping in and allowing them to use the Sex Pistols' backline.

♪♪♪

Up until the 100 Club festival, punk had largely been the preserve of a smattering of disaffected youths and bored middle-class art students, but following Sid's glass-throwing antics during The Damned's performance – which resulted in the 100 Club effecting a blanket-ban on punk – the latest musical craze began to attract some rather more unbalanced characters whose antics would come to be interwoven into punk's bondage-strapped tapestry over the proceeding decades.

When The Clash played the Institute of Contemporary Arts – billed as 'A Night of Pure Energy' – a month or so later on 23 October, Jane Crockford, or 'Mad Jane' as she was more colourfully known to one and all, supposedly got so caught up in the mood that she threw herself at future Pogues frontman Shane MacGowan and tore a chunk from his right ear.

This was also the night that Patti Smith jumped up on stage. Paul has since admitted that he'd been about to swing a paint-splattered boot at the uninvited interloper before realising it was the celebrated punk poetess. Paul was lucky to be on stage himself seeing as he'd come uncomfortably close to spending the night in the cells, as Bernard explained: 'After the soundcheck, Paul and I went out for a walk. Paul found a roll of film screens and he thought he might try sticking them onto his clothes to see what they would look like. We set off up the road but a cop car pulled us up. "What have you got there?" The screens were pornographic. I thought, "Oh no, we've got a gig to do and they're gonna nick my bass player."

'They eventually let us go, but I'd borrowed a friend's car for the night and Paul left the screens in the car. The next day the owner rings up saying his wife had found the screens, and he didn't know where the fuck they'd come from.'

A fortnight later on Guy Fawkes Night The Clash staged their own 'Night of Treason' at the Royal College of Art in Kensington Gore. It would prove a trying time as a section of the crowd were hostile throughout, and expressed their displeasure by pelting the stage with glasses and bottles. The barrage got so bad that Terry was forced to adjust his cymbals. Of course, Mick, Joe, and Paul didn't have the luxury of having cymbals to hide behind and were occasionally called upon to play defensive strokes with their guitars.

The mood was getting uglier by the minute, and when fighting inevitably broke out in front of the stage it seemed as though The Clash would be forced to abandon the show. However, whilst Mick was pondering whether discretion might indeed be the better part of valour, Sid appeared as if out of nowhere and waded into the mêlée with both fists pumping.

Following his recent release from Ashford Remand Centre, where he'd spent several weeks supposedly curbing his enthusiasm for mindless violence, the future Sex Pistol was temporarily bedding down at The Clash's rehearsal space and had realigned his loyalties accordingly. Seeing as the heavily outnumbered Sid was defending their honour, Joe and Paul had felt honour bound to down tools and dive in to even up the numbers. Mick, however, chose to remain a passive spectator.

On returning to the stage once order had been restored Joe and Paul had angrily questioned Mick as to why he hadn't jumped in with them. 'Well, someone's got to keep in tune,' came the reply.

It was at the ICA show that Stephen 'Roadent' Connelly first entered The Clash's domain; his having recently arrived in London from his native Coventry following his release from Winson Green Prison. 'I couldn't go wasting the few quid I had on a ticket, and so I asked Joe if they needed a hand with their gear,' Roadent explained. 'Then when Joe learnt I didn't have anywhere to sleep that night he immediately offered me a mattress at Rehearsals.'

While Roadent is undoubtedly splendid company – especially when he's in his cups – there is neither rhyme nor reason behind Joe's show of benevolence other than his perhaps recognising a kindred spirit. For like Joe, Roadent has tried very hard to distance himself from the privileged private education he received courtesy of a state bursary. Indeed, it is only when he is sufficiently lubricated with gin that the 'H's he drops with deafening regularity deftly take their proper place. But as they say, nothing polishes a diamond quite like its own dust.

Roadent moved into the upstairs space where Paul was already living to share the room's basic amenities – an arrangement which might have proved awkward had it not been for their shared mischievous child-like nature. Indeed, it was Paul who would bestow him his long-standing nickname. He also received a new pair of socks courtesy of The Clash kitty, along with free membership into the group's ever-growing inner-circle.

Roadent says he and Joe also gelled immediately owing to their shared passion for history and politics – not to mention their fascination for European terrorist groups such as the Red Army Faction, Brigate Rosse [Red Brigade] and the Baader-Meinhof Gang. Mick, however, considered him nothing more than a hired-hand. 'The only one I found it hard to get on with was Mick,' he shrugged matter-of-factly. 'But then, didn't everyone…?'

Roadent was only just getting acquainted with Terry when he – having grown weary of Bernard's rhetoric, and the constant inter-group politicking – announced his departure. 'I just thought I'm not happy, and what's the point of being here if I'm not happy,' Terry explained. 'I thought Bernie would be happy, but he wasn't. He said, 'Look, you're the foil. Whenever they [Mick, Joe and Paul] come up with something, you say what the man in the street or the press would say, you immediately confront them with the rational argument against what they're saying. If they can get past you, they can get past the world without being shot down in the first minute.'[8]

Terry, however, remained unmoved by Bernard's argument, though he did agree to honour The Clash's up-and-coming commitments which included their first proper demo session for Polydor Records at the label's Marble Arch studios.

Having lost out to EMI in securing the Sex Pistols' signatures, Polydor's A&R head, Chris Parry, had realigned his sights on the next group on the punk pecking order. Much to Mick's chagrin, the producer Bernard chose to oversee the sessions was none other than Guy Stevens.

'Polydor set us up to do some demo recordings, and Bernie suggested we try working with Guy,' Mick explained. 'We went in and banged out four or five numbers – ('White Riot', 'London's Burning', 'Career Opportunities', 'Janie Jones' and '1977') – which were the first in our live set. I think Guy went to the pub or something and didn't come back, so I don't know how they got finished. 'I was really excited about going into the studio and it was probably overwhelming. I didn't notice anything that was going on in too much detail because I was just getting carried away with it all.'[9]

Guy's going AWOL meant Polydor's resident engineer had to step up to the plate, and his having no idea as to who or what The Clash were – coupled with his insistence that Joe enunciate every syllable – left the group understandably unhappy with the finished results.

– CHAPTER SIX –

WHO NEEDS REMOTE CONTROL...?

*'Well as far as The Clash and songs like "White Riot"
[are concerned], the thing behind it all was Joe. In
that case Joe was the prophet of that, like they talk
about "Cheat The Prophet" and G K Chesterton, it's
a game people play. They recognise what's happening
and imagine it in the future. Well that's it – Joe was the
prophet, I just put the music to it.'*

– Mick Jones

TERRY'S DEPARTURE WAS certainly a blow, but it was far from a
knock-down. Having selected a Sussex University attendee called
Rob Harper from the pool of hopefuls – which included Paul's younger
brother, Nick – The Clash began rehearsing with Harper to put their
new drummer through his paces. Time was of the essence as they
were set to go out on the road on the impending nineteen-date punk-
package tour that Malcolm had put together in order to promote the
Sex Pistols' debut single 'Anarchy In The UK'.

The Anarchy In The UK Tour was set to commence at the
University of East Anglia on Friday, 3 December. Aside from The
Clash, the tour's support bill consisted of ex-New York Doll Johnny
Thunders' new outfit, The Heartbreakers, and The Damned. The
Sex Pistols would be picking up the tab for The Heartbreakers and
The Clash, but as The Damned were signed to Stiff Records – the
recently incorporated independent label set up by Dave Robinson

and Andrew Jakeman, a.k.a Jake Riviera – Malcolm was insistent that they pay their own way.

In a fit of pique, Riviera said that if The Damned were to be treated differently, then they would travel separately.

Malcolm's high-handedness towards The Damned was primarily due to an on-going spat with Riviera in the wake of Stiff's releasing 'New Rose', and yet he'd been forced to invite them onto the tour to assuage worries about the Sex Pistols being a big enough draw to fill some of the larger venues on the tour. But of course, any worries he may have had about the Sex Pistols' pulling power were swept asunder by the ensuing tabloid tsunami following their appearance on Thames TV's weekday magazine news programme *Today*, two days prior to the tour.

With EMI owning a fifty per cent stake in Thames, the Pistols had been hurriedly drafted in to replace the end-of-show screening of the promo video for Queen's latest single 'Somebody To Love', which couldn't be screened owing to the video not having received clearance by the all-important Musicians' Union*. What should have been an innocuous three-minute interview – during which a clip of the promo video to 'Anarchy In The UK' was screened – to allow the Sex Pistols to plug both the single and the tour, descended into four-letter farce when the show's boorish host Bill Grundy wilfully goaded Steve Jones to 'say something outrageous' on prime-time television.

The 'Filth & Fury' headlines of the following morning were a marketing man's dream, and transformed the hitherto relatively unknown Sex Pistols into a household name. Yet the ensuing knee-jerk reactions from various councils, civic leaders, and educational authorities – shamefully aided and abetted by Fleet Street's morality-mongers – left the Anarchy Tour's itinerary in ruins.

'Punk exploded with the Grundy show,' Mick said. 'Then there was the lorry driver who smashed his telly in when the Sex Pistols were on it and the whole thing started to affect us. Loads of dates on the Anarchy Tour were cancelled because of it, but punk was massive by then.'[1]

---

* An alternate version of events has Queen pulling out from appearing on *Today* owing to Freddie Mercury recovering from dental treatment.

Newcastle's outraged councillors had already slapped a banning order on the Sex Pistols crossing the Tyne by the time Frank Thistlewaite, the vice-chancellor at the University of East Anglia, decided to exceed his authority by overriding the Student Union's protests and cancelling the opening show. The tour party had little choice but to make for Derby, the next stop on the itinerary, but this date fell foul of the local council who tried bringing the naughty Sex Pistols to task by insisting they perform a 'behind-closed-doors' matinee for the town's Leisure Committee.

The Leisure Committee had said the other bands on the bill could still play regardless of Malcolm's decision over the matinee, but given that he was picking up The Clash and The Heartbreakers' tabs, both acts told the committee where it could shove its offer. Despite there being little love lost between their respective managers, The Damned would have also shown solidarity had they been given the option. However, as they were charting their own course from venue to venue, they were holed up in a B&B on the other side of town unaware of Malcolm's last-minute subterfuge.

From that point on the tour rapidly descended into pantomimic farce, and despite Malcolm's valiant efforts to find alternate venues, only three of the nineteen dates went ahead as scheduled. Yet while the tour served as the Sex Pistols' tumbrel ride through the streets before being hung out to dry by their corporate paymasters, The Clash came away with plenty of positives. Not only had they played in far-flung places such as Plymouth, Cleethorpes, and Caerphilly, but whilst out on the road the *NME* had devoted a two-page feature to the group entitled 'Eighteen Flight Rock, and the Sound of the Westway'.

The paper had also sent their hip young gunslinger Paul Morley out on the road to cover the tour. Though he would describe The Clash's 'high energy surges of arrangements as being surprisingly only a few steps removed from Showaddywaddy', he was suitably impressed with their 'rhythmically strident sound', and signed off proclaiming them to be 'the best rock 'n' roll band in London.'

With such heady praise ringing in their ears, The Clash returned to London knowing their days of playing second fiddle to the Sex Pistols were over.

♫♫♫

On New Year's Day 1977, The Clash rang the changes with two rhythmically strident performances at London's new premier punk venue, The Roxy. The Covent Garden venue had been staging live shows since mid-December when Tony James' new outfit, Generation X, and Siouxsie and the Banshees had broken in its boards, but the new leaseholder, Andy Czezowski, had designated the opening day of the year as the club's official unveiling.

Czezowski had initially wanted to give the honour of headlining to the Sex Pistols with The Clash in support, but since returning to London Malcolm had now developed something of a siege mentality where his charges were concerned. The Clash, of course, were more than happy to herald in the New Year as it gave them the perfect platform to launch their sonic assault on the year when the two sevens clashed.

According to the Jamaican political leader Marcus Garvey, who'd advocated the return of the African Diaspora to their ancestral lands, 1977 was to be the year of great upheaval. The year the Rastafarians would return to Ethiopia, the spiritual homeland where their ancestors had lived before being dragged off to a life of slavery in the colonies.

Mick must have sensed a portentous whiff in the air as he and Paul had been born the year the two fives had come together, and of course, England had lifted the World Cup eleven years later. So it's ironic that in the opening month of this supposedly apocryphal year when the downtrodden blacks would be symbolically freed, that The Clash signed a recording contract that would enslave them to CBS (Columbia Broadcasting System) for the rest of their career and beyond.

'I don't remember signing anything particularly at CBS – we didn't sign any photos or anything. It seemed to be over so fast,' Mick later reflected. 'I guess Bernie didn't have enough [cash] to organise any stunts to celebrate it, so we went to the pictures.'[2]

As with Joe and Paul, Mick had assumed The Clash would be signing with Polydor, seeing as they'd gone so far as recording some demos for the label. But with CBS offering £100,000 compared to Polydor's

£40,000, just as he had with the Sex Pistols several months earlier, the hapless Chris Parry would see his prize lured elsewhere by more appetising bait.

As they sat in the darkened cinema watching Charlton Heston and Henry Fonda heading a star-studded cast in *Battle Of Midway*, which chronicled the decisive naval battle that proved a turning point in the Pacific theatre during World War II, The Clash could have been forgiven for thinking they'd reached a similar pivotal juncture in their career. Sniffin' Glue's Mark P. wasted little time in accusing The Clash of 'selling out', but it was more a case of them selling their souls because the contract weighed heavily in CBS's favour. Aside from the £100,000 advance having to cover recording costs, hidden away within the legal jargon was an option allowing the label to insist on eight or even ten albums – an option they would exercise in due course. And of course, Bernard, as per his contractual rights, creamed his twenty per cent off the top tax free.

'It's true that Chris Parry had tabled an offer for £40,000, but I wasn't gonna turn down £100,000, was I?' Bernard shrugged. 'Obie [Maurice Oberstein, CBS' CEO] wasn't all that interested in punk, except for the dollars he could add to the balance sheet. I was on my to CBS' offices in Soho Square when I bumped into Malcolm. I knew he was keen to find another label for the Pistols so I invited him to come along. Obie said he'd give us £100,000 to set up our own label and CBS would distribute the records.

'Malcolm said he was interested and that he wanted time to think about it, but as soon as we got outside he changed his tune and said he wasn't going to be held to ransom by CBS. He then asked if he could borrow a fiver for a cab back to the King's Road. I thought, "How can you turn down £100,000 and then ask for a fiver?" But that was Malcolm. I gave him the fiver, went back in to see Obie to explain the situation, and he said I could have the £100,000 for The Clash.'

CBS were naturally keen to start recouping their six-figure outlay, and with Terry Chimes temporarily returned to the fold The Clash shuffled into CBS' compact No. 3 Studio in Whitfield Street (since demolished) on 10 February for the first of three consecutive long weekends, to begin work on their self-titled debut album.

With this being the same studio where Iggy and the Stooges had recorded *Raw Power* some three years earlier, Mick was in his element. 'I was born for this [to make music],' he enthused. 'To tell you the truth it was all I ever wanted to do. I remember going to the career's officer when I was a kid leaving school and the career officer said, "what do you want to do?" and I said, "I want to play in a band" and they said, "Well all we can do is civil service or the armed forces, that's all we have. So good luck to you but we can't help you in any way." But I always knew what I wanted to do.'[3]

The studio offered a reduced rate at the weekend, but with the recording costs coming out of The Clash's collective pocket, speed was again of the essence. To ensure the needle stayed in the red during the marathon sessions, speed of an altogether different nature was thrown into the mix as Mick later revealed to Caroline Coon: 'Two years ago we did the band's first interview on Janet Street-Porter's London Weekend Programme. And me, being all naïve, I blamed bands taking too many drugs for the great mid-Seventies drought in rock. I recall saying it really well and a year or so later I found myself doing just as many drugs as them! I was so into speed, I mean, I don't even recall making the first album!'[4]

The first weekend session was taken up laying down the basic tracks of the thirteen songs slated for the album, but on discovering that the running time was coming in at less than thirty minutes the decision was taken to include their version of Junior Murvin's 'Police & Thieves', which at 6.05 minutes, was three times longer than most of their own compositions. Murvin's lament about gang war and police brutality in his native Kingston – co-written and produced by the legendary Lee 'Scratch' Perry – had proved a hit in Jamaica when it was released the previous year, and The Clash believed its subject matter would strike a similar chord with their audiences.

According to Mick's recollections, Perry initially struggled to grasp what The Clash were attempting. 'Lee had been telling Bob Marley about it, and he was saying, well, I'm not sure about what these punks are about,' he said in November 2007. 'Marley was one of the guys who said, "No, you should see, it's good." He kind of responded by writing that song "Punky Reggae Party". He was asking questions and finding out if we were rebels, too.'[5]

Rather than kid himself that he could emulate Murvin's falsetto range, Joe sang the vocal in his customary gruff style leaving Mick to harmonise the higher notes. And what a perceptive song choice 'Police & Thieves' would prove to be, because the punky/reggae hybrid not only removed any chance of *The Clash* being cynically regarded as the best album the Ramones never made, but it showed the critics that they were a clear cut above the scene's other one-trick ponies.

Prior to releasing the album, CBS tested the water by issuing 'White Riot' as The Clash's debut single on 18 March. With its inflammatory title 'White Riot' was never going to feature on the Radio One daytime play-lists, but thanks to the band's burgeoning fan-base the single did at least manage to scrape into the UK Top 40 (peaking at number 38).

The parent album was released on 8 April; the front cover dominated with a photo of Mick, Joe, and Paul striking a mean and moody pose on the cobbled access ramp of the old Tack Room opposite the entrance to their rehearsal space.

To the uninitiated, the photo – snapped by New York-based photographer Kate Simon – served as a perfect introductory statement of intent for the album's no-nonsense onslaught. From the staccato drumbeat intro to 'Janie Jones' to the lilting melancholic refrain of 'Garageland', the listener is carried along on a ride of relentless rhythms, accentuated with primitive yet proficient rock 'n' roll rebellion.

The Clash fared well with the critics, with the NME's resident Clashophile, Tony Parsons – having echoed Paul Morley's proclamation that The Clash were currently the best rock 'n' roll band in London, lavishing further praise in saying they'd 'made an album consisting of some of the most exciting rock 'n' roll in contemporary music'.

The first 10,000 punters to be swayed into buying the album by Parsons' partisanship could also take advantage of the *NME's* free Clash EP offer by peeling the red sticker from the album's inner sleeve and sending it in coupled with the special 'A Riot Of Your Own' ad which appeared in the paper's 2 April issue (which also featured The Clash on the front cover).

Aside from the subterranean Circle Line interview which Parsons conducted with the group, the give-away flexi-disc also contained hitherto unreleased Clash material – a twenty-eight second edit of 'Listen' and 'Capital Radio'.

Though appreciative of Joe's and Paul's respective worth, the opening paragraph of Parsons' 'Sten Guns In Knightsbridge' interview, which had also appeared in the *NME*'s 2 April issue, reads like an ode to Mick: 'You don't know what total commitment is until you've met Mick Jones of The Clash. He's intense, emotional, manic depressive and plays lead guitar with the kind of suicidal energy that some musicians lose and most musicians never have.'

Nor could Parsons resist borrowing from Giovanni Dadomo's copybook by making mention of Mick's 'uncanny resemblance to a young Keef Richard', and saying the Clash guitarist was possibly leaning on said similitude as a means of relieving an early identity problem.

Mick retorted to the Stone-clone jibe by insisting he didn't believe in guitar heroes. 'I got my self-respect in this group. If I walk out to the front of the stage it's because I wanna reach the audience, I want to communicate with them. I don't want them to suck my guitar off.'[6]

♪♪♪

Joe would subsequently claim that The Clash auditioned every jobbing drummer in London following Terry Chimes' latest departure before finally striking gold with the happy-go-lucky twenty-one-year-old Nicholas Bowen Headon.

The soon-to-be-rechristened 'Topper' (on account of his resemblance to 'Mickey the Monkey' from the *Topper* comic) was already known to Mick from his having auditioned for London SS. Their paths had crossed again at a recent Kinks show at the Rainbow. 'I'd never seen them [The Clash] play, but I was really excited as soon as I did. They are incredible,' he told the *Melody Maker* during his public unveiling. 'I really wanted to join. They are by far the best band in the country.'

'We'd come along a bit, Mick jokingly told *The Telegraph*'s Andrew Perry in Sept 2013. 'So when I asked, he was much more like, "Oh right, I might actually join these guys."'

Born and raised in Kent, Topper had taught himself to play piano before switching to the drums while still at school. His weekends were usually taken up playing with a Dover-based jazz outfit called Force 9, but found he could keep the beat with any form of music.

Upon leaving school with three O-Levels to his name, he'd secured a position as a shipping clerk at the town's docks – where, coincidentally, his boss was the father-in-law of soon-to-be Clash road manager, Johnny Green. But after twelve months of diligently processing outgoing shipments, Topper's mind was beginning to wander – wander all the way to London.

The first thing he did upon arrival in the capital was marry his sweetheart Wendy, and with the nuptials taken care of he then began perusing the 'Musicians Wanted' section in the *Melody Maker* classifieds.

Bernard would, of course, subsequently dismiss Topper as a 'provincial tosser', but there is no truer adage in rock 'n' roll than that of a group being only as good as its drummer. With Topper taking over the drum stool, The Clash's engine room was stoked to the max. They were now ready to take the Westway sound to every point on the compass.

On Sunday, 1 May 1977, just six months on from having been bottom of the pile on the Anarchy Tour, The Clash kick-started their own headline punk-package UK tour to promote *The Clash* at the Guildford Civic Hall. Fellow Anarchy Tour survivors, Buzzcocks, who'd filled in for the expunged Damned for the first of the ill-fated tour's visits to Manchester's Electric Circus, were on the bill, along with The Jam Subway Sect, and The Slits*.

The shambolic Anarchy Tour had served to keep punk rock in the public eye in the wake of the Sex Pistols' teatime contretemps with Bill Grundy, and while the White Riot Tour – as the massive 25-date tour was called – was further evidence that the latest teenage musical trend wasn't a passing phase. For nine months The Clash had been singing about wanting a riot of their own, and with the punk rock genie now out of its bottle they were about to get their wish…

The 3000 all-seater Rainbow Theatre on the Seven Sisters Road was by far the biggest venue The Clash had played to date. In its former

---

* The Birmingham-based Prefects appeared on the billing at several shows.

guise as the Astoria Theatre, the cinema had staged numerous one-off music events during the 1960s – most notably the night Jimi Hendrix first set light to his guitar back in March 1967.

The Clash didn't set fire to their equipment, but the audience's exuberance resulted in some two hundred stall seats being trashed. The ensuing 'Punk Rock Shock Horror!' headlines the following morning were perhaps to be expected given Fleet Street's propensity for never allowing the truth to get in the way of a good story. In this instance, however; the hyperbole was wholly unwarranted as an agreement had been reached beforehand whereby The Clash would cover the cost of any damages incurred during the performance.

The White Riot Tour might have been a success in terms of exposing The Clash to the masses, from a financial point it was an unmitigated disaster as the tour ran up loses estimated at £28,000 – more than a quarter of their CBS advance. A sizeable chunk of said losses came from the impromptu Rainbow renovations, but the majority went on subsidising Subway Sect and The Slits who as yet were both still unsigned acts.

Though initially happy to go along with this show of punk solidarity, it wasn't long before The Jam's management – namely Paul Weller's dad, John – began making grumbling noises about what The Jam were getting in return for the alleged four-figure sum they'd handed over to play the opening ten dates on the tour. As a result, the Woking three-piece, whose debut album *In the City* was holding its own in the album chart despite the critics' tepid response, left the tour immediately after the Rainbow date.

It wasn't only rival acts with whom The Clash now found themselves at loggerheads, however, because midway through the tour CBS decided to ride roughshod over the group's supposed 'complete artistic control' by releasing 'Remote Control' b/w 'London's Burning' as the follow-up single.

Mick had penned 'Remote Control's acerbic lyric about governmental pressure and interference in everyday life shortly after The Clash had returned to London following the ill-fated Anarchy Tour. In light of CBS's high-handed attitude he may well have considered amending a certain line to read: 'they had a meeting in Soho Square' as this was where CBS' London offices were located at the time.

Of course, the silver lining from the 'Remote Control' debacle was that it incited the group to pen 'Complete Control', which is indisputably one of the best songs within the Clash canon.

♫♪

On 20 October, and less than a fortnight since returning to Britain following a mini-European jaunt, The Clash flew to Belfast to kick-start their twenty-one-date Get Out Of Control Tour – with Richard Hell and the Voidoids in support – at the troubled city's Ulster Hall Polytechnic. Or at least that's what they thought...

Their attempt to be the first punk/new wave group to play Belfast would ultimately be thwarted by jobsworth insurance brokers who withdrew the Ulster Hall's policy owing to The Clash supposedly having several outstanding insurance claims against them back on the mainland.

When the spiky-haired, leather-clad throng – which included the then unknown Stiff Little Fingers' frontman Jake Burns – gathering outside the Ulster Hall discovered the show had been cancelled courtesy of periodic announcements on local radio and TV, they marched on the Europa Hotel on Great Victoria Street where The Clash were rumoured to be staying.

When the group emerged out onto the street to try and placate the crowd, several police cars screamed into view with lights flashing and sirens blaring. While the police maintained a healthy distance as though unsure how to handle a hoard of irked punk rockers, The Clash attempted to assuage the irate fans by announcing plans were ongoing to try and re-stage the show at the nearby Queens University. They'd also offered to underwrite any damages incurred, as they had with the Ulster Hall, but such assurances failed to hold sway with the university's faculty. And when the punks lay down in the road in protest pandemonium ensued.

'The most horrible thing was the way the kids were treated – the way they were pushed around,' Mick explained a few days later. 'They didn't have a chance to understand what was happening, so they were disappointed in us. Obviously, it wasn't our fault, but you can't explain that to eight hundred people personally.'[7]

Earlier in the day, Mick and Joe had gone along to the local radio station, Downtown Radio, to give an interview, but had no sooner alighted from the car when they were pounced upon by security officers suspecting them – owing to their zip-infested custom-made 'Street-fighter fatigues' courtesy of Alex Michon – of belonging to the loyalist paramilitary organisation, the UDA (Ulster Defence Association).

This should have been the cue to high-tail it back to the hotel bar until show-time, but someone within The Clash retinue thought it a good idea to take the group on a whirlwind tour of the province's less salubrious sights and have them pose in front of a bomb-damaged pub with its blackened windows boarded up.

The Clash might look menacing strutting about Camden in their urban guerrilla chic, but doing so on the Bogside where people were being maimed and murdered on a near daily basis was outlandish.

Even had the Ulster Hall show gone ahead, The Clash would have faced further ridicule as the stage backdrop they played against was a photographic blow-up of a Belfast street scene, replete with armoured cars and cowering civilians. While one could argue that The Clash were simply adding local flavour to the Rocco Macauley shot depicting the first baton charge by police at the Notting Hill Riot that adorns *The Clash*'s rear cover, the people of Belfast lived with the everyday threat of being struck down by a bullet rather than a baton or bottle.

Mick for one had been harbouring reservations about using the backdrop. 'I didn't think we should put it up here, because they aren't going to particularly want to be reminded of it,' he told Chris Salewitz later in the tour. 'In Bournemouth it's great because everyone is fucking asleep and it's really heavy because everyone is confronted by this stuff. But in Belfast, they don't need to be reminded.'[8]

Mick then went on to say how The Clash were sympathetic to what was going on in Belfast, and that they had empathy for the people. Yet again he was leaving the group open to ridicule, because empathy implies understanding and running the gauntlet at the Electric Circus doesn't even begin to compare to venturing out on the Falls Road after dark.

Aside from being frustrated at the last-ditch cancellation, Mick was disappointed on a personal level. He'd felt the Ulster Hall was going to be a great rock'n'roll show, and that the audience would be one of the best they'd yet played to. 'But of course, the bureaucrats and arseholes put their foot in it,' he lamented. 'But listen, you can be a catholic or a protestant kid, still come along and all be bouncing together. It's a cruel irony, the backdrop being associated with our group, and the authorities stamping on our concert.'[9]

To Mick's delight, his childhood literary hero Lester Bangs was chronicling the Get Out Of Control Tour for the *NME*. Yet while Lester – or 'Mo-lester' as Paul renamed the affable American – would subsequently 'fall in love and see the promised land', Roadent had finally grown weary of Mick's high-handed attitude and duly gave notice.

'It was in Edinburgh,' Roadent shrugged matter-of-factly, as if remembering a tooth extraction. 'It was obviously my job to see that everyone had what they needed for that night's show – strings, skins, plectrums, and what have you. When I got back at the venue – Clouds, I think – Mick came in being his usual self, and shouted, "Where've you been? Have you got my stuff?" He didn't even give me chance to reply before saying something about how I'd asked Richard Hell's people if they needed anything. That was it for me, and of course, that's when I uttered the immortal line: "Fuck off, Mick; you need a valet not a roadie."

'I got my train fare back to London off of Bernie, and the next day I went to the King's Road to see Malcolm and got a job with the Pistols.'

– CHAPTER SEVEN –

AND I LOOK TO MY LEFT...

'I don't know where our sound came from. I think your sound is a reflection of your personality; you'll always sound like you, no matter who you are. When I play you're hearing my whole life.'

– Mick Jones

GIVEN THAT THE CLASH had prophesied 1977 as a ground zero in terms of a musical changing of the guard, it is ironic that they should choose to knowingly lift the readily-recognisable tell-tale riff to The Who's 1964 hit 'I Can't Explain' for the their next single, 'Clash City Rockers'.

Mick was particularly pleased with the new song, possibly owing to it being the first time the group had dipped a toe into Mott The Hoople-esque self-mythology? His euphoria, however, faded away with the chimes of Prince Far-I upon giving the promo copy of the single a spin and discovering to his horror that the final cut had been vari-speeded without his being consulted. Filled with incandescent rage at the 'Pinky & Perky' mix, he set off in search of an explanation for this duplicitous act. Mick's search ended at the first door upon which he knocked as there was only one possible culprit... The Clash's in-house engineer, Micky Foote.

Micky had indeed put his finger to the vari-speeding trigger without first consulting Mick, but he had raised the question of the song's original tempo with Bernard. He'd also proposed that the group return to Whitfield Street to record the song again, but with some four months having passed since The Clash's last release Bernard was anxious to avoid incurring CBS's wrath for failing to deliver a new Clash single within the pre-agreed contractual deadlines.

So while Micky's tempo-tinkering had come with Bernard's approval, the latter – for the time being, at least – was beyond reproach, which left Micky without a chair once the music had stopped.

One could argue that Mick's refusal to budge on his insistence that Micky be expunged forthwith from The Clash's inner-circle was further evidence of the high-handedness that had caused Roadent to serve notice, but justification for the culling came with 'Clash City Rockers' stalling at number 35 on the Singles chart – some seven places lower than 'Complete Control'.

♪♪♪

The Clash's frenetic touring schedule of recent months might have allowed them to fashion a stage show breathtaking to behold, but it wasn't particularly conducive to their coming up with new material for the all-important follow-up album – evidence of which came with their having to co-opt an old 101'ers song (albeit with revised verses) for the B-side of 'Clash City Rockers'.

As a means of getting Mick and Joe's creative juices flowing again, Bernard surprisingly consented to Joe's proposal that the duo fly out to Kingston to get a real understanding of Jamaican culture. 'I only suggested it as a joke,' Joe later told the *Record Mirror*. In hindsight, their going 'to the place where every white face is an invitation to robbery'*, with not even a dog-eared Berlitz travel booklet to guide them along the way was asking for trouble. Indeed, had the locals not mistaken them for a couple of off-duty sailors – as Joe later surmised – then he and Mick may well have come to a sticky end.

Joe's joke would end up backfiring badly as he and Mick returned to London ten days later with precious little in the way of new songs to show for their Jamaican jaunt. 'We only wrote a couple of songs in Jamaica. "Safe European Home" and "Drug Stabbing Time", I think,'

---

* From 'Safe European Home'; the opening track on *Give 'Em Enough Rope*.

Mick later confessed. 'The rest were written in Britain, and even in the studio in New York.'[1]

The paucity of new material wasn't Bernard's only headache in relation to the follow-up album, however. Epic was still refusing to release *The Clash* in the US on the grounds that it wasn't 'radio friendly' (despite it being the best-selling import, shifting upwards of 100,000 in the twelve-month period April 1977 – April 1978) the label was keen to make The Clash's 'Westway sound' AOR (Adult Orientated Rock) friendly, and handed Bernard a short-list of potential producers. 'There was some suggestion at the time that our second album was being geared for the American market, which is why we got an American producer,' Mick reflected. 'But it was Bernie who introduced Sandy to the situation.'[1]

When it was first announced in the music press that Samuel 'Sandy' Pearlman – the power behind Blue Öyster Cult's worldwide success – would be producing the new Clash album, the news was greeted with widespread derision, and yet it's worth noting that Mark P. had deemed the Long Island rockers worthy enough to feature in the first issue of *Sniffin' Glue*.

Blue Öyster Cult may have benefited from being given the 'Pearlman Polish', but the rough-and-ready Clash were a totally different proposition in every sense of the word. And their relationship didn't get off to best of starts owing to Robin Crocker giving Pearlman a smack in the mouth when he tried busting in on the group backstage at the Lanchester Polytechnic.

One of those who witnessed Pearlman's going down for the count was The Clash's new road manager, Johnny Green (a.k.a. John Broad), who'd booked the Anarchy Tour to appear at Lancaster University, where he was enrolled studying Arabic languages, only to have the bra-burning feminists within the Student Union revoke the invitation on the grounds that punk music was sexist.

Johnny would be thrice thwarted in his attempts to see The Clash before he finally got his wish at Dublin's Trinity College on the Get Out Of Control Tour when he secured a ringside seat after being co-opted by the lighting crew to train a spotlight on Joe as he moved about the stage. He performed the task so well that he was asked if he wanted to tag along for the whole tour. Johnny hadn't needed asking twice, but he turned up at the Kinema in Dunfermline three days later only to find the lighting crew hadn't expected him to show and given the job to someone else.

His journey north of the border wasn't to be in vain; however, because the crew belonging to tour support act Richard Hell happened to be a man down. This happenstance of course, meant Johnny was perfectly placed for when Roadent took his official leave of absence from The Clash in Edinburgh two days later.

Johnny was two years older than Joe, and five years older than Paul and Topper, and had packed a lot of living into his twenty-seven years. His being something of a natural raconteur meant he inevitably found himself invited into The Clash's inner-sanctum, and by the tour's finale – which ended with three consecutive shows at the Rainbow – he was chauffeuring the group around in a rented mini-van. At the tour's end Johnny returned to his native Gillingham to spend Christmas with his parents, but the roadying bug had bitten hard and the New Year found him at Rehearsals occupying the grubby mattress vacated by Roadent.

When being interviewed for the *Viva Joe* documentary, Johnny – albeit tongue-in-cheek – says his involvement with The Clash came about owing to Roadent having 'fallen in love with Johnny Rotten.' Yet while Roadent was happy to don a Glitterbest trench coat to undertake certain extra-curricular activities such as the botched attempt to kidnap Nancy Spungen and bundle her on a plane back to New York whilst Sid was at the dentist, nowhere did his duties extend to wet-nursing Rotten or any other Sex Pistol quite like Johnny ended up doing for Mick.

A road manager's duties don't normally extend beyond picking up members of the group and delivering them to wherever they did to be at an appointed hour, but Johnny might as well have donned a butler's uniform before setting off to Pembridge Villas. Led Zeppelin's road manager Richard Cole was happy to chop out a line or roll a joint for Jimmy Page on occasion, but nowhere does he make any mention in his own on-the-road book, *Stairway To Heaven*, of his being called upon to flit about emptying ashtrays and putting the dirty glasses in the sink while Jimmy lounged around in bed sipping ice-chilled Ribena with some tart in his arms.

It could be argued, of course, that Mick's lack of personal restraint came from his having been primped and pampered throughout his formative teens by his doting nan and her sisters, but the rest of the group should all shoulder some of the blame for allowing Mick to repeatedly ignore the idiomatic inch in favour of the infinitely more appealing mile.

♪♪♪

If further proof was needed that The Clash were intent on veering away from the punk pulse beat then it came towards the end of June with the release of '(White Man) In Hammersmith Palais'. Aside from the glaring absence of The Clash's usual machine gun, three-chord thrash, the lyric goes so far as to belittle punk rockers of Everywhere UK for failing to notice what was going on in front of their eyes as they were all 'too busy fighting for a good place under the lighting'. Ironically, when The Clash played the Glasgow Apollo a week into the Out On Parole Tour on 4 July, many amongst the audience suffered a beating at the hands of the venue's bouncers for daring to express themselves under the lighting.

The Apollo's bouncers' notoriety for punching first and evicting second was legendary on the circuit, but while venting his frustrations after the show Joe was arrested for smashing a lemonade bottle. Paul soon followed Joe into the back of the Black Maria for daring to intercede. The coppers were looking to make a clean Clash sweep, but Johnny Green literally carried Topper to safety while Mick scurried back to the hotel to set up an emergency base of operations.

The idea to call The Clash's latest UK jaunt the 'Out On Parole Tour' was in response to Topper and Paul's recent incarceration at HMP Brixton following the fabled pigeon shooting incident that was subsequently mythologised in the song 'Guns On The Roof'.

With lyrics about 'torturing of all the women and children', and of 'putting the men to the gun', one could be forgiven for thinking The Clash had been involved in a siege akin to the one in Balcombe Street in Marylebone in December 1975, when an IRA cell held two hostages at gunpoint for six days within the media glare before surrendering, whereas the truth of the matter was that Paul and Topper had incurred the wrath of the anti-terrorist squad after downing several prized racing pigeons from the roof of their rehearsal space with an air-rifle.

Mick might never have had a cell door slam shut behind him, but he knew only too well from Robin's tales from his time inside what potential horrors awaited his friends the longer they remained detained at Her Majesty's pleasure. Unable to get hold of Bernard he called Caroline Coon, who was well seasoned in dealing with the machinations of the British penal system through her involvement with the charity organisation Release, which she had co-founded in 1967.

Joe and Paul's subsequent arrest in Glasgow had given the tour title an even more prophetic tone, and if Mick was beginning to feel left out then he needn't have worried as he would have his collar tugged after being found in possession of cannabis after the show at the King George's Hall in Blackburn on 13 July.

The group was staying at the long-since demolished Moat House Hotel on the outskirts of Blackburn, close to the M6. While subsequently recounting the tale of Mick's arrest, Johnny Green said that the hotel's irate manager – already getting hot under the collar from The Clash and their entourage wilfully spliffing up in the bar area – finally exploded when a pissed-up Robin Crocker 'pulled out his plonker and pissed in the pocket of the [pool] table.'[2]

With the bar now closed, everyone had begrudgingly made their way up to their rooms. Johnny was disgruntled to find Steve Jones – who'd joined The Clash on stage earlier in the evening for the encore – in his bed with some bird he'd picked up at the venue. This was the second time he'd returned to his room to find the ex-Sex Pistol soiling the bed sheets and was understandably pissed off; his sense of humour diminishing even more when two denim-clad drug squad detectives wrenched him from his slumber a couple of hours later.

The quick-thinking Johnny managed to convince the cops that the stash of white powder they found in his briefcase was chalk dust rather than amphetamine sulphate, and stalled them long enough to enable his sidekick, Baker* (a.k.a Barry Glare) to warn everyone to get rid of any incriminating substances, but he hadn't counted on Mick's inability to flush his entire stash.

Howard 'Mr. Nice' Marks probably has more cannabis resin under his fingernails at any given time than the piddling amount the cops unearthed in one of Mick's socks, but Blackburn CID's very own Starsky and Hutch were honour-bound to haul The Clash guitarist off to the cells. However, it wasn't his getting busted that was uppermost in Mick's mind as he emerged from the police station – ironically located to the rear of King George's Hall – but whether Steve Jones had an ulterior motive for showing up in Blackburn?

Serial ligger Steve had joined them on stage for the encore the previous night at Birmingham's Top Rank, but Mick hadn't thought anything was amiss and was happy to rehearse 'Pretty Vacant' as a special finale. However, when his namesake took to following them around in his battered second-hand black BMW, Mick confronted him and was bemused to hear Steve confess that he'd been under the impression he was auditioning for The Clash.

If Sandy Pearlman is to be believed, Steve was occupying Mick's traditional place to the right of the stage when the producer dropped by the 100 Club where The Clash were rehearsing during his flash visit to the UK at the beginning of the year.[3]

Just why The Clash would have been rehearsing at the 100 Club instead of Rehearsals has never been revealed, but Pearlman says that when he enquired about the situation he was informed that the others were angry with Mick for some reason and had thrown him out of the group. When asked what the reason might have been, Pearlman suggested that it could have been his wanting The Clash to be like Mott The Hoople.[4]

Johnny Green maintains that the reports of Mick's temporary sacking – like Mark Twain's demise – were greatly exaggerated, but of course, his position within the group's inner-circle meant he understood the pressures The Clash were under to come up with the goods for the second album. As Johnny says, you had to know the individual Clash members to understand their idiosyncrasies. Just because they had their rows didn't mean they wouldn't pull together when an outsider tried to interfere. Bernard was far from an outsider, but nor was he one of those going out night after night giving their all.

This was the second time Bernard had thought to bring a Sex Pistol into The Clash fold, but whereas Paul had shrugged off the rumours about his switching places with Glen, Mick took Bernard's meddling personally – very personally indeed. As far as he was concerned, his manager's card was marked.

♪♪♪

While the music press continued their ongoing fixation with John Lydon's post-Sex Pistols group, Public image Limited, following the release of their eponymous debut single, The Clash were ensconced at the Record Plant in New York with Sandy Pearlman adding the final touches to their follow up album which was given the provisional working title *All The Peacemakers* after the line from 'Police And Thieves'. The last-minute tinkerings could have probably been administered much closer to home at Basing Street Studios where the twelve tracks had been recorded, but of course the Portobello Road came in a very poor second compared to hanging out in New York. Mick and Joe had been in America since early August having flown out to San Francisco to link up with Pearlman at the Automatt; the state-of-the-art studio on Folsom Street a spit and a stride from the dock of the bay immortalised in song by Otis Redding. There was some serious work to be done with vocal and guitar overdubs, but the boys still found plenty of time to immerse themselves in all things Americana.

When they weren't making music they could usually be found checking out the likes of the Dead Kennedys, the Avengers, and the Nuns at the Mabuhay Gardens – or the 'Fab Mab' as it was colloquially known. San Francisco may no longer have been at the epicentre of the counter-culture revolution, but the city still enjoyed a vibrant music scene – especially with the advent of punk.

Whilst there they ran into Nick Lowe, the one-time Brinsley Schwartz bassist whose debut 1976 single, 'So It Goes' had provided

Tony Wilson with the name for his late-night TV show, and his current squeeze Carlene Carter, the step-daughter of Johnny Cash.

They also became acquainted with an eighteen-year-old half-Filipino singer called Pearl Gates. Pearl, who'd recently formed her own punk group, and changed her name to 'Pearl Harbor', was already attuned to The Clash's wavelength having bought *The Clash* on import. In the months ahead, Pearl would, of course, become even more ingratiated with The Clash: first by supporting them on US tours, and then by marrying the bass player.

It wasn't all play and no work, of course, and for three weeks Mick and Joe had toiled away doing everything asked of them in the studio. Yet despite Pearlman's subsequent boast of there being 'more guitars per square inch on this record than in anything else in the rest of Western civilisation,' CBS were less than thrilled with the results thus far.

This was the point where Mick and Joe supposedly threw their guitars out of the pram. 'We couldn't stand it any more,' Mick explained. 'We missed the other two [Paul and Topper] so much, and we wanted them to come over. So we went on strike.'[5]

Mick and Joe were obviously frustrated at CBS' nitpicking, but for Mick to say he and Joe 'went on strike' was stretching poetic license somewhat... unless they considered going on strike to mean relocating cross country to the Record Plant in New York where Pearlman had intended on conducting the final mixing?

The manner in which they made the 3000 mile journey betwixt seaboards suggests the two strikers were given a week's paid vacation to tempt them in from the picket line, because while Joe rented a flat-bed pick-up truck and traversed the US seaboards via the more scenic 66 route to New York, Mick accompanied Pearlman to Los Angeles to see Blue Öyster Cult play the Hollywood Palladium, 'I flew in on the Saturday night and saw it [New York] in all its glory at night,' Mick revealed. 'It was fantastically exciting, especially for someone like me who'd grown up watching American TV.'[6]

One of the less appealing attractions New York had to offer at that particular time, was the pitiful sight of Sid Vicious lumbering about the stage during his brief residency at Max's Kansas City; the preferred watering hole of Manhattan's artistic crowd.

Sid had relocated to the city the previous August with Nancy in the forlorn hope of establishing himself as a solo artist. However, while his being an ex-Sex Pistol gave Sid some gravitas amongst the jobbing musicians frequenting the Lower East Side, his inability to string two sentences together without his daily dose of methadone had seen his stock plummet quicker than the Wall Street Crash of seventy years earlier.

Mick would get to see first-hand just how far his one-time squat mate had fallen in the eight months since the Sex Pistols had imploded in San Francisco back in January when – having been cajoled into accepting Nancy's invitation by Joe – he found himself augmenting Sid's ad hoc backing group, The Idols, which did at least include the New York Dolls' rhythm section of Jerry Nolan and Arthur 'Killer' Kane. Aside from two of his one-time heroes, Mick was also familiar with the group's guitarist, Steve Dior, whom he knew from his Warrington Crescent days.

Indeed, Steve recalls seeing Mick playing in an ad hoc outfit calling themselves 'Lipstick Traces' with Eunan Brady, and Honest John Plain play Chiswick Polytechnic circa 1975. Of the songs played that night, Steve remembers the trio opening with the Batman theme, and playing the Stones' 'Midnight Rambler', The Stooges' 'I'm Sick On You', and the New York Dolls' 'Subway Train' and 'Looking For A Kiss'. He was also with Mick and Paul at the 101'ers Aklam Hall gig the night preceding their fabled encounter with Joe at the Lissom Grove Labour Exchange.

Sex Pistols die-hards continue to wax lyrical about how great the 21 September show was, but the bemused expression on Mick's face in Eileen Polk's photograph taken in the dressing room area after the show tells its own story. 'We just about managed five songs. Five songs for five bucks,' he subsequently reflected on his less than auspicious US live debut. 'It was a nightmare between shows (Sid was required to play two shows per night), it was full on. Sid was sort of semi there. It was a serious drug thing. Me and Joe kept looking at each other 'cos we couldn't believe it. The people there were as far out of it as you can be without actually being dead.'[7]

Little could Mick have imagined as he shared a backstage beer with Sid and Nancy that within a month Nancy would indeed be dead, and Sid would be facing a second degree murder charge.

Sid's fate was to be deemed vicious by nature as well as in name, but when speaking about his old friend in 2011, Mick remembered a very different Sid. '[He] could be quite an intimidating guy but when you got to know him he was a beautiful intelligent guy – and no one ever really says that much,' he said. 'We were really good friends me and Sid. We were in a squat together and were really close. We [The Clash] were the only ones who stuck up for him when it all happened in New York.

'As I say he was an intelligent guy but so much of it is like being a boiled sweet and getting sucked down to the inner, he was a much more complex guy than how he was perceived to be.'[8]

New York was in similarly sad shape to the somnambulistic Sid having narrowly staved off bankruptcy three years earlier, yet Mick and Joe were hopelessly seduced by its jaded glory. They saw beyond the decaying brownstones and boarded up shops, and in their minds eye saw spectral cinematic images of Marilyn flashing her panties in *Some Like It Hot*, Marlon Brando making an offer no one could refuse in *The Godfather*, Travis Bickle cruising the streets in *Taxi Driver*, and *King Kong* scaling the Empire State Building. Indeed, such was their childish enthusiasm at working in the city that never sleeps, when Paul and Topper flew out on 23 September to add their input on the album's final mixes they found Mick and Joe with a yellow cab waiting kerbside outside JFK so they could witness their Clash compadres expressions when they caught their first glimpse of the Manhattan skyline.

Despite their grumblings over the rough mixes, the suits at CBS/ Epic were keen to bring The Clash over to America in the coming year to promote the new album. They were also making noises about releasing *The Clash*, albeit with an alternate track-listing to make the album more appealing to mainstream America.

All that was needed now was for CBS/Epic to put their full weight behind *Give 'Em Enough Rope* – as the album was to be called – and the rock 'n' roll fantasies Mick had enacted in his mind's eye whilst practising daily in his bedroom at Wilmcote House would become realities; the icing on the Clash cake – at least as far as he was concerned – coming with Bernard hoisting himself with his own petard…

♪♪♪

Mick and Joe were still in San Francisco when Bernard attempted to reclaim the 'complete control' he'd demanded some two years earlier by announcing via the music press that The Clash were to play a show at the Harlesden New Roxy on 9 September without bothering to consult the group beforehand.

The Clash hadn't performed live in the capital since the end of July and the sixteen hundred tickets sold out within days of going on sale. This was fantastic news in terms of confirming the group's popularity, but Mick and Joe suddenly found themselves lodged between the fabled rock and hard place. On the one hand they wanted to continue working on the album, yet neither wanted to disappoint their fans. Bernard might have viewed their accompanying Pearlman to San Francisco as an unnecessary 'silly indulgence', but they were naturally anxious to ensure the new album was the best it could possibly be.

Mick viewed Bernard's actions as nothing short of an ultimatum and treated them as such, and although Joe wasn't yet ready to contemplate a future away from Bernard he nevertheless agreed with Mick that they should stay put in San Francisco and see out their obligations. Their refusal to come home like dutiful lapdogs not only forced Bernard into postponing the Roxy date, it also caused a stalemate within the Clash camp.

Instead of flying out and confronting his rebellious charges, however, Bernard misguidedly added insult to injury be issuing a statement whereby he claimed The Clash were postponing the Roxy date to Saturday, 23 September as a protest against the minimal airplay their records were being afforded.

This would prove sufficient to shatter the faith Joe and Paul had continued to show in their manager – with the normally taciturn Paul going so far as to phone the *NME*'s offices and openly challenge Bernard's authority. Any remaining shreds of credibility Bernard had were trampled into the tarmac at Heathrow as Paul and Topper flew out to New York to join Mick and Joe the same day as the rearranged Roxy date.

Paul and Topper had ostensibly flown out to New York to hear the latest mixes of *Give 'Em Enough Rope*, but a discussion as to what they should do about Bernard's recent actions was also high on the agenda. On 26 September, with both *NME* and *Sounds* hinting that The Clash were set to part company with their manager over the Roxy fiasco, Bernard flew out to New York for showdown talks.

Bernard would be the first to admit that he was more interested in conjuring up scams to subvert the music industry than managing a rock 'n' roll group per se, so seeing his charges flying halfway across the world to perform tasks that they could just as easily be carried out in London was anathema to his mind. The debut album had been recorded over three weekends with minimum of fuss and even less layout, and yet here they were recording in flash studios, staying in big hotels, and acting like the pampered rock stars they'd supposedly set out to topple from their pedestals.

As far as he was concerned, it wasn't so much America that was casting a spell on Mick and Joe, but rather the record company. Indeed, Bernard has always maintained that CBS had bribed The Clash to get rid of him. Yet while Maurice Oberstein and the rest of the CBS board would have undoubtedly found Bernard's unorthodox managerial style contrary to the norm, his argument doesn't stand up given that he would be subsequently be reinstated to the managerial role – albeit with diminished powers.

The showdown talks failed to resolve the fractious situation, but with the new album in the can, and the European leg of the self-explanatory-titled Sort It Out Tour set to commence with a show at the Belfast Queen's Hall on 13 October, The Clash returned to London. However, their attempt to right Bernard's wrongdoings by honouring the Roxy date before flying out to Belfast was scuppered by the GLC (Greater London Council), who restricted the admittance to just nine hundred – despite the Roxy's management having removed some five hundred seats to create a dance area.

Unable to reach a compromise, The Clash had little option but to postpone the show yet again – as well as add a second date to accommodate all sixteen hundred ticket holders. By the time news of the cancellation went out on local radio, however, hundreds of fans were already en route to the venue.

The Clash could have simply beat a hasty retreat and left the Roxy's management to take the flak, but instead they dutifully hung around to explain the situation, as well as give away promotional 'Tommy Gun' T-shirts to those fans left the most out of pocket. (The rearranged shows were played on 25/26 October)

Bernard couldn't be held responsible for the GLC's restriction policy, but as far as The Clash were concerned he was fundamentally to blame for the fiasco. Upon their return to London after the final show of the clutch of European dates at the El Paradiso in Amsterdam on 23 October, the group – via a solicitor's letter – informed Bernard that his managerial contract would be rendered null and void as of 1 December.

Unsurprisingly, Bernard didn't take kindly to the officious missive and issued his version of events via a press statement that appeared in the following week's edition of *Melody Maker*. 'I have been given the elbow by the band,' he grumbled. 'I took them off the street and made them what they are, and now I'm out.' After saying he'd been left out of pocket, and taking a parting pot shot at The Clash by accusing them of drifting into what he called 'rock 'n' roll nonsense', he added 'I know I've been painted as a horrible ogre-like figure, not letting the band have any fun, but that's not what it was about. I didn't view my job as being here to subsidise their silly indulgences, like recording in big New York studios, and staying in top New York hotels. That's basically what the split is all about.'

Having vented his spleen, Bernard then unleashed his own solicitors and obtained a court order whereby all Clash earnings were to be paid directly into his account. The Clash tried countering by accusing Bernard of having adopted the Malcolm McLaren's 'one-up-the-trouser-leg' approach to accountancy.

The Clash first approached the *NME*'s Clash-friendly journalist Barry Miles – to see if he'd be interested sharing managerial duties with CBS' Head of Publicity, Elle Smith. Miles would go on record saying the figures The Clash provided for analysis proved beyond doubt that Bernard had 'ripped them off something rotten, before saying he and Elle had passed on the offer because their efforts would have been exhausted with trying to recoup some of the money, rather than in taking the group to the next level.

The Clash next turned to Caroline Coon, whose interest in the group had crossed over from professional to personal now that she was seeing Paul. Mick was initially sceptical about letting one of group's girlfriends oversee their affairs, but as they'd elected to give the gig to someone they already knew and trusted, rather than bring in an outsider, Caroline had all the necessary credentials.

♪♪♪

Give 'Em Enough Rope – with a cover designed by CBS' groovy in-house graphic designer Gene Greif, and based on a Chinese government propaganda postcard titled 'The End Of The Trail'*, which depicts the end of Capitalism in the form of two vultures feasting on a cowboy corpse as the Red Army advances – was released on Friday, 10 November 1978.

Regardless of the less-than-complementary reviews, *Give 'Em Enough Rope* surpassed both the group and record company's expectations by reaching number two on the UK chart – and would surely have claimed the top spot had the UK not been in the grip of *Grease*-mania.

The criticisms regarding the supposed 'overproduction' were largely unjust because while The Clash were one of the finest live acts around, not even their most die-hard fans would have wanted the album to sound like a live show. It's also worth remembering that an album is quite literally a 'record' of where a group is at in terms of musical ability/creativity at that particular juncture in their career.

In the eighteen months since the release of their eponymous debut, Mick, Joe, Paul, and Topper had not only matured both as people they'd worked hard at perfecting their craft. *The Clash* was rightfully lauded as being one of the most pivotal albums of the punk period, but without *Give 'Em Enough Rope* there could have been no *London Calling*, and ergo, no multi-million-selling *Combat Rock*.

– CHAPTER EIGHT –

ELEVATOR GOING UP...

'I can't remember many of the gigs on that first tour, which was really short. I just remember the bus and watching America go by outside like some big movie.'
— Mick Jones

THE CLASH WERE THE MOST exciting rock 'n' roll act in Britain, and with Give 'Em Enough Rope having been custom-made to appeal to the US mainstream market it was only natural they began focusing their energies on conquering America. They might still be railing against the USA in song, but away from the mic, Mick – as indeed were Joe, Paul, and Topper – was hopelessly enamoured with America and looking forward to playing some shows stateside.

Epic, however, were rather less enthused with the idea of bringing The Clash to America as *Give 'Em Enough Rope* was treading water in the lower reaches of the US chart, and from a financial viewpoint, bringing The Clash over to promote an album that had as yet failed to crack the *Billboard* 100* would simply be throwing good money after bad. Such was the label's reticence that had it not been for Caroline Coon's dogged negotiating skills in cajoling the label into providing the funding the tour would not have gone ahead.

'The Clash were close to breaking up because of the problems with Bernard Rhodes and we faced all sorts of other difficulties,' she told *Q* magazine for its May 2001 retrospective on the tour. 'Our record

---

* The album would peak at No. 128

company refused to finance an American tour. Luckily, our American label, Epic, although a little afraid of the politics, knew this band could be huge, so I spent £3000 of my own money flying to New York where I arranged for Epic to give us $30,000 to fund the tour.'

Caroline had pulled off an impressive coup in getting Epic to capitulate, but rather than bask in their manager's victory The Clash upped the antipathy by insisting on calling their inaugural US outing the Pearl Harbor '79 Tour. Needless to say, the inflammatory title brought about further unrest at Epic HQ. It might have been nigh on four decades since the Imperial Japanese Navy's premeditated strike on the US pacific Fleet stationed at Pearl Harbor, Hawaii, in December 1941, but it was still a livid scar on the US psyche.

Believing The Clash would see the error of their ways; Epic's marketing team got on with promoting the trip as the *Give 'Em Enough Rope* Tour. They hadn't counted on the group's obduracy, however, and even as the logistics were being mapped out in New York, back in London the Camden-based Fifth Column T-shirt company – owned by Clash fan Chris Townsend – was busy running up a batch of T-shirts featuring a kamikaze pilot and rising sun on the front, and a foundering American battleship adorning the back.

Epic had acquiesced, but the tour almost fell through owing to the US Immigration Department dragging its feet in issuing the group with their all-important work visas. The initial fear was that The Clash had fallen victim to a US Government clampdown, but even though this wasn't the case as the festive break had created a serious backlog. With less than a week to go before the opening tour date their American booking agent, Wayne Forte, was forced to apply for priority status.

Unlike Epic, Forte had no illusions regarding The Clash's stateside appeal. 'I thought the Pistols, The Clash and The Jam were like The Beatles, the Stones, and The Who,' he told Randal Doane in *Stealing All Transmissions*. 'The Clash were the bad boys, these dirty grimy guys, but the kids still loved 'em.'

Having cut his teeth with the William Morris Agency, Forte was savvy enough to know how to best play his hand. He knew there was little point in trying to sell The Clash to the whole country at this stage in their career, and instead targeted America's musical and cultural epicentres such as San Francisco, Washington D.C., Boston and New York. When Forte called Ron Delsner, New York's 'Big Cheese' in terms of concert promotion, to enquire about putting The Clash on at the 3,000-capacity Palladium on East 14th Street, the latter thought him insane but Forte had already done his homework.

A few months earlier he'd spoken with Bob Plotnick, owner of Bleecker Bob's in Greenwich Village. When Plotnick said how he'd sold 1,000 import copies of *The Clash*, Forte guestimated that while 1,000 domestic LP sales would equate to a concert-going audience of around 300, 1,000 import sales meant one thousand devoted fans; fans who wouldn't just buy a ticket to see The Clash, they'd be sure to bring a friend.

While Forte was doing his utmost to chivvy the US Immigration Department along, The Clash headed into Wessex Studios in Highbury New Park to record the tracks that would subsequently make up the *Cost Of Living* EP*; including a rabble-rousing version of the 'I Fought The Law'. Sonny Curtis' classic had been one of the discs Mick and Joe had regularly spun on the Automatt's jukebox during their time at the studio, and both had made a mental note to give the song a run through at rehearsals on returning to London.

The initial reaction wasn't as they'd hoped, however, as when Mick first played the song to Paul on acoustic guitar he'd thought it a terrible idea. Thankfully, he underwent a change of heart once Mick plugged in his Les Paul and Topper jumped behind the kit.

♪♪♪

A warm-up show had been booked at the Commodore Ballroom in Vancouver on 31 January. Steve Jones had no doubt regaled The Clash with harrowing tales of the harsh treatment Noel Monk's team of Vietnam vets had meted out when he or any of the other Sex Pistols dared step too far out of line on their ill-fated inaugural US tour some twelve months earlier, The Clash thought it prudent to stick with the mischievous devils they knew and trusted.

---

* The *Cost Of Living* EP was released on 11 May 1979.

Coming to America under the 'Pearl Harbor '79 banner undoubtedly put a few corporate noses out of joint, but contrary to what their stateside detractors were saying The Clash weren't coming to America to bury rock 'n' roll, but rather to reclaim it; evidence of which came with the no-expense-spared hiring of pioneering rhythm and blues legend Bo Diddley as support. The idea being, that having Bo open proceedings would not only serve as a reference point for The Clash's own fusion of R&B, punk and reggae, but would also familiarise America's youth with its own forgotten culture.

The idea was hardly innovative, given that the Rolling Stones – having achieved their initial flush of success on the back of the 'Bo Diddley Beat' – had invited Bo to accompany them on several of their US tours, but Mick and Joe were at least being mindful to pay their own dues. Once Caroline had dutifully tracked the guitar legend down in Australia, they gave her full remit to have the Oz promoter offer Bo whatever it would take to get him on an aeroplane – the inducement being a reported $20,000.

'In America, the record company said we could have anybody we wanted to support us,' Mick explained. 'We said, "Can we have Bo Diddley?" They said, "Ooh, we don't know about that." He was fantastic! We had Lee Dorsey as well. And Screamin' Jay Hawkins— he came out of a coffin every night.'[1]

Epic had been worried that Diddley would be bottled off the stage owing to the colour of his skin, but in Vancouver it was the headliners who suddenly found themselves under fire from a barrage of cans, bottles, and other projectiles when they tried to leave the stage – despite having played three encores.

The Clash had hired a luxury touring bus hired from country singer Waylon Jennings, but rather than make a straight run for California they stopped off in Seattle to enjoy a good night's rest in a bed that didn't move before continuing onto San Francisco. Whenever The Clash were out on the road Johnny would arrange for an early morning call. The call which roused him from his slumber the following morning wasn't from the concierge, however; but rather Bob Gruen informing him Sid Vicious was dead. The mood was understandably sombre for the rest of the day.

The Berkeley College Campus was famous for its student riots of a decade earlier, but the show at the campus' community theatre proved a rather tepid affair with Joe – in his garbled tour diary for the *NME* – going so far as to liken the audience's reciprocation to the onstage antics never getting beyond their politely 'tapping their biology books in time to the tunes.' Even opening with 'I'm So Bored With The USA' failed to elicit much of a response.

With the audience appearing to be as equally bored with The Clash, Joe had enquired of Johnny Green who was responsible for 'putting us here with these dozeys'. When Johnny pointedly jabbed a finger at his backstage pass which read: 'Bill Graham Presents', Joe had then turned his attention to Caroline to ask why she'd booked the Berkeley show through Graham, and was told in return that those bands who don't cosy up with Graham didn't get to play California, let alone San Francisco.

Joe was still absorbing this information, Johnny relented to the repeated pestering of a 'mixed bag of people in tie-dyed sarongs and saris, and bizarre baseball caps with and animals and propellers on top, and allowed them backstage to meet and greet The Clash in return for their bizarre headgear.

On overhearing Joe grumbling about Graham's domination of the local scene, the interlopers told him that if The Clash wanted to play to a real audience they were staging a benefit show at the Geary Temple for an organisation intent on breaking Graham's monopoly.

The Clash were expected in Los Angeles in two days time, and the American road crew weren't overly keen at the idea of remaining in San Francisco to play a benefit show – especially seeing as Graham would get to hear about their wilfully biting the hand that would be feeding them this particular evening. After all, The Clash could split up and never return to California, whereas they would all still need to make a living.

Johnny Green remembers the Geary Theatre show as being a 'storming gig from the second the band ran on to the disintegrating stage,'[2] but The Clash couldn't hang around to rejoice in stealing some of Graham's thunder owing to their having a four-hundred-mile drive to Los Angeles to navigate. 'The drive takes all night an' we test out the bunks which are like comfy shelves,' Joe reported in his *NME* tour diary. 'We hit LA in the morning and we gotta play the Santa Monica Centre the same night. Me an' Mick try to get a look at Hollywood but we collapse instead. Later, Mick tells me his hotel bed just kept moving all the time, just like mine, and we work out it's because we were on the bus all night.'

The Clash managed to arrive at the Santa Monica Civic Auditorium by the skin of their teeth, but the truck ferrying their gear was less fortunate and with the clock ticking Johnny Green was forced to reach for the phone book. The replacement PA was set up on stage ready to go when the missing truck finally pulled up outside the venue. The road crew were happy to leave the group's gear where it was, but Mick was having none of it and insisted they make the changeover.

It was at the Santa Monica show that the group came face-to-face with their employers. Several Epic execs had flown in from New York with no other agenda than to pose for a photograph with The Clash before sloping off for a night on the company credit card. The Clash, however, had no intention of allowing themselves to be seen as label puppets, and just as the photographer had been about to snap the shutter they'd walked out of the room leaving the dumbstruck executives catching flies – much to Caroline's chagrin. 'All the top record company people came to that gig, the very people I'd had to get the money from to make the tour possible,' she explained. 'I really wanted the band to meet with them and say thank you, but The Clash were determined to be as rude as possible.'[3]

Epic's red-faced press officer, Susan Blond, who'd painstakingly arranged the sycophantic suits into a neatly defined group, had pleaded with Caroline to get them to come back into the room, but in Elvis parlance, The Clash had already left the building.

The next scheduled pit-stop was Cleveland, Ohio, where The Clash were set to appear at the Agora Ballroom on 13 February. Joe's old Newport buddy Allan Jones was covering the tour for *Melody Maker*, but arrived in town only to discover the group had disappeared from the radar somewhere near the Oklahoma State line owing to the fierce snowstorms that had brought the Midwest to a standstill. The

Welshman was slightly anxious as to how The Clash would greet him when they did arrive as he'd yet to pen a favourable review.

The Agora Ballroom date was a designated benefit show in aid of a local US Army veteran called Larry McIntyre who'd lost both his legs in Vietnam. McIntyre had apparently incurred the displeasure of his neighbours after having had the audacity to go swimming in the pool at the complex where he was living. It would seem losing one's body parts for Uncle Sam is acceptable practice as long as one keeps the scars under wraps. Swimming was one of the few recreations left to him, and McIntyre was suing his not-so-amiable neighbours.

The benefit was to raise funds for McIntyre's legal fees and The Clash were to have been introduced to the beneficiary after the show, but the double amputee gave back-word after hearing Joe forget his name in the heat of the moment thanking the crowd for being 'so free with your money for this guy what's got no legs'.[4]

The following morning The Clash awoke to discover they were the ones in need of a benefit as there wasn't enough in the kitty to cover the hotel bill. Caroline had been on the phone to Epic all morning trying to speak with the person who could authorise the payment who, like their opposite number at Soho Square, was tied up in a meeting. With no show until the following night in Washington D.C., there was no immediate hurry, but unless someone at Epic came through and settled the bill, there was every chance that the tour party would have to do a runner. 'I told Epic that they could meet us at the state border,' Caroline dead-panned. 'We'd be the bus with the Highway patrol chasing it…'[5]

To add to the irony of the situation, Topper caught a feature on the previous night's show on the local TV station, Channel 8 (Owned by CBS). According to the feature, it was Bo Diddley who'd headlined the show and The Clash didn't get so much as a mention.

Despite their having endured a ten-hour drive to Washington D.C., in one of those 'we're-here-so-we-might-as-well-go-see-it' moments, the tour party decided to drive over to 1600 Pennsylvania Avenue in the early hours of the morning to see the White House. Joe's immediate reaction on seeing America's most famous residence was to rue not having a bazooka close to hand.

At the show itself Mick could have been forgiven for thinking he was under attack as he kept getting electric shocks from his Les Paul copy. His frustration finally spilled over during 'London's Burning', and he unslung the offending Gibson and smashed the neck against the stage. 'I thought it was a good gig,' he reflected. 'I thought it was alright in the end; smashed the neck right off my fuckin' guitar, though. Funny, I used to hate groups that smashed their instruments.'[6]

Following the penultimate show at the Harvard Square Theatre in Cambridge, Massachusetts, where the 1800 capacity venue had sold out in under an hour despite The Clash only receiving airplay on one Boston radio station, the tour wended its way down the eastern seaboard to New York.

The Big Apple was already abuzz about The Clash when the group arrived in town, but those lucky 3,800 ticket-holders crammed into the former cinema on West 14th Street were in for a night they would never forget. The group was well aware that this was the night that would go a long way to breaking them in America. Aside from the leading lights of New York's glitterati, including Andy Warhol, Robert De Niro, and Carrie Fisher wandering around backstage, the cream of America's rock cognoscenti were also in attendance; and the enigmatic Lester Bangs went so far as to cite the Palladium show as one of the best rock 'n' roll shows he'd ever witnessed.

The day after the Palladium triumph Mick took time out to speak with Ira Robbins from the underground newspaper, *Trouser Press*. The interview starts off well enough with Mick chatting about his personal musical heroes including Mott The Hoople. Indeed, it's only when Robbins alludes to the accusatory fingers pointed at The Clash by certain sections of the British music weeklies in that they'd suffered from 'Mott The Hoople Syndrome' whilst penning *Give 'Em Enough Rope* that the temperature drops dramatically.

'I was very fond of Mott,' Mick responded testily. 'No, we didn't name "All the Young Punks" for him [Ian Hunter] — that was something else. It was nothing to do with "Dudes". And the whole "New Boots" thing was a joke with Ian Dury — that was a mistake as well. You can call that number anything; it's kind of a statement like "Garageland" was on the first album. It's our message of what's happening with us.

'But it's important that people don't see it as a kind of corny biopic,' he continued. 'Some do see it as a system of living. That's not all it is, we're more than that. It's all for them as well as us; it's for their imaginations. We're raising consciousness. It's the only thing that young people can do for other young people that's worth doing.'

One song on the album which clearly proved a hit with Robbins was 'Stay Free', which Mick had playfully introduced from the Palladium stage as their 'wimpoid ballad'. 'Even the skinheads cry over it,' Mick chuckled. 'It really moves them. It's very difficult to do it every night; we certainly don't always do it. When we do it, it changes the whole tone of the set.'

Bringing the interview to a close, Robbins asked Mick if he and the rest of The Clash had been wary of coming to the US and the tour ending up a failure. Mick responded by saying – albeit tongue-in-cheek – that 'it would just have meant we wouldn't come back.'

When Robbins says that Mick had looked like he was enjoying himself on the Palladium's stage, Mick replied: 'It was real nice. We had a big stage to fill and we wanted everyone to feel a part of it which is really difficult. You couldn't do it if the audience was any larger. That is the most you can do it to and still communicate effectively.'

Having confessed to an aversion to The Clash ever playing Wembley Stadium, and citing the 'Rock Against Racism' show at London's Victoria Park the previous April as being their biggest outdoor crowd, Mick candidly admitted that The Clash's live show was more effective at indoor venues such as the Palladium. 'We've worked those bigger places, but bigger shows aren't communication shows,' he explained. 'I can't see it working. The last time they asked us to headline the Reading Festival we told them to stick it, so they got Tom Robinson or somebody like that.'

♪♪♪

The simmering unrest between The Clash and those operating within Epic's corridors of power, which the group had wilfully exacerbated by refusing to pose for the obligatory 'meet and greet' photo backstage at the Santa Monica Civic Centre, was alleviated somewhat when both parties came together to work a happy compromise over Epic's decision to belatedly release an amended version of *The Clash* in America. The 100,000+ import sales of the original album suggested that Epic's decision would be handsomely remunerated and the group reluctantly agreed to the label dropping several songs from the UK track-listing and replacing them with non-album UK singles as yet previously unreleased in the US, coupled with a promotional single: 'I Fought The Law' and '(White Man) In Hammersmith Palais'.

As both of these tracks featured on the revised album, Epic complied with the group's demand that a freebie forty-five featuring 'Groovy Times' and 'Gates Of The West' to be included with the album.

CBS' then Head of A&R, Muff Winwood (renamed 'Duff Windbag' by The Clash), believes the majority of The Clash's internecine struggles with Epic around this time were the result of the label's strategy on how best to market the group in America. 'In Britain, they [The Clash] could use the media, and do the bizarre things that British groups have always done with the media because the country's small enough to be able to do it, but in America it's much more difficult,' Muff explained. 'You just can't replicate how you do things in England. You have to do it in a different way. You need big business to flow things through.'[7]

Muff then goes on to reveal that he and the rest of CBS UK team who were working for the greater good of The Clash experienced a more uneasy relationship with Caroline than they ever did with Bernard.

Having said that, however, he was keen to stress that whereas Bernard had been his own man, Caroline had the distinct disadvantage of trying to operate within the strict 'dos and don'ts' mandate that The Clash had given her. One of the do's was to keep the record company at arm's length, but in order to maintain a steady cash flow so that The Clash could function like any other group Caroline was forced into holding regular consultations with CBS UK regarding their plans.

Owing to the slipshod care and attention paid to the small print in their recording contract before putting pen to paper, The Clash were expected to deliver a new album each year. This wasn't per calendar year, as the eighteen-month gap between *The Clash* and *Give 'Em Enough Rope* demonstrates, but the group would have to deliver new product before the end of the year.

Upon the group's return to London Caroline had drawn up a four-pronged plan for The Clash. While plotting a return to the US was part of her strategy, delivering a new album as per contractual obligations took priority. However, if The Clash were to deliver a new album by the year's end they would need time to write new songs, and in order to be in any fit state to pen new material they needed some downtime to recharge the batteries.

Getting The Clash to drop down a couple of gears was no easy thing, but Caroline was determined that with royalties coming in from the records, Joe, Mick, and Paul – being the group's three main shareholders so to speak – put at least some of their hard-gotten gains into bricks and mortar. Paul was the only one to follow Caroline's advice – possibly because he'd come to trust her business acumen more than the others – by putting a mortgage down on a basement flat in Oxford Gardens.

Mick had been forced to retreat to his old bedroom at Wilmcote House after returning from America to find thieves had ransacked the flat at Pembridge Villas and made off with his guitars and video-recording machine, and was therefore delighted when Caroline secured a lease on small mews house on Simon Close, just off Portobello Road. Joe typically chose to ignore Caroline's advice and continued his transient existence living out of a suitcase at his girlfriend mother's World's End council flat. Topper, who wasn't yet officially considered a full equal member of The Clash, had little option but to continue renting.

The next item on Caroline's four-prong agenda came in finding The Clash a more permanent replacement to Rehearsals where they could concentrate on writing in a relaxed atmosphere free from the worry of having to pack their gear away at the end of each day as they'd had to do at Nomis, Black Hole, and several other pay-per-hour rehearsal spaces of varying refinement in and around London. Johnny Green remembers that it was he and Baker who made the pilgrimage to Pimlico after coming across Vanilla's 'studio-to-let' amongst the *Melody Maker* classifieds, but it was undoubtedly Caroline who arranged for the funding through Peter Quinnell, the accountant she'd brought in to help sort out the group's finances in the wake of Bernard's departure.

Caroline never consciously strayed beyond her remit as the 'non-manager manager of The Clash', as she jokingly referred to her role on occasion, but her authoritarian, no-nonsense approach inevitably began to grate. Some have pointed to Caroline's relationship with Paul adding a 'John and Yoko frisson' as the reason for her expulsion, while Johnny Green says Joe and Mick either didn't think she was up to the task, or that she was 'on the make'.[8]

Appointing the girlfriend of one of the group as manager was perhaps a tad too *Spinal Tap*-esque, but suggesting Caroline was lining her own pockets at The Clash's expense is ludicrous as she didn't even seek recompense for the £3,000 she'd laid out while arranging the US tour. Indeed, the only accusation The Clash could possibly throw in Caroline's direction was that she perhaps took her eye off the ball to enter discussions about her being appointed creative consultant for Lou Adler's punk-themed film *All Washed Up** which was then at the pre-production stage.

---

* By the of its release in 1981, the film had been re-titled *Ladies And Gentlemen, The Fabulous Stains*.

– CHAPTER NINE –

DON'T TOUCH THAT DIAL

'By the third album we were still learning, still developing and we developed our musical style. There was a point where punk was getting narrower and narrower in terms of what it could achieve and where it could go. It was like painting itself into a corner and we wanted to do anything and everything. We thought you could make any kind of music.'

– Mick Jones

THE LONG-SINCE DEMOLISHED Vanilla Studios* in Pimlico more than lived up to its lacklustre name, but Johnny Green says he knew instantly the moment he walked up the stairwell and into the cramped low-ceilinged, windowless womb that he'd found The Clash somewhere they could call home. The familiarity stemmed from 36 Causton Street providing floor space for cars and guitars in a near-identical situation as the British Rail yards at Camden Lock, which housed Harry's Garage and Rehearsal Rehearsals. The rectangular room also had a six-inch platform running down one wall and across the far end that could serve as a stage. The subtle difference between Rehearsals and Vanilla being that the latter was owned by a shady Iranian clique sporting Arthur Daley-esque camel coats that had a posse of minders on

---

* The garage/studios were demolished in 1993, and standing on the site now is the London Diocesan House.

call should anyone start asking uncomfortable questions about the garage's car-spraying operation.

Johnny had two questions for the Iranians: was the studio available for extended lease; and could The Clash have the place solely for their own use? The Iranians had just the one: could The Clash pay up front?

Johnny may have been given the mandate of finding the group a new home, but that didn't mean to say CBS would okay the cost without consultation, and the people he needed to speak with at Soho Square suddenly became unavailable whenever money was mentioned. Fortunately for The Clash, however, their accountant Peter 'Quister the Twister' Quinnell understood the urgency of getting his clients back into the studio and OK'd the cheque. While the money worked its silent magic, Johnny and Baker set about ferrying the group's gear over to its new home and setting it up on the raised area as close as possible to how they liked to work – with Joe, Mick, and Paul all facing Topper.

Having procured a table, a few chairs, and the all-important tea-making utensils, Johnny and Baker set the amps to stand-by, plugged in the kettle, and awaited the group's arrival. Johnny knew from experience that Vanilla was custom-made for The Clash. Not only did it resemble the archetypal gang hideaway from an Ealing crime caper, it was also off the beaten track which would hopefully deter friends and record company personnel from dropping by. Other sundry benefits that the new locale offered were the studio being situated within walking distance of a pub [The White Swan], and a sandwich bar – both of which were to become regular haunts.

'Vanilla was very, very secluded and not many people came to see us because it wasn't easy to find the place,' Mick explained. 'It was in the back of a garage and you wouldn't know there was anything there so we were cut off from everyone. You had to come by prior appointment.'[1]

While close friends such as Robin Crocker, Barry 'Scratchy' Myers, and Rude Boy actor Terry McQuade, did indeed come by prior appointment, instead of being ushered into studio, more often than not they would be taken over the road to the Causton Street Children's Playground for a game of 'Crombies for goalposts' football.

Judging from Johnny's recollections, the four members of The Clash played football pretty much the same way they did their respective instruments: Topper and Mick possessing the artistic flair, Joe as being a 'head-down-and-charge-for-goal'[2] kinda guy, while Paul was an out-and-out clogger.

These not-so-genteel kick-abouts weren't simply designated exercise breaks to give all concerned an hour in the open air before going back inside to nail another song, but rather no quarter contests played out on an equally unforgiving asphalt pitch that could have resulted in one of the group being carted off to hospital. The news that Joe or Mick had an arm or ankle in plaster from playing footie might have shocked those music journos who were monitoring the new album's progress, but the same disclosure would have been met with bemused resignation over in Soho Square as Muff Winwood and the other CBS suits who'd visited Vanilla of late had also been press-ganged into playing and had the bumps and bruises to prove it.

Johnny Green remembers The Clash's work ethic at Vanilla as 'extremely disciplined', and with their having finally made the conscious decision to move away from punk's rigid 4/4 pulse beat they could play around with the rocking rhythms that had stirred them in their youth. During the recording of *Give 'Em Enough Rope* Sandy Pearlman had proclaimed Topper a 'human drum machine' owing to his unerring ability to play any style or mode without dropping a beat, and Topper's dexterity, coupled with Mick's unerring knack for finding a melody, allowed them to throw some Clash chords at any musical genre that took their fancy.

Coming up with new material for *Give 'Em Enough Rope* had proved taxing, but having shaken off the shackles of their self-imposed restraints, the songs were coming thick and fast. 'I don't think the first American tour was the inspiration for "*London Calling*", Mick revealed. 'A few of the songs on the second album had talked about that, [but] I think by this time the lyrics were actually the spur to start doing different kinds of music.'[3]

Johnny and Baker could, of course, always be counted on to serve as an in-house sounding board, but The Clash knew the tried and tested means of gauging any new song's worth was in front of a live audience. They were already scheduled to headline the second of two Rock Against Racism orchestrated Southall Defence Fund benefit shows over consecutive evenings at the Rainbow Theatre in Finsbury Park on 13/14 July, but it was decided to book a couple of low-key shows at the Notre Dame Hall in Leicester Place the week prior to their Rainbow date.

The Clash hadn't graced a British stage since the beginning of January, but both shows sold out within hours of word hitting the street. At the opening show, rather than charge straight in with the new stuff, The Clash elected to get the crowd rocking with a trio of familiar tunes 'Clash City Rockers', '(White Man) In Hammersmith Palais', and 'Safe European Home', before tentatively sliding into the new material.

With their appetites whetted for playing live again, The Clash were suddenly keen to play other one-off dates – regardless of the logistics involved. There was talk of their flying out to Cuba for a one-off show, but the idea quickly floundered over safety issues.

Another occasion where they were forced to revise their thinking came following an invitation from the Undertones to headline a festival in their native Derry. Though it wasn't made public at the time, Joe had received a death threat (via the *NME*) from the Red Hand Commandos, a splinter group from the Protestant Ulster Defence Association (UDA), over his having sported a T-shirt declaring support for the ongoing H-Block hunger strikes at the Harlesden Roxy show the previous October.

Revised thinking would be the order of the day when it came to who might be called upon to produce the new album. *Give 'Em Enough Rope* had received a harsh reception at the hands of the British music media, but it was still generally assumed within The Clash camp that Sandy Pearlman would be recalled to duty. Indeed, the proposal got as far as the discussion stage before Pearlman took himself out of the equation following the death of his father.

In accordance with their new wide-ranging repertoire The Clash began mooting producers they believed were capable of appreciating, harnessing, and transferring the melody-fused magic onto vinyl. CBS would have already had a list of producers capable of delivering such a remit at their disposal, so given the underwhelming in-house response to Guy's production work on the group's Polydor demos back in November 1976, hearing that Joe was out trawling the darkest recesses of Soho in search of the mercurial maverick would have surely had everyone at Soho Square reaching for the smelling salts.

Muff Winwood was particularly aghast at the news and put forward a compromise whereby The Clash could have Guy, so long as CBS could nominate a third party who was capable of grabbing the tiller should Guy stray off course. The 'third party' they called upon was Bill Price, whom the group were already familiar with from their working together on the *Cost Of Living* sessions back in January.

Bill's appointment didn't get everyone's vote, however, as Joe was keen to record the new album on a couple of Teac machines at Vanilla so as to reduce studio costs, which in turn would keep the album's retail price at a minimum. On this occasion, however, he was outvoted and The Clash block-booked Wessex's Studio One for a calendar month.

After several months of seemingly aimless meandering in the wake of Bernard's dismissal, The Clash appeared to have their career firmly back on track. They'd written enough new material for two albums and Epic were making positive noises about getting the group back to America at the earliest opportunity to promote the US friendly version of *The Clash*.

Another unexpected boon came with their being approached with a last-minute, cash-in-hand support slot at the Ruisrock Festival in Turku, Finland; the £7,500 fee going a long way to easing any immediate personal financial worries they may have had.

♪♪♪

With The Clash having been booked to appear at the Tribal Stomp II Festival in Monterey, California, on 8 September, it made sense to follow the US jaunt on from there. Organising a US tour, of course, was infinitely more complex than arranging a couple of low-key dates in Leicester Square. Realising they needed professional expertise, the group began pondering their options. Joe had apparently been plucking up the courage to throw Bernard's hat back into the ring, while Mick was being courted by Andrew King and Pete Jenner of Blackhill Enterprises. Blackhill got the vote; the deciding factor being Blackhill had Ian Dury and the Blockheads on its roster.

Blackhill's initial introduction to The Clash had come via their resident PR guru Kosmo Vinyl (a.k.a Mark Dunk) who'd served his public relations apprenticeship with the legendary Keith Altham, before taking a job with the newly incorporated Stiff Records in 1976; serving as MC on the first month-long Stiff package tour featuring Elvis Costello and the Attractions, and Ian Dury's Blockheads before gravitating towards Blackhill so that he might concentrate his not-inconsiderable energies in promoting Dury.

Mick had first encountered Kosmo during the spring of 1977, whilst the latter was running a record stall on Portobello Market. Having spotted a copy of the 'Remote Control' single amongst his wares, Mick had asked Kosmo to remove it from sale as he 'weren't into it'. The rest of the Clash readily welcomed Kosmo with open arms, but others within the group's inner-sanctum weren't quite so receptive. Despite the barely concealed antipathy, with Blackhill taking over the managerial reigns Kosmo quickly became a semi-permanent fixture in the Clash camp and would come to take on PR duties similar to those he'd performed for the Blockheads.

The Clash had opted for Guy Stevens because they believed he still possessed the 'X' factor; that indefinable talent for recognising a hit record the moment he first heard the song on a tape machine. Much to everyone's amusement, however, Guy didn't actually own a tape machine and Johnny Green was charged with remedying the situation.

Guy's unorthodox approach to producing has become part of the *London Calling* legend, and the first hint that he had scant regard for normal recording procedures came with his insisting 'Brand New Cadillac' was a wrap after the first take – regardless of it speeding up towards the end. Further mad-cap behaviour came with his wrestling Bill Price to the floor over a fader, pouring a bottle of wine into the studio's Bösendorfer Grand piano to improve the sound, having the cab driver charged with delivering him to the studio on time sit in on the sessions with his meter running; lying prostrate in front of a visiting Maurice Oberstein's Rolls Royce and refusing to get up until Obie had declared the album to be 'magnificent'.

Under normal circumstances any one of the erratic episodes would be deemed a dismissible offence, but as The Clash knew, of course, Mr. Stevens was no ordinary Guy.

Diversifying into different musical genres had worked well enough back at Vanilla, but it soon became obvious to one and all that some of the new songs would require a broader format than guitar, bass, and drums. With The Clash signed to Blackhill, it was easy enough for Kosmo to call in Blockheads' organ player, Mickey Gallagher, while his previous good standing with Jake Riviera and Dave Robinson over at Stiff Records allowed him to call upon Graham Parker and the Rumour's brass section – credited as 'the Irish horns' on the album – to further flesh out the sound.

Bringing in the extra help, however, meant The Clash would overrun their allotted time at Wessex.

Working to their usual six-week turnaround mandate, CBS had been aiming for a mid-October release date. In order to have the album in the shops by that date, the label needed the finished album in the can by the end of August at the latest, but The Clash were on a roll and had little interest in keeping to mandates.

In keeping with Joe's earlier proclamation to the *Melody Maker* that 'there will be no six-quid Clash LP ever!' the group first of all got CBS to agree to release the album at £5 (the lowest UK price category for a single album at that time), and then inveigled the label into including a free two-track seven-inch single, which was subsequently augmented to a four-track twelve-inch EP.

The Clash hadn't finished with their wheeling, however, and with CBS forced to concede that a 33rpm twelve-inch cost no more to manufacture than a 45rpm four-track twelve-inch EP, the company quickly realised it had been hoodwinked into giving The Clash what they'd wanted all along – a double album retailing for the same price as a single. The Clash may have scored a value-for-money victory for the fans, but the sting in the tail came with CBS insisting the proposed double album would count only as a single album so far as the group's contract was concerned.

With the Ruisrock readies having long-since been used up, The Clash were forced to take the begging bowl round to Soho Square in order to get the eighteen songs as near perfect as possible before heading for the airport. That they didn't leave Wessex until two hours before departure time suggests it was a very close run thing.

With Bill Price left to get on with mixing the tracks slated for *London Calling*, The Clash flew out to California for the Tribal Stomp II Festival, which would serve as a warm-up show of sorts for the impending twenty-three-date 'Take The Fifth Tour'. The tour was by far The Clash's biggest undertaking, yet despite the ever-present lack of funds, as far as they were concerned a bigger tour meant a bigger entourage and aside from Kosmo, Johnny Green, Baker, and the rest of their tried and trusted crew, each member also insisted on bringing along a travelling companion to lighten the mood. Joe, Paul, and Topper naturally opted for their girlfriends (Gabby, Debbie, and Dee respectively), while Mick – having recently split from Viv Albertine – invited his LA-based pal Rory Johnston along to serve as his personal tour manager.

Johnston was hardly what one could call a novice in the tour management department as he'd cut his teeth babysitting the Sex Pistols on their January '78 US tour, but the rest of the group saw his inclusion as yet another show of Mick's diva-esque behaviour – especially as he hadn't thought to discuss it beforehand. There was, however, little danger of Johnson being allowed to exceed whatever authority Mick might give him as Epic had already installed their guy, Mark Wissing, to serve as their on-the-road liaison, and Andrew King and Pete Jenner were also coming along to ensure the tour proceeded as smoothly as possible.

The *NME*'s in-house cartoonist Ray Lowry, who'd befriended The Clash after seeing them at the Electric Circus in Manchester on the Anarchy Tour, was invited along to provide the paper with a pictorial narrative of the tour, while his fellow *NME* staffer Pennie Smith would be joining up with the tour to capture the mood through her lens. CBS were already baulking at the escalating costs, and for a while it looked as though Ray would have to pay his own way before a revision of the budget freed up enough cash to allow his inclusion.

Ever anxious to ensure that the tour got rave reviews all round, Kosmo had arranged for *Sounds* and *Melody Maker* to send out their own Clash-friendly reporters – Pete Silverton and Allan Jones respectively – to cover 'The Quest' as he'd dubbed The Clash's mission to convert America to their particular brand of five-star rock 'n' roll.

♪♪♪

'Taking the Fifth' is the colloquial term for when an American citizen invokes the Fifth Amendment of the US Constitution which protects against abuse of government authority in a legal procedure, but The Clash's use of the axiom could well have applied to their recruiting Mickey Gallagher as a temporary fifth member for the tour. Typically, Mickey didn't receive the call until the day before The Clash were due to leave for America. Mickey had been thinking of taking his family away on holiday when Joe called out of the blue with the group's proposition. When Mickey explained his thinking, Joe simply told him to bring the wife and kids along. Though it was too late in the day for Mickey to accompany The Clash from the off, he and the rest of the Gallagher clan joined up with the tour in Boston the following week.

The cost of the wide-ranging support acts would also take a large bite out of whatever money The Clash were set to make on the tour. Just as they had done on the Pearl Harbor '79 Tour, they invited Bo Diddley onto the bill for the 14 September Chicago show, while Sam and Dave, and Screamin' Jay Hawkins were to be reintroduced to American audiences at various junctures.

The Clash also paid their dues to the New York Dolls by inviting David Johansen to open proceedings on the tour's official opening night at the St. Paul Civic Centre in Minnesota, while Johnny Thunders' latest outfit 'Gang War' – which also featured former MC5 guitarist Wayne Kramer* in the line-up – appeared as special guests at the show in Worcester, Massachusetts.

The Tribal Stomp II Festival was the brainchild of Chet Helms, the colourful Bay Area music promoter who'd made his name promoting a wide range of artists in San Francisco during the mid-to-late Sixties. Helms had also managed psychedelic rock outfit Big Brother and Holding Company, and was responsible for turning the group's mixed fortunes around by recruiting an unknown singer called Janis Joplin.

Helms was hoping the festival would recreate the mystique of the legendary Monterey International Pop Festival of June 1967, but despite repeated assurances that the festival would be a resounding success, Helms' aspirations didn't quite live up to everyone else's expectations as only 500 of the 12,000 tickets available had been sold. Adding insult to the general air of despondency looming large over the carnival was the fact that those Californians that had deemed the festival's billing worthy of the $12.50 admission fee were all decked out in a kaleidoscopic array of kaftans, tie-dyed dresses, love beads, and other hippie ephemera.

The Clash were included in the festival's opening afternoon bill along with Soul Syndicate, and the Chambers Brothers. Also playing that day was Joe Ely, whom The Clash had befriended the previous summer while the Country rocker was in London promoting his second album, *Honky Tonk Masquerade*.

Somewhat surprisingly, given that they'd spent the last six weeks or so playing and listening to the songs intended for the new album, the only one to feature in the festival set-list was the title track itself, 'London Calling'.

Four days later The Clash took the fifth for real at the Saint Paul Civic Centre; one of those soulless, circular concrete wombs that are woefully unsuited for rock 'n' roll – regardless of Elvis having played there back in the day. The vacuous setting certainly didn't do the group any favours, and served to stifle their onstage creativity.

---

* In 1975 Kramer was caught selling cocaine to undercover federal agents and given a two-year prison sentence. In 'Jail Guitar Doors' The Clash name-check him with the couplet: 'Let me tell you about Wayne and his deals in cocaine...'

The American media had the grace to put The Clash's flat-lining down to opening night nerves, but Pete Silverton of *Sounds* chose to lay the blame squarely at Joe and Paul's door for being a 'sideshow to the main action which is Mick running the show from the centre of the stage, arguing with the roadies, chivvying the sound guys, and deciding which song they're gonna run through next.' Unbeknown to Silverton, Mick had been throwing his weight around behind the scenes by rejecting the tour backdrop that Paul had conceived back in London. The backdrop, which depicted WWII American B52 bombers with their bay doors open, raining their cargo of death down in the direction of Topper's kit, had set The Clash back £1,500, yet despite having raised no objections to playing under the Pearl Harbor '79 Tour banner at the beginning of the year, just as with Rocco McCauley's Belfast street scene backdrop, Mick now rejected the new backdrop on account of it 'promoting violence'.[4]

Ray Lowry was dutifully commissioned to come up with a less-confrontational replacement, and the cartoonist would spend a frustratingly fruitless couple of days dashing around Manhattan flitting from art loft to art loft with a huge canvas under his arm. His efforts would come to nought, however, for as soon as he mentioned why he needed their studio space, the proprietor would bump up the price. As a result, the multi-flag backdrop that had first been unfurled at the Harlesden Roxy shows the previous October was hurriedly flown over and pressed into service.

The collective mood wasn't improved when the tour rolled into Chicago two days later only to discover Epic hadn't as yet stumped up the $20,000 Blackhill had requested the label contribute towards the tour. What had initially seemed an administrative oversight was soon seen for what it was when CBS suggested they be allowed to release the US version of *The Clash* in the UK, and advance the group moneys from the royalties they could expect to earn in order to finance the tour.

The Clash, however, refused point blank, and it was only when they threatened to hail a cab to O'Hare International that Epic relented and released the promised funds.

The tour might have been back on, but having suffered The Clash's sling and arrow insults during the subsidy stand-off with Epic proved too much for the hapless Mark Wissing, who tended his resignation as liaison between the two forthwith.

On the day of the show itself a local celebrity DJ failed to show at the hotel to interview Mick owing to his having spent the previous night out on the tiles with a bag of coke and a local hooker. His subsequent attempt to assuage The Clash guitarist's feelings by turning up backstage at the Aragon Ballroom and presenting Mick with two of the hooker's friends only served to heighten The Clash's increasing sense of estrangement.

Following shows in Detroit, Cleveland, and Boston the tour bus wended its way down the Eastern seaboard to New York for two sold-out shows over consecutive nights at the Palladium. *Trouser Press*' Ira Robbins was once again in attendance to commit his thoughts on the evening's events to paper. Having opined there was little chance of a Clash show 'being [either] slick or standard', went on to add that the 'fearsome foursome – survivors of enough self induced setbacks to stop an army – [had] reached a level where it's not how good they are at any particular gig, it's how hard they work to make it good.'

From the moment The Clash hit the stage and blasted into the opening three-song salvo: 'Safe European Home', 'I'm So Bored With The USA' and 'Complete Control' they worked at a frenetic pace to ensure everyone within the converted theatre – be it the ordinary fans, the press, or the celebrity 'glitterati' – would be talking about the show for months to come. Robbins certainly went away happy, believing The Clash could be both fun and exciting having 'maintained their unique ethics while adopting enough conventional technique to make a concert fully satisfying, for critics and paying customers alike.'

It is the following night's Palladium outing, which, thanks to a certain photograph, has served to earn The Clash a lasting place in rock 'n' roll legend.

Smashing up instruments during a show had become almost as passé as the trashing of hotel rooms by the late-Seventies. So much so, that it took Sid Vicious' bludgeoning of a heckler with his bass midway through the Sex Pistols' show in San Antonio for people to sit up and take notice again. Yet while Pete Townshend has the honour of the first accredited onstage guitar-smash from his trashing his Rickenbacker at the Railway Hotel back in September 1964, it was Pennie Smith's snap-photo of Paul slamming his Fender Precession bass into the Palladium stage which the Rock and Roll Hall of Fame subsequently inducted as the 'ultimate rock 'n' roll rock photo'.

The Pearl Harbor '79 Tour may have given The Clash a taste of touring America, but on that occasion they'd only been called upon to play nine shows in three weeks and with this latest jaunt cramming twenty-three dates into five weeks it was inevitable that the Groundhog Day existence of traversing the vast expanse that is the continental USA would gradually begin to wear everyone down.

Joe cracked as early as Detroit when he smashed a reporter's tape recorder, whereas the smashed Fender Precision residing in the bus' cargo hold bore silent testimony that the normally placid Paul was feeling the strain. When Mick finally succumbed to a bout of cabin fever following a show at the O'Keefe Centre in Toronto, rather than target a tape recorder or guitar, he made everyone suffer by refusing to board the bus until someone procured him a spliff.

Under normal circumstances this wouldn't have seemed a strange request, but this was Canada not Camden Town. With Mick still refusing to budge, someone pointed out that scoring weed would be less of a problem once they were back across the border. Mick wasn't interested and staged a one-man sit-in while a couple of obliging fans hurried off in a cab to score some weed. Mickey Gallagher was gob-smacked and couldn't work out who to consider the worse offender: Mick for holding everyone up for the sake of a spliff, or the rest of the group putting up with his tantrum.

It wasn't only the musicians' moods that were wearing thin by this juncture, however, as The Clash's purse was also near empty and Epic were refusing to get out their chequebook. Johnny and the Baker were accustomed to working with little or no money, but the American road crew didn't know Mick Jones from Casey Jones and went on strike.

Kosmo tried to intervene, but to the Americans he was just the fast-talking Limy in a loud suit that got in their way prancing around at the side of the stage during showtime. Thankfully, Johnny Green knew how to walk their walk and got them to retire to a room with a few bottles of whichever southern comfort took their fancy while the cash-flow problems were sorted out.

♪♪♪

Upon their return to London, The Clash reconvened at Wessex Studio with Mickey Gallagher once again providing piano. They were there primarily to oversee the overdubs and remixes for *London Calling*, as well as record Wilbert 'Willi' Williams' 'Armagideon Time', which The Clash had introduced into the set at the Tribal Stomp II festival, and was now earmarked as the B-side of 'London Calling'; the introductory single that would serve as a tantalising taster for the album.

Prior to leaving for America Kosmo had entered negotiations with the *NME* to look at repeating the flexi-disc single idea that had proved so successful with *The Clash* to promote *London Calling*. By the time he'd finally cajoled the paper into agreeing The Clash had just twenty-four hours to come up with a new song if they were to meet the deadline. This was a big ask, but Mick returned the next afternoon with both the tune and finished lyric to 'Train In Vain'; a funky, soul-pop ode to his lost love, Viv Albertine.

Although Mick and Viv had enjoyed an on/off and oft tempestuous relationship, Viv had moved into Simon Close with Mick earlier in the year. However, with The Slits' star rising in ascendancy thanks in part to their ongoing association with The Clash, the pressure of trying to maintain their relationship finally became too much for her.

'Mick used to cry and cry about Viv,' Johnny Green revealed. 'She was quite hard on him. He rarely behaved like that with other women. He played the rock star normally, but with Viv, no. It's the only time I've ever seen him like that. She broke his heart. He was in love with her.'[5]

The Slits' debut album, *Cut*, had been released on Polydor whilst The Clash were in America, and Mick returned to find that Viv had twisted the knife in the track 'Ping Pong Affair'. Though she's careful not to mention him by name, with the song's lyric referring to the female protagonist declaring that her jilted lover – who is left sulking in his room – can have his records and comics back while she heads off down Ladbroke Grove to have some fun, leaves little doubt as to who the song is about.

A far more personal revelation came in 2014 with the publication of her autobiography, *Clothes, Clothes, Clothes, Music, Music, Music, Boys, Boys, Boys*, in which Viv confesses to having aborted Mick's unborn child sometime during 1978.

Having booked herself into a clinic in Brighton with just two days to spare before she'd be over the legal voluntary termination limit, Viv had called Mick to drop the bombshell. 'Before I leave I tell Mick over the phone that I'm pregnant and I'm off to the hospital to deal with it on my own. He offers to come with me but I don't want him to. I don't want to feel anything. If he's there I might feel something.'[6]

In the book Viv ends her narrative on the subject by saying although she didn't regret having the abortion for twenty years, and still believes it a woman's fundamental right to choose, she did eventually come to regret her decision, and wishes she had kept the baby.

Bill Price has always maintained that the tune to 'Train In Vain' – if only as a backing-track – had been laid down before The Clash flew out to America. Even if this were true, it was still an exceptional effort on Mick's part. Joe would subsequently claim his aversion to 'jealousy and heterosexual complaining songs' as the reason for his allowing Mick the honour of singing lead vocal on the song, but Mick's burning the midnight oil to meet the deadline must surely have figured in his decision.[7]

Despite pulling out all the stops, Kosmo's strategy came to nought when the *NME*'s parent company IPC rejected the flexi-single idea out of hand. The Clash could, of course, have tucked the new song in the vault for a later day, but as the initial idea had been to give the fans a freebie, it was decided to tag the uncredited track onto the end of *London Calling*.

– CHAPTER TEN –

ANOTHER DAY OLDER AND DEEPER IN DEBT

'I actually like pop art, I like pop music, and I like pop culture. There wouldn't be any of the other stuff without it. We shouldn't look down on it. Pop's more about ideas. That's where it's interesting. The important thing is not who's doing what, but the overall impression, where ideas jump out. Rock would seem a bit more laboured.'

– Mick Jones

B LACKHILL HAD BEEN EQUALLY busy upon their return, and while The Clash were holed up at Wessex recording 'Armageddon Time' and 'Train In Vain', their management were frantically finalising a forty-date UK tour to promote London Calling, set to commence with a warm-up show at the Friars, Aylesbury, on 5 January. The group were itching to get out on the road again, so much so they decided to spice up Christmas by booking two festive dates at the 250-capacity Aklam Hall – a Ladbroke Grove community centre situated directly beneath the Westway – for Christmas Day and Boxing Day – 'to play for all them who don't have a family blow-out and a kip during the James Bond film,' as Mick sold the idea to a bemused Johnny Green.

In keeping with the festive spirit, the admission price for their 'Christmas Dinner Dance' was set at 50p, and the Xmas card-style flyers featured two Pennie Smith pics: one of Mick sporting a straw boater and red nose, and the other of The Clash posing in Stella's living room dressed in their Americana finery. Alas, the festive cheer didn't extend to Soho Square, and with no money forthcoming the group were forced to scrimp on the PA, while Kosmo paid for the flyers out of his own pocket.

With Christmas Day being the one day of the year when all was still and not a creature stirred, those who happened upon one of the eye-catching flyers simply assumed some wag was pulling a festive hoax. Regardless of the hall being less than half-full, however, The Clash played as if their lives depended on it and gave those hardy souls that had abandoned their sofas and leftover turkey in favour of chancing their arm a Christmas night to savour.

Needless to say, with the word that The Clash's Christmas extravaganza was genuine spreading quicker than the flu, the Boxing Night bash was packed to the rafters.

The Clash made it a hat-trick of London dates when – billed as 'mystery guests' – they played alongside Ian Dury & the Blockheads and Matumbi on the second night of a four-show Benefit for Kampuchea at the Hammersmith Odeon. Following the recent fall of the Pol Pot regime, refugees from the former Cambodia were pouring into neighbouring Thailand. Although new crops would be harvested in the summer, in the interim 1,000 tonnes of food and emergency supplies would need to be airlifted into the country each day if disaster was to be averted.

Adding their name to what was undoubtedly a noble cause was part and parcel to being in The Clash, but it would prove a night of mixed fortunes for Mick owing to his relenting to Kosmo's badgering and joining the Ian Dury and the Blockheads on stage for 'Sweet Gene Vincent'. This show of grandstanding didn't sit well with the rest of the group. Joe was particularly incensed and tore into Mick backstage for getting ideas above his station. Mick was said to be so upset that he burst into tears, but went on anyway.

The Clash had taken to the Odeon stage sporting the new bowling shirts (once again designed by the group's in-house seamstress, Alex Michon) they were set to wear on the forthcoming UK tour.

The shirts – predominantly black with front panels in contrasting colours – were worn rocker style with the sleeves rolled up high on the bicep and served to heighten Rob Harper's observation that The Clash live spectacle was akin to watching three Eddie Cochrans. When the time came for Mick to join the Blockheads, however, he'd changed into tight-fitting black leathers.

To compound his folly of donning leathers to play pantomimic popstar, just before going out on stage to join Dury, Mick ran across to Johnny Green and told him to 'stick a fag in me mouth'[1] so as to complete his Brando-esque bad boy image.

Yet while Mick could easily shrug off Joe and Paul's grumblings as sour grapes, the *NME*'s Paul Rambali referring to him as 'a lead guitarist of tireless vanity' whilst penning his review of The Clash's performance would have found a chink in his armour.

♪♪♪

The Clash had named the forty-date UK tour '16 Tons' after the Tennessee Ernie Ford song of the same name. It was meant as a tongue-in-cheek reference to their owing their soul to the CBS company store, but the true irony lay in their ongoing failure to realise their worth. They might not have been the biggest group in the world in terms of record sales, but with three albums and two successful US tours under their belt they should have raised their game and booked bigger venues instead of returning to the same low-rent halls they'd played on the White Riot Tour some three years earlier.

As they had done in the US, The Clash were keen to have one of the acts that had proved an inspiration to them to serve as main support. Toots and the Maytals, the originators of 'Pressure Drop' – which had been a perennial feature in the set, and had also featured as the B-side to 'English Civil War' – were duly invited only to pull out again offering neither explanation nor apology just days before the tour was set to commence. Following some frenzied phone calls, Joe Ely was drafted in to play the last ten dates, whilst renowned reggae DJ, producer and toaster, Mikey Dread, was booked for the majority of the dates.

The Sixteen Tons Tour officially got underway at the Odeon in Canterbury the following night, but within days of their going back out on the road for real The Clash's policy of spending every available minute rehearsing, recording, or playing, began to exact a heavy toll. Jock Scott, another of the group's inner-circle associates, recalls Mick threatening to quit the tour early on, but although his mood was mollified on that particular occasion, he became increasingly withdrawn as the dates rolled by and rarely ventured out of his hotel room.

The flip side of embarking on another full-scale UK tour, of course, was that it put The Clash centre stage in terms of media exposure. This time around it wasn't only the music press who were keen to record the group's on-the-road shenanigans as the BBC's flagship early evening news magazine programme, *Nationwide*, sent a film crew along to the Caird Hall in Dundee (18 January).

Aside from footage of them performing 'Clampdown' and 'Revolution Rock', and walking from the coach to the hotel, the report featured Mick and Joe relating their respective brushes with the law during the Out On Parole Tour – and the accompanying police harassment (as they saw it) – before then laying out The Clash's VFM manifesto in that they'd released a double album for the price of a single, and kept ticket prices to an absolute minimum. To emphasise the point that The Clash were always willing to go that extra mile for their fans, the report finished with footage of Joe and Terry McQuade assisting ticketless youngsters in through the dressing room window.

What the *Nationwide* exposé failed to pick up, of course, was the slow-burning fuse on the fractious relationship between Mick and Joe that had been festering away since the Kampuchea benefit. With Paul – and possibly Topper – also believing Mick had been wrong to accept the guest spot with the Blockheads; it was only a matter of time that matters came to a head.

The Clash were catching their breath backstage at the Sheffield Top Rank (27 January), and with the South Yorkshire crowd baying for more, Joe suggested they really bring the curtain down in style by playing 'White Riot' at the end of the three-song encore. Mick refused point blank. To his mind, 1980 wasn't only a new year; it was the beginning to a new decade, and therefore high time they dispensed with 'White Riot', and the rest of the three-chord thrashers that made up the first album.

When speaking to *Uncut* some nineteen years after the events in Sheffield, Joe said how it was a coupling of Mick telling him he didn't respect the stage and hurling a vodka and orange in his face that had caused him to give Mick a smack in the mouth. When giving his version of events, however, Johnny Green makes no mention of Mick's put-down, or of his hurling a drink in Joe's face. Only that Joe 'slammed him [Mick] with his fist, full in the face.'[2]

Mick was supposedly still lying prostrate upon the dressing room floor when Joe, Paul, and Topper headed back out on stage, and Johnny says how he hurriedly helped Mick to his feet, wiped the blood from his face, and popped on a pair of sunglasses. Just what Mick or anyone else within The Clash's retinue would need of sunglasses in January, Johnny doesn't say, but their pal Mo Armstrong had sent over several FSLN* bandannas from San Francisco, and Johnny tied one of the red and black bandannas about the lower half of Mick's face before guiding him out towards the stage.

He was still clearly dazed, but Mick dutifully dropped note perfect into 'Garageland' and bounced about the stage throwing his customary shapes. However, while he ploughed into 'White Riot' with his usual gusto, at the end of the first verse he unslung his Les Paul, propped it against a speaker and strolled off stage.

Mick's show of defiance could well have led to further fisticuffs, but in typical Clash style, neither the backstage fight, nor his abandoning the stage during the encore, was ever mentioned; though a tacit reminder came with 'White Riot' being dropped from the set until much later in the tour.

♪♪♪

With 'London Calling' having given The Clash their best placing on the UK Singles chart to date (No. 11), Kosmo – aided and abetted by

---

* The Frente Sandinista de Liberación Nacional had overthrown Nicaraguan dictator Anastasio Somoza Debayle the previous July, thus forever ending the tyrannical Somoza dynasty.

the group themselves – came up with the idea of launching a non-stop assault on the UK Singles chart by releasing a brand-new Clash single each and every month; the idea being that a new record would be issued once the previous single began dropping out of the chart.

With the 1 February date at the Victoria Hall in Stoke-on-Trent having been cancelled, and their having a couple of days off before the first of two consecutive nights at Manchester's Apollo Theatre, The Clash, together with Mikey Dread, Bill Price and Jerry Green (who'd both come up from London by train) set up home in Pluto Studios to record 'Bankrobber', which had been slated as the first of the mooted 'Clash Singles Bonanza'.

Surprisingly, not everyone was happy with The Clash's marketing strategy, as Mick explained. 'We had a big row at Heathrow airport with the head of CBS, Maurice Oberstein, who was there with his dog and lady chauffeur. He didn't want to put out twelve singles. But eventually "Bankrobber" came out in England, so we got one single out in twelve months.'[3]

CBS' reluctance to put out 'Bankrobber' stemmed – according to Paul – because they thought the mixes 'sounded like David Bowie backwards.'[4] With the label flatly refusing to release the single, and The Clash doggedly refusing to record an alternate song, the ensuing stalemate killed off any hopes of the singles campaign.

CBS did eventually relent to releasing 'Bankrobber' in the UK (8 August), and despite minimal daytime airplay, coupled with The Clash's ongoing refusal to appear on *Top Of The Pops*, the single reached No. 12 on the chart. 'We'd never appear on *Top Of The Pops* because it was rubbish, so they got their [in-house] dance troupe, Legs & Co, to do a routine to it,' Mick said. 'They were all dressed up as bankrobbers wearing masks and hats and did a hilarious dance.'[5]

Two others who donned hats and masks in the 'Bankrobber' cause were Johnny Green and Baker who posed as villains faking a bank robbery on Lewisham High Street as part of Don Letts' promo video. During the filming Don, Johnny, and Baker were stopped and questioned by the cops who reluctantly accepted their tale that they were 'art students working on a project for our final grades.'

'They (Johnny and Baker) were standing outside a bank wearing hats, long coats, and masks like gangsters from an American movie and the police pulled them because they thought they looked dodgy,' Mick chuckled. 'As if robbers would be that stupid!'[6]

On 27 February, *Rude Boy* received its premiere at the Zoo Palast, as the official British entry at that year's Berlin Film Festival. With the exception of Johnny Green and Baker – who'd both impishly disregarded Mick's order to the contrary – no one from either The Clash or Blackhill were in attendance. Their joint refusal stemming from The Clash having distanced themselves from the film – despite having pocketed some £2,550 of the £4,000 advance as per the contract the outgoing Bernard had signed with Dave Mingay and Jack Hazen back in October 1978. Also in accordance with the contract, the group would receive ten per cent of the net profits over £25,000.

Rude Boy received tepid reviews within the mainstream press, but the music critics were at least all agreed that the live footage of The Clash was worthy of the admission price. This didn't cut any ice with the group, however, and upon their return to London following the final date of the US leg of the Sixteen Tons Tour at the Motor City Roller Rink in Detroit, they sought an injunction to prevent the film being screened; their chief objection being the film's sub-plot which revolved around the experiences of a black youth being arrested for pick-pocketing, as they felt it reinforced the stereotype that all black teenagers were thieves.

Mingay would later defend the film's sub-plot by saying how four white kids such as The Clash could – in late-Seventies Britain at any rate – make a million pounds from misleading the youth, supporting drug-taking and creating anarchy, whereas a black kid would be arrested and imprisoned for stealing a quid.

At the time of The Clash's injunction, he and Hazen were left somewhat perplexed at The Clash's standpoint as the scenes in question were not only amongst the first to be shot, but were shot prior to their approaching the group to appear in the film.

As with the vast majority of rock 'n' roll films, The Clash's off-stage acting left much to be desired, they were musicians not actors after all.

When penning his review for the *NME*, Neil Norman opined that Mick 'is the actor playing his part to the hilt, whether it's on the steps of Clerkenwell Magistrates Court or in the studio laying down the vocal to "Stay Free"'.

Johnny Green, however, says Mick was unhappy at the way he came across on screen, and suggests this was due to Mingay and Hazen's going out of their way to create a huge discrepancy between Mick's self-image and his screen-image after tiring of his playing the rock star. 'I think what you see in the film is the result of their low opinion of Mick,' he says. 'There was some really nice stuff of him in the rushes, but that all ended up on the cutting room floor.'[7]

Rude Boy certainly didn't have much in the way of a storyline, but one of the more interesting sub-plots was Mick's obvious antipathy towards the seemingly hapless Ray Gange, who was only following direction from Mingay and Hazen.

The film struck a chord with Johnny Green as it allowed him the chance to sit back and really savour The Clash live experience free from the worry of things going wrong. Yet betwixt the Berlin premiere and the film's London airing Johnny had come to realise that very little was going wrong with The Clash of late. 'Train In Vain' had been released as a single in the US to coincide with the Sixteen Tons Tour and was doing nicely, while *London Calling* was shifting product on both sides of the Atlantic. That The Clash had become a streamlined operation was very much down to Johnny's competence, but it had been the map-cap, flying-by-the-seat-of-your-pants roller-coaster ride that had made being with The Clash so much fun. In recent months he'd become increasingly bored by the predictability of it all, and with Kosmo having effectively taken over the more creative aspects of his role, he gave notice in Boston that he'd accepted a job working with Joe Ely in Texas.

With the European leg of the Sixteen Tons Tour set to kick-off at the Markthalle in Hamburg on 12 May, Johnny could have been forgiven for thinking Joe (whom he'd always been closest to within The Clash) would try twisting his arm into accompanying them on one last Bash Street Kids beano, but Joe merely shrugged it off with a casual 'yeah, alright'.

If Johnny was expecting a similar reaction from Mick he was in for a surprise, however. Despite his having pandered to Mick's every whim during the guitarist's pampered rock star phase, the two had never enjoyed a particularly close relationship and yet it was Mick who took Johnny's departure the hardest.

No sooner had The Clash served their injunction on *Rude Boy*, they accompanied Mikey Dread to Jamaica and booked time at the island's legendary Channel One studio in Maxfield Park; the idea being they might expand on the rock/reggae crossover they'd started back at Pluto whilst recording 'Bankrobber'.

Mikey had come to know the individual Clash members quite well by now. Perhaps not surprisingly, it was the reggae-loving Paul with whom he forged the closest bond, but though he came to understand Topper and Joe, he never quite got where Mick was coming from. 'I could never figure [Mick] out in all the time I was there,' he explained. 'He was the one who was picking on everyone else. I'm not being negative. He was a very chilled guy. But he was more like a superstar, you know?'[8]

Being in the company of Mikey Dread afforded The Clash a certain amount of protection, but with Jamaica in the grip of an economic meltdown that made Britain's financial woes seem a mislaid wallet, it wasn't long before the locals came a calling looking for handouts. After all, the Rolling Stones always ensured everybody had a dollar in their pocket whenever they were in town. The Clash could argue they were on a parallel with the Stones in musical terms, but they were poles apart financially. If it hadn't been for Blackhill managing to cajole CBS into providing money to cover the cost of the studio they wouldn't be there in the first place, and all other costs were being taken care of courtesy of Paul's girlfriend Debbie's credit card.

Of course, that mattered little to the local populace: The Clash were white men, ergo they had money. Though Mikey was himself threatened on occasion, he didn't think anyone would go so far as to physically harm the group. However, rather than risk being proved wrong, he advised his friends to pack up their gear and get the hell out of Dodge.

A boy with a dream...

Rock, rock, Clash City Rockers.

Got a spare bottom E string? Mick and Joe on stage.

Helping out a mate: Mick on stage with The Rich Kids circa early '78.

Mick with Ellen Foley circa 1981.

It's official: the 10 September 1983 issue of the *NME* confirming Mick's dismissal from The Clash.

The horses are on the track: the cover of *Big Audio Dynamite*, released in October 1985.

Long overdue: Mick, Joe, Paul, and Topper at the 2001 Ivor Novello Awards.

BAD looking good second time around for the 2011 reunion.

Mick onstage with Pete Wylie and Peter Hooton at Liverpool Olympia on 24 September 2011.

Do you remember this one? Paul joins Mick on stage at The Scala during the Justice Tonight Tour of December 2011.

Copyright: Peter Stevens – www.peterstevensphotography.co.uk

Mick and Pete Wylie on stage during the Justice Tonight Band tour.

Master and pupil: Mick jamming with his long-time hero Ian Hunter at the lock-up studio in East Acton in November 2013.

I think I've got one in the back: Mick at his Rock 'N' Roll Library.

Watch out for the caretaker. Mick enjoying a sneaky fag in the toilets.

Come on you 'R's: Mick and Glen outside QPR's Loftus Road ground on match day.

With Paul set to fly up to British Columbia to commence filming on *All Washed Up*, rather than head for the airport immediately, the group further availed themselves of Debbie's credit card unwinding with Mikey in Montego Bay until it was time for Paul to dust off his equity card.

London Calling was still riding high in the charts on both sides of the Atlantic, but while Blackhill believed themselves to be a forward thinking management company, they were still old school enough to insist The Clash have a new album out in time for the pre-Christmas shopping frenzy. Paul was in Vancouver with Steve Jones and Paul Cook giving the camera a taste of how the Sex Pistols' backline might have looked had Bernard and Malcolm been allowed to carry out their Machiavellian scheme, but Mick, Joe, and Topper – with Mikey Dread and Bill Price also in tow – flew to New York and settled themselves into the Power Station on 53rd Street where they messed around giving the Clash treatment to songs such as the Equals' 'Police On My Back', and Prince Buster's 'Madness'.

With the constant lack of money something of a continuing thread in The Clash story, one has to wonder why they flew out to New York when a recording studio closer to home would have equally suited their purpose – especially as the money CBS had provided for the Power Station sessions lasted but a few days? Rather than return home the group compounded their lunacy by begging CBS to allow them to remain in New York.

What was even more surprising, however, was that Maurice Oberstein relented to their cap-in-hand demands and released sufficient funding for Kosmo to secure a cut-price, three-week block booking at Jimi Hendrix' old haunt, Electric Lady, on West 8th Street. What Oberstein didn't know at the time of signing the cheque was that in-betwixt all Kosmo's transatlantic pleadings Mick and Joe had formulated a new battle strategy... and when the temporarily-truncated Clash set up house at Electric Lady, they did so to write and record the mooted new album.

♪♪♪

The behemoth that would become *Sandinista!* began with another transatlantic plea, this time requesting Mickey Gallagher's presence in the studio. Mickey was also asked to bring over his fellow Blockhead Norman Watt-Roy as Paul was still away filming. While awaiting the two Blockheads arrival, Mick and Joe put the word out on the street that they were keen to meet with Ivan Julian; the ex-Voidoids' guitarist having obviously impressed them on the Out Of Control Tour.

Thinking The Clash merely wanted to renew their acquaintanceship, Ivan dutifully dropped by the studio expecting nothing more than to wile away an hour shooting the breeze over a couple beers. However, on hearing the basic backing track to one of the new songs ('The Call Up') he grabbed up a guitar and jammed some chord changes over the main riff. In the two-and-a-half years since the Out Of Control Tour, Ivan would have monitored The Clash's career upward trajectory with more than a passing interest. He would have also gained an insight into the dynamic between Mick and Joe, and although he still regarded Joe as the group's anchor in terms of creativity, he was left in little doubt that Mick was the one calling the shots.

Being a jobbing musician, Ivan understood how tension can quickly build up when the dollars are disappearing with each tick of the clock, but he was struck by Mick's domineering personality. 'There weren't any rows as such, [but] Mick would push people when it was sometimes uncalled for,' he revealed. 'There'd be a time when the guys would feel like breaking out, and Mick would be insisting we carry on. It was like, "Come on, what's your problem?"'[9]

Ivan might not have witnessed any serious disputes between Mick and Joe, but by the time The Clash reconvened at Wessex in mid-August following the Sixteen Tons European dates cracks were beginning to appear in the group's creative partnership. Evidence that Joe was feeling the strain came at the opening European date in Hamburg with his smashing a young German skinhead about the head with his Telecaster in retaliation for the skinhead using the lad in front of him as a human punch-bag. Joe was lucky to escape serious charges, but instead of taking a much-needed break he agreed to assist Mick with the song-writing on *Spirit Of St Louis*, the second album by Mick's Epic label mate and new girlfriend Ellen Foley* (Seven of the songs making up the final track-listing are credited as Strummer-Jones compositions). All four members of The Clash would make guest appearances on the album, and Mick would also take over the production chair at Wessex where Ellen recorded the album.

It was whilst The Clash were recording in New York that Mick first became hip to the new music that was buzzing around the Big Apple. Although Joe and Paul were happy to borrow a little of what was going down with the kids in Harlem and the South Bronx on songs such as 'The Magnificent Seven', Mick embraced rap with a passion, as he later revealed to Paulo Hewitt: 'Ever since I hit that New York club for the first time, I thought, "God, beatbox", that was it for me. I knew I was still a guitar player and I stuck that on top of it.'[10]

'C'mon Every Beatbox' was still several years hence, yet while Mick saw the endless possibilities available to The Clash if he could only persuade Joe and Paul to give up rioting in favour of dancing, he has always maintained that he didn't view the group's experimentation with rap as particularly ground-breaking. 'We never thought that, at any time,' he subsequently revealed to Kris Needs. 'We were just sort of knocking out some numbers. It's like that's all we wanted to do; to do our thing. We didn't necessarily wanna be part of this big, happening thing that was so cool. We just did what we wanted to do. I guess it's because we had that kind of attitude.'[11]

Mick might have been the one espousing hip-hop, but it was Joe who first mooted the idea of The Clash trying their hand at some rap rock. 'Well, the thing was… it was just all around us,' Mick said in November 2007. 'Joe went like this, "Let's do a rap tune." Even though I was the one who was most enthusiastic about what seemed to be coming off the radio at the time, [and] excited about it. But it was actually Joe who went, "Uh, let's do a rap tune." When we did "The Magnificent Seven", which was going to be called "Magnificent Rappo Clappers", I think we just got swept away. We took on what

---

* Despite having roles in films such as *Tootsie*, *Fatal Attraction*, *King Of Comedy*, *Cocktail*, and *Married To The Mob*, Foley is perhaps still best known for her duet with Meat Loaf on 'Paradise By The Dashboard Light' from the latter's squillion-selling 1977 album, *Bat Out Of Hell* (Though Karla DeVito features in the promo video, she is lip-syncing to Foley's vocal).

was going on around us. And by that time we'd been to a few places, so we didn't have such a narrow view of things, and it had an affect on us, and we changed. We were constantly changing.'[12]

The Clash undoubtedly benefited from copping an attitude in terms of their refusal to be pigeon-holed when it came to making music, but by adopting a similar stance when it came to ignoring wiser counsel they left themselves open to ridicule. And there was no greater example of this than their insistence on *Sandinista!* being a triple album.

While it might be just another urban myth, legend has it that upon discovering The Clash were intent on releasing *London Calling* as a double album, Bruce Springsteen had stormed into Epic's New York offices demanding that he be allowed to follow suit with his own latest album. And that it was upon subsequently hearing Springsteen boasting that his double offering, *The River*, would put 'those Limeys' in their place that The Clash decided to let Bruce suck on his ego by going one further and releasing a triple album.

Regardless of where the idea for releasing a triple album came from, it should have been disregarded just as quickly. The 1980-era Clash was a far more erudite creature to the one that had come crash, bang, walloping out of the stalls four years earlier, but they weren't so far removed from punk's original ethos to know triple albums reeked of the worst possible excesses of rock; the hitherto reserve of prog-rockers and other self-absorbed arseholes. To compound their folly, The Clash were equally insistent that *Sandinista!* be retailed at the same price as a single album.

Blackhill thought the whole idea idiocy incarnate and wasted little time in voicing their opinion. Financial suicide aside, they argued – rightfully – that simply because there were enough songs in the can to warrant a triple album, didn't necessarily mean the songs were worthy of committing to vinyl.

It's easy to pass judgement long after the fact, but the general consensus amongst The Clash cognoscenti is that while *Sandinista!* would have made a passable double album, it would have made a blinding single. Even, today, some thirty-odd years on, one has to argue that the album has enough padding to warrant it being re-titled *Sandbaginista!*

Disregarding the sagacious advice of his former mentors at Blackhill, Kosmo headed over to Soho Square to thrash out a deal with CBS on the group's behalf. Surprisingly, Maurice Oberstein consented to the triple… but only on the proviso The Clash agreed to waive royalties on the first 200,000 copies sold in the UK.

Given that *London Calling* had fallen some 20,000 short of this mooted figure in UK sales, unless it surpassed expectations in America then The Clash would be plunging themselves deeper in debt.

Andrew King and Pete Jenner have always believed CBS had long been chiselling away at The Clash to drop them, but this was the juncture when they realised the futility of trying to oversee the business affairs of four young men who eschewed all forms of authority.

When signing Pink Floyd, King and Jenner had boasted they'd make them 'bigger than The Beatles', and though they were pragmatic enough to accept The Clash were never likely to emulate the unit-shifting potential of the Dave Gilmore-era Pink Floyd, let alone the Fab Four, they had at least formulated a business plan that was beginning to make some headway with the group's crippling £250,000 debt to CBS.

In ploughing ahead with the three-for-one album deal and forgoing their UK royalties, The Clash wilfully holed the Blackhill business plan beneath the waterline.

– CHAPTER ELEVEN –

THE REBELS WERE DANCING ON AIR

'I don't worry about making it; I worry about not making it. If I don't make it, then all the kids who are watching can say to themselves, "Well, shit, they didn't make it, they didn't get out. What hope is there for us to make it?" If we make it, then those kids know that they've got a chance too.'

– Mick Jones

IN TERMS OF 'MAKING IT', prior to the release of Sandinista! The Clash could rightfully claim to have seen it, done it, and had the obligatory T-shirt to prove as much. Post Sandinista!, however, it was a different story, and following the mauling the album received at the hands of the music press – with several notable Clash aficionados such as Ian Penman, Nick Kent, and Paul Morley happily adopting an 'et tu, Brutus' stance in twisting the knife – the group retreated from public view to lick their wounded pride.

Mick, perhaps feeling the sting more than the others seeing as he'd been the one to suggest a triple album, fled to New York to be with Ellen Foley. It would prove something of a fillip for his bruised ego as The Clash's American fan-base tended to be infinitely more AOR orientated than their British counterparts. So much so, that *Sandinista!* reached a highly respectable #24 on the Billboard chart – three places higher than *London Calling* had managed. The feat was even more remarkable given that the album retailed for $15, had received little of no promotion from Epic, and the majority of American music lovers were snapping up anything and everything relating to John Lennon following the ex-Beatle's murder four days earlier on 8 December.

Mick had also come in for criticism over the production on *Sandinista!* so the offer from Ian Hunter for him to join his one-time idol at the Power Station where the ex-Mott The Hoople frontman was recording his latest solo album proved most welcoming. Mick Ronson would be producing the album, but as Hunter had penned 'Theatre Of The Absurd' following a conversation he'd had with Mick about the reggae-rock crossover The Clash had helped bring about.

Following further sessions at Electric Lady, Mick – with Ellen Foley in tow – accompanied Hunter and Ronson back to London and into Wessex Studios where the album was to be completed under Bill Price's tutorship. Hunter would subsequently admit in Campbell Devine's *All The Young Dudes* that he and Ronson had both been 'lacking in focus' at the time, and were therefore happy to take a back seat. Aside from inspiring two now songs by coaxing Hunter to set two of his poems – 'Central Park 'n' West' and 'Noises' to music, Mick (though uncredited) laid down guitar parts, joined Ellen on backing vocals, and brought in Topper and Tymon Dogg to add drums and violin respectively.

One final input – albeit inadvertently – came with the album title. The initial working title back in New York had been *Theatre Of The Absurd*, but Mick had playfully renamed the album '*Haircut*' owing to Hunter having had his trademark curly locks shorn at a local barbers. When it came time for the finished masters to go to press Ian kept the tonsorial theme in naming the album, *Short Back 'n' Sides*.

While discussing the album with Campbell Devine, Hunter admitted to being somewhat intimidated by Mick's 'very strong personality in the studio'. Another who saw a different side to Mick during the Wessex sessions was his old friend John Brown. Calling out of the blue after several years of silence, Mick told John how he was looking to put a backing group together for when Ellen went out promoting *Spirit Of St Louis* sometime in the spring and asked if John was interested in strapping on his bass.

John, of course, already knew Hunter well enough, and with Robin Crocker being an ever-present at Wessex during the sessions Mick not only invited him to come along to the studio, but offered to pick him up en route.

John's wife had recently given birth to their first child, a daughter, and John was naturally cock of the hoop and keen for Mick to meet his new family. The meet and greet didn't go according to plan, however, as Mick walked straight past John, had a quick look around the room, before announcing it was time to go.

The studio reunion didn't live up to John's expectations either, as Mick kept his thoughts and his stash of weed to himself.

There was no one within Mick's immediate sphere that hadn't bore the brunt of his aloofness of late, and if John came away from Wessex that day thinking his old friend needed bringing down a peg or two then his wish was already on the wind.

Things had not been going well for The Clash of late. Not only had CBS pulled the plug on a UK tour to promote *Sandinista!* but they'd received yet another battering from the critics following the release of 'Hitsville UK', with Ian Penman calling it the group's 'creative nadir' and labelling them 'Third world guerrillas with quiffs'.

Mick simply immersed himself in Hunter's solo album, but Joe didn't have Wessex's walls to hide behind. He knew he was just as much to blame as Mick for the mess The Clash found themselves in, and would trudge the streets racking his brains seeking a solution to their current ills. It was on one of late evening soul searches that the answer seemingly presented itself outside a Wimpy bar in Notting Hill…

Bernard had hardly been idle since parting company with The Clash as his involvement with Subway Sect, the Specials and Dexys Midnight Runners readily testifies. Yet while he was still brimming with ideas, he was also at something of a loose end at the time of his happenstance encounter with Joe and therefore willing to listen to Joe's overtures.

Paul says he fully supported Joe's proposal that Bernard be reinstated – if only because he missed the anarchic environment within which The Clash had existed first time around, while Topper didn't appear to have an opinion one way or the other – despite Bernard having branded him a 'provincial tosser' – just so long as whatever agenda Joe had in mind didn't interfere with his drug-stabbing time.

Mick, of course, was abhorred by the news. 'I could quite easily have walked out then,' he told Paulo Hewitt in 1986.[1] 'But it's like a marriage, or the people you love: you cling on hoping it's going to work out.'

The socialist-minded Joe had always maintained that The Clash was a democracy, but whilst he allowed Paul and Topper an equal say in any decision making, with Mick being his partner in the metaphorical 'marriage' – the McCartney to his Lennon, as it were – there really was only one vote he needed to snag to gain a majority.

Mick may have become a bit of an autocrat in the studio and rehearsal room, but he rarely opposed Joe when it came to Clash policy and yet the mere thought of bringing back the guy who'd tried to oust him from the group stuck in his craw. He was struggling to fathom how Joe could even contemplate the idea, let alone put it to a vote. This was one instance when he was prepared to stand his ground, but Joe pulled the rug out from under his feet by threatening to quit The Clash unless his demand was met. It was a niggardly ultimatum, and Mick could, and perhaps should, have called Joe's bluff by throwing down his own gauntlet – that he would quit if Bernard came back.

Whilst on the road during the Take The Fifth Tour Mick had told Paul Morley that The Clash were everything to him, and that as he had nothing else in his life apart from the group, he'd sort of come to resent The Clash.

Considering Mick was alone in unfamiliar surroundings thousands of miles from home this rare outpouring has to be taken in context because occasional flashes of resentment aside, he loved being in The Clash, and like a disheartened spouse he elected to cling on and hope for the best.

♪♪♪

In order to maximise sales of *Sandinista!* in the UK, The Clash agreed to CBS' suggestion of releasing an unprecedented third single from the album. The suits at Soho Square were pleased The Clash were proving compliant for once, but they were less thrilled at the group's preferred choice as 'The Magnificent Seven' was some six minutes long, and therefore unlikely to gain much Radio One daytime airplay.

Fearing CBS would disregard their artistic control as they had when releasing 'Remote Control', The Clash put forward a compromise. Taking their lead from the New York rap artists who were bringing in outside DJs to produce twelve-inch extended dance remixes of their songs that were proving a hit in the clubs, they offered to supply an edited version of 'The Magnificent Seven' coupled with a longer instrumental remix which they called 'The Magnificent Dance'.

'"Magnificent Dance" was another signpost to the direction we were going in,' Mick explained. 'We always took on board the music that was happening around us, made it part of our thing.'[2]

Production was becoming very much Mick's 'thing' around this time as he was invited to oversee the twiddling and the fiddling on Theatre Of Hate's* debut album, *Westworld*; even coming out front of shop to add guitar parts to several of the songs, including the title track. And yet, somewhat surprisingly, he was absent when it came to the remixing of 'The Magnificent Seven' at Wessex.

Much has been made of the 'Pepe Unidos' production credits on 'The Magnificent Seven', as the mythical Puerto Rican producer, who was also in the chair during the recording and mixing of *Cut The Crap*, was – according to the sleeve-notes accompanying the 1999 reissue of *Super Black Market Clash* – a collective consisting of Joe, Paul, and the recently reinstated Bernard. But with his now taking his managerial cut from The Clash's net earnings, rather than their gross income, Bernard was hardly likely to sit in silence and allow The Clash to carry on digging when they were wallowing in a financial hole. If that meant having an equal say in the studio, then so be it.

Mick may have had serious reservations about the situation, but even he had to admit Bernard made an immediate impact upon his return. 'Bernie came back on the scene because people thought we'd gotten out of control,' he subsequently offered. 'The first thing he wanted to do was book us for seven nights in New York.'[3]

---

* Mick also took the production chair for Theatre Of Hate's follow-up album, *Aria Of The Devil*, the following year. However, owing to the group's affable frontman Kurt Brandon mislaying the master tapes the album wouldn't see the light of day until 1998.

Like the rest of the group, Mick was already disheartened from CBS having refused to finance a UK tour, so when Epic pulled the plug on the proposed sixty-date US tour to promote *Sandinista!* The Clash were left wondering what their next move – if any – might be. Without label support, Bernard knew touring in the traditional sense was no longer viable, and with this in mind he hit on the idea of the group securing prestigious week-long residencies; not only in New York, but also in other major cities around the world such as London and Paris.

Bernard has received plenty of kudos for thinking up the 'Clash city residency' plan, but the honour of being the first-ever rockers to set up a Broadway block-booking – as Mick would surely have known – goes to Mott The Hoople who played five consecutive nights at New York's Uris Theatre in May 1974.

Being something of a forward thinker, Bernard knew The Clash well enough to know familiarity rarely bred contempt. Again, with this in mind, he booked the group back into Vanilla Studios, and despatched Baker to seek out Johnny Green – who'd recently returned from Texas – to offer him his old job back.

Finding Johnny proved easy enough, but regardless of the change in management he sensed The Clash had drifted further apart during his absence and politely declined the invitation.

The UK and US tours had foundered on Epic's fiscal reef, but having booked the now-defunct Bond's International Casino on Times Square to serve as the venue for The Clash's week-long residency in New York commencing on 25 May, Bernard put together a month-long European tour – billed as the 'Mission Impossible Tour' – starting in Barcelona on 27 April.

When reminiscing about this period in *The Clash*, Paul says that Mick – despite Bernard's presence – was still prone to tantrums; one such occasion occurred in Germany when Mick threw his toys out of the pram saying he wasn't prepared to continue with the tour and wanted to go to New York instead.

Jock Scott was another who witnessed Mick's bloody-mindedness first hand. 'We're playing at [the] Real Madrid basketball stadium, a huge gig, loads of punters, and Jonesy would go, "I want egg and chips,"' he explained. 'Everyone would be saying, "Look, we're in

Spain, they don't have egg and chips." But Mick would be determined: "I want egg and chips or I'm not doing the gig."[4]

♪♪♪

Despite its glamorous name, Bond's International Casino was in fact a discotheque, and the only time money changed ever hands was at the front door. With The Clash having sold out the Palladium at each time of asking, when Bernard and Kosmo visited the city to peruse prospective venues for the residency the local promoters put forward the proposal of the group playing a one-off date at the 16,000 capacity Madison Square Garden. However, with the group having previously refused to play New York again unless they could do so in an unseated venue, Bernard had a set mandate in mind. Bond's, therefore, with its makeshift stage, and a dance floor that could comfortably hold 4000 punters, seemed the perfect choice.

The venue certainly appealed to The Clash as it featured in the opening scenes of *Taxi Driver*; the 1977 Martin Scorsese film starring Robert De Niro in the lead role of Travis Bickle. Mick was a huge fan of the film, and it seemed as though life was imitating art when Scorsese – a long-time Clash aficionado – invited the group to make a cameo appearance in *The King of Comedy*, the film he was currently shooting with De Niro in the lead role.

Before setting off for Heathrow The Clash had promised New York to expect 'something special', and come showtime they certainly didn't disappoint. Bounding out onto the stage to Ennio Morricone's '60 Seconds To What?' from *For A Few Dollars More*, the second film in the Clint Eastwood 'man-with-no-name' Spaghetti Western trilogy, they had the audience eating out of their hand from first note to last during the twenty-six song, two-hour long set.

Triumph, however, would soon turn to fiasco when the city's fire marshals – responding to an anonymous call – arrived the next day to enforce the club's fire safety capacity of 1750 – despite The Ramones and The Plasmatics having both played to 4,000 crowds in recent weeks. Following an emergency summit meeting between Bernard and Kosmo, Bond's management, and fire chiefs, a compromise was reached whereby The Clash agreed to play sixteen shows so that each and every ticket holder would still get to see them play.

The first of the amended shows went according to plan, but the following day the city's building department – having come to the conclusion that Bond's was a disaster waiting to happen – slapped a court order on the club, closing it indefinitely. Of course, by this time, the majority of the 'bridge-and-tunnel' out-of-towners were already en route to the venue for the originally scheduled Saturday matinee. The ticket-holders didn't take the news kindly and chaos ensued as hundreds of irate fans took to the street to bring Times Square to a standstill.

The ensuing media coverage would provide The Clash front-page headlines around the globe, but at the time the Fire Marshal's enforcement presented Bernard with a very serious problem seeing as Bond's had taken in excess of $250,000 in tickets sales, which prevented The Clash from playing an alternate venue – such as Madison Square Garden – until all the money had been refunded.

Thankfully, the New York Building Commissioner – having been browbeaten into submission by his Clash-loving offspring – put forward a second compromise whereby the rescheduled shows could proceed so long as Bond's beefed up their security, and revised their emergency evacuation procedures.

In spite of the chaos, Mick would have fond memories of the Bonds run. 'We ran this town.' He told reporters when returning to New York with Big Audio Dynamite several years later. 'We took Broadway. De Niro was bringing his kids to see us. The city stopped cos The Clash were in town.'

The Clash had indeed taken New York, but their prolonged stay in the Big Apple only served to heighten Mick's resolve to guide the group's hip-pop direction. As with every other musical craze that caught his ear over the years he threw himself into hip-hop with a passion. Seeing him strutting about town with a beatbox permanently pressed to his ear, and his wearing a baseball cap on back-to-front, the rest of the group took to calling him 'Wack Attack'.

♪♪♪

When The Clash returned to London towards the end of June they were still walking tall from having brought Times square to a standstill, but the mini-riot they'd inadvertently caused outside Bond's Casino was put a scuffle compared to the 'plight riots' that were sporadically breaking out in towns and cities across Britain.

The long-simmering resentment of the unemployed and underprivileged in the inner-cities had first spilled over into violence back in April in Brixton following the stabbing of a black youth. The youth in question had been attacked by three other black youths, but trouble flared following rumours that the youth had been left to die by the policemen responding at the scene. During the ensuing carnage some 300 police officers were injured, and scores of properties and cars were destroyed.

London hadn't witnessed such scenes of carnage since the Gordon Riots of 1780, and the government was quick to react by commissioning Lord Scarman to look into the causes of the riots, as well make recommendations to prevent such occurrences happening again.

In his report, Scarman expressed his concerns with the plight of the ethnic minorities within London and other major inner-cities, and their relationship with the rest of the community. He felt it essential that people be encouraged to have a sense of responsibility for their own area, and called for a policy of 'direct coordinated attack on racial disadvantage.' That further rioting broke out in London, Leeds, Liverpool, Birmingham and Sheffield, and other underprivileged areas was evidence that his concerns went unheeded.

The Clash hadn't played live in their homeland since the previous summer, yet still came under sniper fire from certain quarters over the perceived irony of their giving 'White Riot' repeated airings on Broadway while London was burning. The incongruity especially wasn't lost on Mick, given his long-standing reticence over 'White Riot' still featuring in The Clash live repertoire.

'I don't think I'd make a good rioter. I don't think I even agree with them,' he told the *NME*'s Paul Rambali. 'Destroying your own places, especially when the government ain't gonna give you another one, seems really double dumb. I do my thing, and it's a creative thing, that's how I feel I contribute. And if my absence is conspicuous on these occasions, then I say, "Don't look to me in the first place." I'm not a street-fighting man. I still gotta belief in the power of reason. I think I'd be really stupid to go out and think I could lead the people.'

The one person Mick wished would take his lead on occasion, of course, was Bernard. Having decided the time was right to begin knocking the new song ideas The Clash had been working on throughout the summer – 'Straight To Hell', 'Ghetto Defendant', 'Inoculated City', and 'Know Your Rights' – into shape Mick presumed they'd be returning to New York to begin work on the new album. Bernard, however, had other ideas. Not only did he concur with the criticisms of self-indulgence over the expense and time The Clash had devoted to *Sandinista!* he was triply determined that any new Clash product would be recorded with minimum fuss and within a set budget.

Mick would succeed in keeping Bernard at bay while he and Jerry Green booked time at Air Studios to work on alternative DJ mixes of The Clash's next intended single, 'This Is Radio Clash' ('Outside Broadcast' and 'Radio 5'), but he was less successful when it came to recording the new album.

When speaking to *Rolling Stone* in 1986, Mick said how Joe and Paul were sick of Mick 'bringing my New York environment everywhere I went with them.' Bernard was equally exasperated, and had little trouble convincing Joe that the new album be recorded quickly and cheaply to maximise profits. With the argument settled, The Clash moved their gear – along with the Rolling Stones' mobile studio – into Ear Studios, located in the People's Hall on Freston Road, and set within the shadow of the Westway.

Another gnawing bone of contention between Mick and Bernard came over the appointment of Mick's new guitar tech. Shortly after the group's return to London Mick's guitar tech had quit, and Bernard was duly charged with finding a replacement. Mick had repeatedly insisted that he wanted said replacement be a girl, yet while female guitar technicians were something of a rarity within the male-dominated rock 'n' roll roadie world, there were several that Bernard could have approached. Instead, however, he purposely hired an ex-Wishbone Ash roadie called Digby Cleaver.

Digby had apparently satisfied Bernard's requirements by professing a liking for the American psychedelic punk outfit, The Cramps, but regardless of whatever capabilities he may have had Mick – albeit initially – took Digby's appointment as a personal affront. He was well within his rights to do so because if Bernard was unwilling to meet him on this seemingly trivial point, then what chance his having his views and opinions on Clash policy respected? It wasn't only Digby's sex that annoyed Mick, but also his waistband-length hair.

The irony wouldn't have been lost on the rest of the group given that Mick's nickname back in the *Give 'Em Enough Rope days* had been 'Poodle' owing to his own shoulder-length tresses. Joe and Paul simply looked on in amused silence, but Topper took Digby to one side and suggested he take a trip to the barbers if he wanted to remain on the Clash payroll.

As with Rehearsals and Vanilla, Ear Studios was a secluded, out of the way space where The Clash could get to work without the inherent distractions that came with more upmarket studios such as those in New York. There was even a patch of scrub wasteland to the rear of the building where the team-building football matches of Vanilla could be recreated.

Jerry Green's serving as engineer was another reminder of that halcyon period when The Clash were at the creative pinnacle, but any thoughts of inviting Guy Stevens in from the cold again to sprinkle more of his madcap magic over proceedings were scotched when Guy's luck finally run out and he accidentally overdosed on the pills prescribed to combat his chronic alcoholism. As a fitting tribute, The Clash wrote and recorded 'Midnight To Stevens'* as their personal tribute to Guy.

Recording of the as yet untitled new album was put on hold for the second of The Clash's much-vaunted week-long residencies at the Théâtre Mogador in Paris, with the Mighty Wah! (Featuring Mick's future Justice Tonight collaborator, Pete Wylie, on lead vocals), and The Beat providing support.

---

* 'Midnight To Stevens' wouldn't see the light of day until the release of *Clash On Broadway* in 1991.

As with Bond's in New York, the Paris residency was restricted solely to the Théâtre Mogador, but when The Clash hit the stage on the opening night of their third and final magnificent seven-day residency of the year at the Lyceum Ballroom on 18 October, they did so upon the back of a mini-UK tour to promote the forthcoming release of 'This Is Radio Clash'.

In keeping with the new material slowly being stockpiled for the new album, the Lyceum stage (as it had been in Paris) was set to create an 'urban Vietnam' feel with tiger-striped checkpoint barriers. And as he had done in New York and Paris, New York graffiti artist Futura 2000 did his Rolf Harris-esque 'can-you-guess-what-it-is-yet?' aerosol artistry on the huge backdrop while The Clash went about their business.

The British music press were the usual discourteous selves when penning their respective reviews, but the fans – oblivious to both Mick's resentment of Bernard's retaking the managerial reins, and his determination to steer The Clash away from traditional rock 'n' roll into more experimental waters – were happy to pay homage to their homecoming heroes.

True, The Clash were still lagging behind The Jam in the polls, were viewed as yesterday's trend by those courting Spandau Ballet, Duran Duran and the other New Romantics, and were no longer troubling the upper reaches of the UK singles chart, but in the eyes of their hardcore following they could do no wrong.

With the live commitments over for the year, the intention – or so Bernard, Joe, and Paul believed – was to return to Freston Road and pick up where they'd left off writing and recording demos for the new album. Mick, however, had other ideas, and having gotten Topper on side, he played Joe at his own game by refusing to continue with the sessions unless they reconvened to New York.

Mick would later claim to have been joking about the move, and while Pearl Harbor would subsequently play down the supposed rift that his ultimatum caused within The Clash, Mick's further insistence that they record everything again from scratch once they'd moved into Electric Lady in mid-November must have left Joe and Paul wondering how many other hoops they'd have to jump through in order to hear the emperor's new chords?

In hindsight, we know now that the underlying reason for Mick's insistence they record the album in New York was that it allowed him to be closer to Ellen Foley. That their relationship had taken something of a downturn of late is evidenced with Mick having already penned the lyric to 'Should I Stay Or Should I Go?', but his reaction at losing the silver bullet pendant Ellen had given him whilst on stage at the Glasgow Apollo suggests he was hoping their being in the same city again would rekindle the flame.

Despite Mick's churlish insistence that they start from scratch on the new album – tentatively titled 'Rat Patrol From Fort Bragg' – the work rate at Electric Lady was prodigious with 'Rock The Casbah' being completed in a single afternoon. Such was their collective drive that they quickly racked up seventeen songs. Much to Bernard's chagrin, however, rather than 'let the ragas drop', all the new songs were coming in around the six minute mark, which meant The Clash were looking at another double album.

If it can be said that Mick was already on the paradoxical path to becoming the irresistible force to match Joe and Paul's immoveable object in terms of where each wanted to take The Clash, neither party was – at least at this juncture – contemplating a Clash without Topper. Yet that very reality was thrust upon them when Topper – who by his own estimation was spending £100 a day to feed his habit – was caught in possession of heroin at Heathrow in the midst of a foolhardy twenty-four hour mercy-mission stopover in London to deliver some gear to his girlfriend who was facing a cold-turkey Christmas owing to there being a drought in the capital.

With a twenty-five date tour of the Far East – including another seven-date residency at the Capitol Theatre in Sydney – set to get underway with a show at the Shibuya Kohkaido in Tokyo on 24 January, Topper's lawyers used this as the fulcrum of their argument against a custodial sentence when the drummer went before the bench at Uxbridge Magistrates Court on 17 December.

Topper escaped with a £500 fine (coupled with the judge's recommendation that he seek professional help for his addiction), but his conviction would prove problematic for The Clash as a whole. From now on they would suffer the indignity of being stopped and searched at airports. For a group that had always been vociferously anti-heroin in public, having to acknowledge they'd been papering over the cracks of their drummer's addiction for some time would have been exasperating.

– CHAPTER TWELVE –

YOU DON'T UNDERSTAND MY POINT OF VIEW

'We always got criticism in The Clash but we always thought "you should be happy. We've gone a long way and it represents what you can do", you know what I mean? We took it all the way to Broadway and that meant something.'

– Mick Jones

THE CLASH RETURNED TO Electric Lady in early January, but whilst New York was still aglow with fading festive cheer, there was little bonhomie inside the studio. Mick could barely stand to be in the studio at the same as Joe, and would usually have laid down his guitar overdubs and disappeared off into the night again before Joe arrived. According to Jerry Green, Mick was also no longer willing to suffer Paul's rudimentary musicianship in the studio, even to the point of bringing in Electric lady's in-house tape-operator Jerry Garcia to play bass on occasion.

When reflecting on the recording sessions, Mick says that the producer's cap was kind of thrust at him by the others, and that it was his having to try and make some sense out of the 'big sprawling mess' that was responsible for his surly moods.[1]

With the clock counting down on the opening date of the Far East tour at the Shibuya Kohkaido in Tokyo on 24 January, Mick was too wrapped up in trying to bring the finished album in on time before hailing a cab to JFK to worry about what effect his high-handed attitude was having on the rest of the group. However, when he proudly presented Joe, Paul, and Topper with his fifteen-track, sixty-five minute masterpiece he received his comeuppance when they collectively dismissed the mix out of hand.

When speaking about the *Rat Patrol...* mix with *Creem* magazine's Bill Holdship in 1984, Joe uncharitably likened it to a 'home movie mix', before going on to opine that he didn't believe anyone can be so great that they didn't occasionally put in a bad shift. 'Mick wouldn't have that,' he continued. 'In his mind, he was a great artist, and great artists don't write crap. It was dangerous. I think Mick's got a tendency to bring yes-men close to him, and shut out people who will tell him the damn truth. Remember, I'm supposed to be his buddy and partner, and I said to him, "Mick, I don't think you can produce." What I meant was that you can't just sit in the chair, move some faders, and claim to be a producer. And it was, "You bastard! I thought you were my friend!"'

Listening to the *Rat Patrol From Fort Bragg* bootleg today provides a fascinating insight into what Mick was trying to achieve with the album, but with Topper having sided with Joe and Paul he was reluctantly forced to concede defeat. CBS were already making noises about album being long overdue, and so rather than risk further displeasure The Clash opted to book some studio time in Sydney in the hope of their being able to bring the album in for the label's rescheduled end of April release date.

♪♪♪

Mick may well have preferred the production chair over the tour bus, but with The Clash never having played anywhere further east than Vienna there was undoubtedly a spring in his step as he set off for the airport: 'It was pretty crazy when we arrived in Japan,' he said. 'It felt very strange – we were chased around like we were The Beatles or something, with lots of screaming and people throwing presents to us. It was beautiful.'[2]

The Clash were indeed treated like visiting royalty by the Japanese, and the demand for tickets proved so great that two further dates were added in Osaka and Tokyo before they bid their hosts sayonara and flew to Sydney where they staged a press conference to promote the impending seven night residency at the Capitol Theatre. They then flew on to the New Zealand capital, Auckland, where they experienced the realities of Topper's drug conviction when the equipment was impounded and searched for drugs. As with the Japanese dates, The Clash received a hero's welcome in both New Zealand and Australia. To outward appearances – Joe's onstage collapse from heat exhaustion in Perth aside – the group were solid and giving their all, but away from the stage and the media glare it was a different story.

Legend has it that Joe had once drawn a metaphorical Alamo-esque line in the sand; the demarcation depicting Mick and Topper as the musicians in the group, while he and Paul were the entertainers. In days gone by when The Clash lived by an 'all-for-one-and-one-for-all' ethic had the allegorical line existed for real it wouldn't have been visible to the naked eye, but in recent weeks it had grown into an impassable chasm.

Following the penultimate show at the AC Hall in Hong Kong, The Clash flew on to Bangkok where they would be bringing the tour to a close with a show at the Thammasat University. Despite the ever-mounting tension, with the new album brimming with urban [Vietnam]erican vibes The Clash couldn't help but allow their imaginations run wild. 'We went mad in Thailand,' Mick told the NME's James Brown in 1991. 'It was like *Apocalypse Now*. When you go that far away, it takes a long time to get back. One great thing that happened was we were out in the bars dressed like *The Deer Hunter*, and they have these girls in the really heavy places dancing on the bar. Joe and Kosmo got up and did the frug on the bar with these girls. When you come back from that, it's hard to get back into normal life. It was a fantastic adventure.'

Mick's fond memories of The Clash's Far Eastern fling were no doubt coloured by the fact they arrived in Bangkok to find they were sitting at the top of the local hit parade. However, by the time of the NME interview he was pragmatic enough to admit that every visiting western group probably enjoyed a similar status whilst in Thailand. 'I think it's quite corrupt, like the police chief and the guy in charge of the music industry are the same man,' he pondered. 'They don't have real records, just bootleg tapes.'

Although their having failed to make much progress on the new album whilst in Sydney meant The Clash were still some way away from being able to present a 'real record' to CBS, they were at least unanimous on bringing Pennie Smith (who'd covered the Japanese leg of tour for the *NME*) over to Bangkok, where they would be bringing the tour to a close with a show at the Thammasat University, to shoot the cover.

Pennie had barely time to unpack her camera when Bernard inexplicably went Thai boxing, leaving the group without any money. The Clash, of course, were well versed in having empty pockets, but where they would have once found other ways to amuse themselves they now preferred to sit around in brooding silence. Although Pennie got the group to pose by a deserted railway line, she came away again sensing the images she'd captured in her lens were of four individuals who were no longer willing to even fake a show of togetherness. The Clash may have been beyond faking a sense of togetherness for the cameras, but the unity of old came to the fore when Paul was rushed to hospital with a mystery ailment. A couple of days earlier he'd jumped into what appeared to a mud puddle, only to be instantly engulfed by a swarm of flies. Paul had laughed it off at the time, but no one was laughing when the doctors diagnosed a twisted colon and recommended immediate surgery to remove part of his intestine.

Fearing Paul was dying, the others were seriously contemplating allowing the doctors to wield their scalpel, but thankfully the tour manager went in search of a second opinion. The Swiss doctor he brought in assured them there was nothing wrong with Paul's colon and that he'd merely caught a bug of some kind; the evidence of which came with his making a complete recovery.

'We had a good time because Paul got hospitalized,' Mick explained in November 2007. 'We all stayed and hung out there for a bit, so we went a little mad. That was one of the best times, I think, where we were really together. 'Strange when you go that far away, you feel differently, and when you go back you're shouting from the top of the houses for a few days before you slump back down. We were really together, even though that was when we were on our way to the end.'[3]

Owing to their unexpected prolonged sojourn in Thailand, The Clash returned to London in mid-March no nearer to reaching a compromise over the new album than when they'd left New York. Mick was stubbornly refusing to discuss the situation, but with CBS/Epic expressing serious concerns about the group releasing another cut-price double album, Bernard called everyone together and – after a show of hands – the decision was made to bring in a seasoned producer to give Mick's Electric Lady mix a serious overhaul; preferably one with previous experience in snatching victory from the jaws of defeat operations, and someone both immune to outside influences and capable of dealing with bruised egos.

Several names were mooted, but there really was only one candidate that ticked all the boxes – Glyn Johns. Aside from boasting a CV that included production credits with the Rolling Stones, The Faces, The Who, and The Beatles, the forty-year-old Glyn had been brought in to perform similar salvage operations with the latter two acts. Though his work on the warring Fab Four's unreleased 1969 *Get Back** album would ultimately be deemed a tad too austere, his no-nonsense approach while renovating Pete Townsend's bloated and over-ambitious *Lifehouse* project into the infinitely more robust *Who's Next* undoubtedly spared The Who's guitarist from a nervous breakdown.

Glyn appreciated the hard work Mick had put in on the album, but he too believed it to be too self-indulgent and too drawn out. Given the remit of sorting the wheat from the chaff, Glyn invited Mick and Joe to his home studio in Warnford, West Sussex, and with his being both a strict timekeeper and a teetotaller; he informed them that the sessions would begin at 11 a.m. sharp.

Joe responded to the call and duly arrived at Glyn's door bright and bushy-tailed the following morning. Such was his enthusiasm that he and Glyn had three remixed tracks in the can by the time Mick deigned them with his presence. Perhaps not surprisingly, Mick didn't think

---

* The album was released in 1970 as *Let It Be*.

168

much of the remixes and voiced his opinions. Glyn, of course, had had to put up with the quirks and foibles of Keith Richards, Ronnie Wood, and Keith Moon et al, so while he was politeness personified he let Mick know in no uncertain terms that if he wasn't willing to get there on time then his opinions would count for naught.

Being truculent in the studio had become second nature to Mick, but Glyn had little truck with discourtesy. The following morning he phoned Joe to tell him that he wasn't prepared to continue working on the album if Mick was going to throw a tantrum at every turn. Joe reportedly blew his top and promised Glyn all would be sorted. True enough, when Mick arrived at the studio some time later that day he did so fully chastised and ready to get to work.

Over the next three days the *Rat Patrol From Fort Bragg* suffered near fifty per cent casualties, and once Glyn, Mick and Joe had completed their triangular triage 'Kill Time', 'Walk Evil Walk', and 'The Beautiful People Are Ugly Too' had been given the last rites, while 'First Night Back In London', and 'Cool Confusion' were sent back behind the lines and placed in reserve. Nor did the remaining twelve tracks come away unscathed as 'Straight To Hell', 'Red Angel Dragnet', 'Ghetto Defendant', and 'Sean Flynn' all underwent major surgery in keeping with the snappy new title Joe had decided upon, *Combat Rock*.

When speaking about the possibility of his *Rat Patrol…* mix receiving an official release in November 2007, Mick had the grace to admit Glyn John's mix was better. 'It was painful at the time for me to admit that it was, but in the end it turned out fine, and no one remembers all the little finicky bits,' he revealed. 'It was a little bit more of a contemporary, "what-was-going-on-at-the-time-type of thing", but the end record turned out to be a more lasting record, I think.'[4]

♪♪♪

On 23 April, CBS released 'Know Your Rights' b/w 'First Night Back In London' as the opening salvo from the forthcoming *Combat Rock* which was set to follow the single into the shops on 14 May. Keeping with tradition, The Clash arranged a corresponding nineteen-date UK tour starting in Aberdeen on Monday, 26 April, and knuckled down to some serious rehearsals ahead of it. However, five days prior to the Aberdeen date Joe suddenly went missing.

Mick, Paul, and Topper were completely in the dark as to why Joe would abandon his post, but his going AWOL left them with little option but to postpone the opening dates of the tour while they awaited news of their frontman.

It was a plotline worthy of Agatha Christie, and like all mystery thrillers the tale had a cunning arch villain in plain view to the audience throughout...

Worried about poor advance ticket sales for the opening dates of the tour, Bernard suggested Joe slip off the grid for a few days by visiting Joe Ely in Texas, but not tell anybody where he was going. Joe knew Bernard was worrying unnecessarily over the advance ticket sales as The Clash could always rely on a big walk up on the night – i.e. fans turning up at the venue cash-in-hand – but went along with the scam regardless.

However, somewhere betwixt his leaving Bernard and going home to pack a bag Joe decided to add a further twist to the storyline, and instead of flying out to Texas, he booked seats for him and his partner Gabby on the next available boat train to Paris.

With Epic having booked two month-long US tours to promote the album stateside, Joe's genuine disappearance not only threw The Clash's tour diary into confusion, but threatened their very existence. It was going to cost a pretty enough penny settling the cancellation fees for the UK tour dates, but American promoters wouldn't be quite so magnanimous, and should they elect to enforce the cancellation penalties set within the contractual terms and conditions The Clash would incur such debts they would have little option but to cease trading.

The Clash were also set to headline the Lochem Festival in Holland on Thursday, 20 May, having secured a 'not-to-be-sniffed-at' $75,000 fee plus expenses, and the festival's promoter Frank Zanhorn was also left pondering his options when ticket sales for the festival dropped dramatically in the wake of the announcement of Joe's vanishing act in the *NME*.

Joe was no doubt aware of the potential consequences of his actions yet although he was thoughtful enough to let certain people, such as his mum and CBS' Kit Buckler, know he was alive and well he chose to remain in Paris playing catch-me-if-you-can.

Although he was hardly inconspicuous given that he participated in the Paris marathon, it was only owing to a Dutch journalist friend of Zanhorn's (who was supposedly unaware of the furore surrounding Joe's disappearance) mentioning his having happened upon The Clash frontman in a Paris bar a few days earlier that a very much relieved Kosmo was finally able to run Joe to ground.

Though Joe was back in time for The Clash to honour their commitments at the Lochem Festival, within days of their return to London Clash fans everywhere were rocked with the news that Topper had quit the group over 'a difference of opinion over the political direction the [Clash] will be taking.'

Eager for a chance to give their version of the tumultuous events of recent weeks, Mick, Joe, and Paul accepted an invitation from the NME's Charles Shaar Murray – yes, the same Charles Shaar Murray that had suggested The Clash be returned to the garage with the motor running whilst reviewing *The Clash* five years earlier – to share a pot of coffee at a Portobello Road café.

Having sat patiently while Joe cobbled together a couple of philosophical clichés such as the need to prove to himself that he was a human being rather than a robot, as a means of rationalising his Lord Lucan act, Murray naturally wanted to know whether Mick and Paul had adopted a similar stoical approach to their singer's Parisian pilgrimage.

'Well, I felt that anything he [Joe] does is alright,' Mick responded with a shrug, before going on to contradict the general conception within the Clash camp that Mick no longer cared for touring by saying he was disappointed that they'd had to postpone the UK tour. 'I felt sure that he had a good reason, and he's such an extraordinary person that it was fine; we could handle it. Hold the fort is what we did.'

When Murray enquired as to the reasons for Topper's surprise departure, Mick, Joe and Paul abided by The Clash's official communiqué – that appeared within the same 29 May issue as the interview – by saying it had been Topper's decision in that he'd wanted to 'strike out in another direction' having supposedly tired of adhering to The Clash's party political line.

In terms of 'worst kept secrets', Topper's spiralling addiction has to rank alongside the British government's insistence it knew nothing about Argentina's plans to invade the Falkland Islands* until the Bandera Oficial de Ceremonia was flying over Port Stanley, but Murray was gracious enough to ignore the elephant sitting in the corner.

Whilst raking over the coals of Topper's sacking in *The Clash* (during which Mick was conspicuously silent), Joe hit the nail squarely on the head in saying that it was pointless trying to pretend that he, Mick, and Paul could mask Topper's failings either on stage or in the studio because with their drummer falling apart everything else would indeed 'fall apart like a house without any foundations.'

By his own admission, Topper says he was completely off his gourd during the Far East tour, but even then, Mick was seemingly prepared to soldier on, clinging to the hope that he'd experience a Damascene revelation and drag himself back from the edge. The realisation that he was – as indeed were Joe and Paul – chasing a Chinese rocks-infused chimera came at the Lochem Festival.

Prior to going out on stage Joe was in the dressing room doing some last-minute preening in the full-length mirror when Topper came bursting in, grabbed the mirror and began chopping out several lines of cocaine... and he wasn't for sharing.

With the opening date of the Casbah Club USA Tour in New Jersey a little over a week away, The Clash knew they could no longer keep ignoring what was going on under their drummer's nose. Immediately upon the group's return to London an emergency meeting was convened at Paul's flat in Oxford Gardens where Topper was given the news. In typical fashion, however, rather than sack Topper straight off, he was informed he was being temporarily suspended (the media would be told Topper was suffering from nervous exhaustion), but that if he managed to clean up his act by the time they came off the road after the second leg of the US tour then he would be welcomed back with open arms.

Given that his brush with the law back in December had failed to serve as a wake-up call, it's questionable whether Topper would have been able to shake the monkey from his back without professional

---

* Argentina invaded the Falklands on 2 April 1982.

help. Mick, it seems, was still willing to allow him the chance, but Joe now saw him as a liability, and within days of the meeting he blithely informed the media that Topper had been sacked because of his heroin addiction.

This would prove a callous act with serious repercussions, because prior to Joe's public denouncement Topper had only chased the dragon. It was only upon realising there would be no reunion waiting at the end of the rehabilitation rainbow that he first began using intravenously.

From there the downward slope became ever more slippery. In 1987 he was jailed for eighteen months for supplying heroin, and upon his release was reduced to driving a mini-cab to feed his own habit. But of course, being the best drummer driving a cab was obviously preferable to being the best drummer in a coffin, which was the fate the judge presiding over his initial court appearance in December 1981 had envisaged unless he mended his ways. Thankfully, the moneys he received from the advance for *From Here To Eternity* in 1999 would allow Topper to purchase a house in his native Dover where he entered a methadone programme and finally got himself clean.

Whether Bernard played any part in Topper's dismissal is neither here nor there, of course, because no group – let alone an international act like The Clash – can hope to function with a hop-head keeping the beat.

♫♫♫

Within a week of its release *Combat Rock* emulated the feat of *Give 'Em Enough Rope* by slamming onto the UK albums chart at number two – being denied the top spot by Paul McCartney's *Tug Of War* – and with *London Calling* and *Sandinista!* having now accrued enough sales to finally balance The Clash's debit sheet at Soho Square, the future looked rosier than it had for quite some time. Of more immediate concern, however, was finding a new drummer. With the opening date of the US tour almost upon them and no time to stage auditions, there was really only one viable option… give Terry Chimes a call.

Though Terry responded to the call, he made it abundantly clear that he was doing so on a temporary basis to enable The Clash to fulfil their touring commitments for the remainder of the year. Even though Terry was available, there was still plenty of hard work to do – especially as Paul had already left for New York to liaise with Alex Michon in designing some new *Combat Rock*–themed Clash clothing to sell in America.

In the five years or so since his last tour of duty with The Clash, Terry had kept the beat for The Heartbreakers and Generation X, as well as doing session work in the wake of the latter group's demise following Billy Idol's decision to relocate to America to launch his solo career. Terry was accustomed to hitting the ground running and threw himself wholeheartedly into learning the principle songs from *Combat Rock*, as well those from *Give 'Em Enough Rope*, *London Calling* and *Sandinista!* that made up the forty-song pool from which The Clash would compile their nightly set-lists.

Mick, of course, had made consigning songs from *The Clash* to history something of a personal crusade of late, but given Terry's obvious familiarity with the first album the American audiences would receive an unexpected bonus.

The first leg of the US tour included five consecutive sell-out shows at the Hollywood Palladium, but Mick's embarrassment at playing 'Career Opportunities' and 'Garageland' in such salubrious surroundings, was assuaged somewhat when Joe held out an olive branch by inviting him to remix 'Rock The Casbah' for US release.

The second leg was initially supposed to reach its *Combat Rock* climax in Boston on 8 September, but unexpectedly ended up being extended another six weeks owing to The Clash accepting Pete Townshend's offer for them to fill the main support slot on The Who's supposed farewell tour.

Needless to say, the news provoked varying reactions back in the UK for while Townshend's generous gesture could be construed as a symbolic passing of the baton; those dyed-in-the-wool fans that had followed The Clash from their conception viewed it as a betrayal. True, The Who were the backstreet kids of their own g-g-g-generation, which perhaps explains why they had fared better than

Elvis, The Beatles, and the Rolling Stones in The Clash's apocalyptic '1977' cull, but they still represented the old order that punk rock had set out to destroy.

Mick, however, saw the clutch of stadium dates – which included two sell-out appearances at the William A. Shea Stadium in Queens, New York – as an opportunity to spread The Clash credo to a larger audience. Indeed, such was the demand for tickets that special seating erected on the New York Mets' hallowed infield for the first time in the stadium's eighteen year history. 'It was a great honour for us to be asked to do it. It was brilliant, actually,' he said. 'We were very excited about it. It helped us immensely.'[4]

This was evidenced by Mick's remixed version of 'Rock The Casbah' climbing to a staggering number seven on the Billboard 200 following its release towards the end of October. And with *Combat Rock* still laying siege to the Billboard album chart it really did appear that The Clash were set to reap the rewards from their kow-towing to The Who.

On Saturday, 27 November, The Clash fulfilled the last date in their '82 tour diary by appearing on the bill of the third and final day of the three-day Jamaica World Music Festival – staged at the newly constructed Bob Marley Performing Arts Centre in Montego Bay – alongside Rick James, The English Beat, Jimmy Buffett, and Rita Marley and the Melody Makers.

Owing to poor planning on the part of the organisers The Clash didn't go on stage till 4 a.m., and such was the somnambulistic state of the crowd by this hour that Joe jokingly tried provoking the audience into life by threatening to bring the Grateful Dead on. Bernard had reportedly done some threatening of his own backstage by threatening to withdraw his charges from the festival unless they were paid $200,000.

According to despatches, The Clash opted on a reggae-tinged set to compliment the laid-back attitude of the audience, but a cursory glance at the track-listing on the *From London To Jamaica* bootleg there's little to differentiate from any other show from 1982. What is noticeable from the recording, however, is how uncomplimentary Mick's BAD-esque guitar sound is to Joe's vocal.

It had proved a frenetic year both on and off stage for The Clash, and on their return to London Mick, Joe, and Paul retreated to their respective bolt-holes to enjoy some much-needed downtime. However, though Mick was barely speaking to Joe and Paul, and vice-versa, the three went into Wessex Studio at the end of December – with Mickey Gallagher and Blockheads' drummer Charley Charles in tow – to record 'House Of The Ju-Ju Queen'; the song Mick and Joe had penned for Janie Jones* to prove they were still in love with the recently-released cabaret singer cum vice queen's world. During the session they also recorded a version of James Brown's 1970 hit 'Sex Machine' for the B-side of the single that would supposedly relaunch Janie's pop career. (The single would eventually be released via the Big Beat label in December the following year).

The 'House Of The Ju-Ju Queen' was a Clash release in all but name, but Mick, Joe, and Paul insisted on giving Janie top billing and mischievously credited themselves as 'The Lash'.

Terry Chimes may have been absent from the Wessex session, but he'd enjoyed playing with The Clash again and may well have accepted the offer to join the group full time had such an offer been forthcoming. Realising that he faced an indeterminate period of inactivity twiddling his drumsticks while waiting to see whether Mick and Joe would act like adults and finally have a 'clear-the-air' discussion for the good of The Clash, he accepted Billy Idol's offer to join him in LA, before subsequently going on to work with Hanoi Rocks.

♪♪♪

1 January 1983 is the day generally credited with being the birth of the 'true internet' following the completion of the migration of the ARPANET to TCP/IP, while the recently-released 'New Year's Day' gave The Clash-inspired U2 their first international hit single. The following month saw the Dublin outfit's third album, *War*; slam straight in at number one on the UK album chart, but as for The Clash themselves, the world heard nothing until April when it was

---

* Janie – born Marion Mitchell – was jailed in 1973 for seven years (serving three) for 'controlling prostitutes', as well as for her involvement in the BBC Radio One 'sex for airplay' Payola scandal.

announced they'd been approached by Unison (an acronym for 'Unite Us In Song') the organisers of the second Us Festival in Glen Helen Regional Park, in San Bernardino, California, to headline the opening New Music Day on 28 May.

The overall Memorial Day weekend audience was expected to be in the region of 700,000, while The Clash could expect to play in front of an estimated 150,000, and pick up a whopping $500,000 pay check.

Mick shared Joe and Paul's reservations about whether The Clash should accept the invitation, but his qualms were that the group needed more time away from each other before reconvening to plot a viable strategy for taking The Clash forward, whereas Joe and Paul were more concerned about the potential UK media backlash of them playing what was little more than a corporate sponsorship love-in.

'That was our big problem all the time, really,' Mick explained. 'The bigger we got the worse it seemed to get for us. It is a very strange irony. You'd think we'd be getting on great, but it got scary.

'We were always battling with contradictions, but when we got big, we were faced with big contradictions. It was almost at the point of compromise, and that was a big factor towards breaking up. That, and we never had any time off, and we lived on top of each other for like six or seven years. We got dog tired and fed up. When we were struggling, it definitely held us together. "Come on! Where are we going? We're going to the top!" We had all that drive, and just like anybody we had good intentions. But you get compromised. You can't beat it. We did okay, considering the things we had to contend with.

'Compared to most groups, we did great. But trying to deal with those contradictions was the worst. On the one hand, there was what we were singing about, and then we were becoming more and more, and bigger and bigger. And it's like, what's there? There's more. And then there's more after that. And then it is like, well hold on a minute, don't we have enough? So we were in crisis most of the time. The more we worked, the more screwed we were.' [5]

The contradictions Mick spoke about may have been playing havoc internally, but they were at least paying dividends. With the royalties flowing into The Clash coffers from the sales of *Combat Rock* and

'Rock The Casbah', for the first time since putting pen to paper at Soho Square some six years earlier the group were at long last in a position where they could pick and choose their options.

The Us Festival was far removed from The Clash's mid-Seventies manifesto, but Bernard believed that his warring charges should accept the invitation – if only as a means of getting them functioning as a cohesive unit again.

This, of course, meant finding a new drummer, and with this in mind Bernard placed the following ad in the 23 April issue of *Melody Maker*: 'YOUNG DRUMMER WANTED: Internationally successful group Recording and concert appearances immediately'.

One of the three hundred or so who responded to the ad, and was deemed worthy of being invited back to play on stage with Joe and Paul (Mick was in New York at the time) was future Stiff Little Fingers drummer, Steve Grantley.

Playing on the same stage with Joe Strummer and Paul Simonon was a dream come true for any wannabe musician and Steve was certainly no different as he'd grown up listening to The Clash. Now, as any SLF fan will happily testify, Steve is one of the best drummers around – and indeed, one of a handful of drummers worthy of polishing Topper's drum stool. Following a run through on stage, Joe and Paul were of a similar opinion and invited Steve back to go head-to-head with another drummer called Pete Howard.

This time, however, Mick would also be on stage, and the fact that Pete got the nod kind of gives the outcome away. 'Playing with Joe and Paul was a doddle,' Steve reflected whilst on tour with SLF in 2002. 'Joe had even given me the nod that I'd impressed them more than Pete, and I thought, "This is it, I'm gonna be in the Clash!" But seeing Mick standing there on stage dressed head to toe in leather and looking cool as fuck, I just went to pieces and missed my timing on "London Calling".

'Joe was great and said we could start again, but I was so overawed that I dropped one of my sticks. It just got worse from there. And all the while I could see Mick glaring at Joe as if to say, "You brought me back from New York for this!" Christ, it was embarrassing.'

Having road-tested Pete Howard with four warm-up shows in Texas and Arizona, The Clash arrived in Los Angeles to hold a press conference to promote the festival. According to *Pulse Magazine*, former Apple genius Steve Wozniak – the brainchild behind the Us Festivals – reportedly paid $21,000 for a private-hire jet to fly The Clash in from Tucson, Arizona. If that were true, then Wozniak was soon regretting laying on the five-star treatment as not only did they deride the festival for being marketed in the manner of 'cat food', they also engaged Wozniak in a little last-minute horse-trading at the festival itself by refusing to perform unless Wozniak agreed to donate $100,000 to a Southern Californian summer camp for disadvantaged children.

'We're trying to get Mr. Wozniak, who started this whole thing off in the name of money, to put some money back into California,' Bernard told those reporters who'd responded to the emergency press conference he staged some two hours before The Clash were due on stage. 'With a figure of $18 million being spent we figure he could give ten per cent of that towards some organisation.'

Bernard then announced The Clash would be willing to match Wozniak's benevolence by donating ten per cent of the group's earnings to help the poor, but his suggestion that the other acts follow suit was met with disdain – particularly by Van Halen frontman, David Lee Roth, despite the poodle rockers being paid $1 million (plus substantial add-ons) for their troubles.

Unison begrudgingly agreed to donate $32,000, but its enraged president, Dr. Peter Ellis, declared The Clash's demands 'simple extortion'. Bernard, however, has always maintained that it was his stance that night in San Bernardino that laid the foundations for Live Aid two years later.

When The Clash went on stage two hours later than billed, they did so in front of a banner proclaiming 'The Clash Are Not For Sale', yet while their ongoing fight to keep album prices and concert tickets to a minimum went some way to supporting such a declaration, their mere presence at the festival showed they weren't above prostituting themselves for a couple of hours if the price was right.

Perhaps not unsurprisingly, the backstage bartering beforehand made for a highly-charged atmosphere front of house. So much so, that when the DJ at the side of the stage immediately began addressing the 140,000-strong crowd the moment The Clash finished 'Clampdown', the last number of their scheduled twenty-song set, Kosmo took this to mean The Clash weren't going to be allowed an encore and ran across and punched the bemused DJ full in the face.

Kosmo soon found himself under attack from a bevy of security personnel, and to everyone's surprise it was Mick who leapt to his defence. This in turn saw Paul and Joe jump in to save Mick, with Paul getting a sprained thumb for his pains. The fracas was over pretty quickly, but for a few frenetic heartbeats pandemonium reigned as The Clash vented their in-house frustrations on anyone who strayed into range.

Those closest to The Clash would have no doubt taken seeing Paul and Joe rush to Mick's defence as a sign that the brotherly bond that had carried them from the back room at Davis Road to Broadway was stretched to breaking yet still intact.

Little could anyone know, however, that the three Eddie Cochrans would never perform on the same stage together again.

– CHAPTER THIRTEEN –

WHAT AM I GONNA DO NOW?

'I really think it was musical differences, although there was a set-up to cause musical differences. Bernie's suggestion that we all try to play New Orleans music could have been setting things up so that he could say it was musical differences...'

– Mick Jones

FOLLOWING THE EXALTED HIGH of playing to 140,000 people, upon their return to London The Clash quickly descended to more run-of-the-mill mundanity of everyday life. Said mundanity, of course, only applied to Mick, Joe, and Paul, whereas Pete Howard viewed it as all part of what was already promising to be an incredible journey; or at least it would have been had the 'kick-one-and-we-all-cry' camaraderie evidenced on stage in San Bernardino not evaporated into the ether at Heathrow arrivals.

Now that he'd experienced life on the road with The Clash, Pete no doubt imagined that group rehearsals would consist of their warming up by running through a couple of Clash standards, then working on song ideas before adjourning to the nearest pub where his new bandmates would regale him with stories and anecdotes well into the evening. He soon came to realise, however, that the reality was somewhat different...

With Mick's tardiness when it came to rehearsing being an old and familiar tale Pete quickly became accustomed to Mick showing up as and when he pleased. However, whereas Joe and Paul would have once sat around kicking their heels waiting for Mick to deign them with his presence, they now simply adopted a 'if he comes, he comes' attitude and got on with the job. And on the rare occasions Mick did show his face, Pete couldn't help but notice the difference in ambience than when it was just himself, Joe, and Paul.

Another eye-opener for the new boy, was that while Kosmo had gone to great lengths bigging up The Clash's supposed 'gang mentality', while Joe and Paul did indeed spend most evenings socialising together with their respective partners, Gabby and Pearl*, Mick was nowhere to be seen. Mick had never been much of a drinker anyway, and much preferred staying home and smoking dope with his own circle of friends. He was also still playing 'getting to know you' with his new girlfriend Daisy Lawrence, and so an evening down the pub swapping war stories with the guys with whom you've spent the last six years living in and out of each other's pockets came in a very poor third.

The fundamental problem facing The Clash was that Mick was keen to embrace new technology whereas Joe and Paul appeared content to keep reinventing the wheel. Indeed, their relationship had disintegrated to the point where Joe had taken to posting lyrics through Mick's door rather than deal with him face-to-face.

Another niggling gripe causing unrest was that Mick had recently hired New York attorney Elliot Hoffman to oversee his interests. In hindsight, this doesn't seem unreasonable given that The Clash were finally making some real money – especially given that a sizeable chunk of the $500,000 from their appearance at the Us Festival was still forthcoming, owing to IRS' complicated tax procedures with moneys leaving the US. Bernard, however, took this as a personal sleight, and his mood wasn't improved when Mick subsequently refused to sign his copy of the managerial contract he'd had drawn up until his lawyer had cast an eye over it.

Again, in retrospect, this doesn't seem an excessive request seeing as Hoffman could have withdrawn his services had Mick signed the contract without first seeking his expertise. Joe and Paul, however, were now way beyond such rationale, and with Bernard playing devil's advocate there was only likely to be one outcome...

---

* Paul had married Pearl in New York the previous May.

What Am I Gonna Do Now?

♫♫♫

Those closest to The Clash had been hearing rumours for several weeks, but it wasn't until Saturday, 1 September that the rumours were confirmed via a 'Clash Communiqué' from Bernard and Kosmo stating that Mick had been sacked owing to his having 'drifted apart from the original idea of The Clash'. The missive ended by saying that Mick's departure would 'allow Joe and Paul to get on with the job that The Clash set out to do from the beginning.'

It wasn't until the announcement appeared in the *NME*'s 10 September issue that the world at large first learned of the latest power play, or of Mick's response to his being sacked. Via a CBS press release, Mick challenged The Clash communiqué by saying how there had been 'no discussion with Strummer and Simonon prior to his sacking,' and that nor did he feel that he'd 'drifted apart from the original idea of The Clash' as Joe and Paul claimed. He brought his own communiqué to a close by saying he would be 'carrying on with the same dedication as in the beginning.'

Mick's sacking would have Clash fans the world over poring over the lyrics to 'Should I Stay Or Should I go?' looking for subliminal hints as to Mick's state of mind in regard to his position in The Clash. But while he was probably already harbouring doubts about the group's long-term future, it's a matter of record that the song was a lament to his then failing relationship with Ellen Foley.

Mick was quite correct in saying there hadn't been any discussion with him prior to his sacking, but there had been plenty of debate during his continued absence, as Paul revealed to *Mojo* in 1999: 'Me and Joe had been talking about it, and it got to the point where I said, "We're grown men, I can't take any more of this", and Joe agreed. We were both in agreement that we were fed up, we wanted to get on with the job, rather than waiting around for Mick.'

When reaffirming his and Joe's position at the time of Mick's sacking in *The Clash*, Paul elaborated on what he'd meant by their 'getting on with the job' by saying he'd thought The Clash should carry on touring because the transatlantic success of *Combat Rock* saw them on the verge of making a serious dent on the music charts, while Mick supposedly wanted to stay at home.

In the same tome, Mick admits to being 'surprised they put up with me as long as they did, really,'[6] but such musings, of course, came long after bridges had been rebuilt.

Back in 1984, it was a different tale entirely, and whilst venting his spleen to the *NME*, Joe claimed that he'd practically had to beg Mick to play guitar, and that trying to get him to do anything was 'like dragging a dead dog around on a piece of string.' The final insult, however, came with Mick supposedly saying that he didn't care what The Clash did as long as he could run it past his lawyer first.

An incensed Joe supposedly told Mick to 'piss off, and write songs with your lawyer.' What he should have done, of course, is stop to consider that Mick's diva demeanour was down to nurture rather than nature. After all, aside from a few father/son outings, Mick's upbringing – as he revealed during the *Sabotage Times* interview – was overseen by a 'completely matriarchal society'; one that pampered his every whim. Indeed, the first 'adult' male to exert any influence on Mick's development was Guy Stevens, who was only twelve years older, and far from what one might describe as a role model.

His being sacked from Violent Luck on account of his perceived lack of musicianship would prove instrumental in affecting his state of mind when putting The Clash together. Because by co-writing, arranging, and subsequently producing he – in his mind at least – pretty much made himself indispensable... Or gave him 'the best seat in the house'[7] as he subsequently put it to Lisa Robinson in 1986.

Mick is the first to admit that he lacked self-control during this period, but Joe and Paul were equally culpable for meekly acquiescing to his Elizabeth Taylor-esque whims instead of yelling 'cut' and demanding a retake. If Joe had stood up to Mick on occasion there would have been no need to bring Bernard back in from the cold – especially when he knew better than anyone that Mick and Bernard were cut from the same uncompromising cloth.

Bernard is first and foremost an ideas man, which is the only reason he agreed to manage London SS in the first place. If he'd have thought for a heartbeat that Mick wanted London SS to become the next

Rolling Stones he'd have ripped the 'What Side Of The Bed...' T-shirt from Mick's back that night at the Nashville.

As Don Letts says in his highly-informative 2007 autobiography, *Culture Clash*, it was Bernard's knowledge of the underground cultures that had gone before The Clash that gave them added depth. 'They [The Clash] could see the tradition that they were following,' he explained. 'They made music as a way of communicating ideas as a protest thing, rather than just having an agenda of making music to just sell records.'

Conversely, of course, no matter how much The Clash tried to adhere to Bernard's underground culture credo, while eschewing said agenda of making music simply to sell records, such was the brilliance of the music that it was inevitable they would by assimilated into the mainstream.

It was Bernard who also set The Clash on their personal-political path by steering them away from Mick's paeans to teenage lust and getting them to write about what was affecting their lives. However, while such sagacious advice worked when penning the songs that made up the track-listing on *The Clash*, and possibly *Give 'Em Enough Rope*, by the time of *London Calling* their songwriting had inevitably come to encompass their on-the-road experiences, as did the more pertinent material on *Sandinista!*, but it could be argued that *Combat Rock* was a soundtrack-in-waiting should Francis Ford Coppola decide to direct *Apocalypse Now II: Travis Bickle Gets Drafted*.

It's even questionable whether *London Calling* or *Sandinista!* would have seen the light of day – at least in their existing formats – had Bernard remained in charge of The Clash's affairs throughout. However, just because he called it right in suggesting bringing in Glynn Johns to jettison the *Rat Patrol* ragas didn't mean he was interested in making The Clash commercially viable second time around.

If making money for The Clash was all Bernard had been interested in he would surely never have agreed to their signing their lives away on the CBS' £100,000 contract back in 1977.

Like Robert Johnson, The Clash had reached a crossroads. However, whereas Johnson supposedly traded his immortal soul in return for some juicy Johnny B. Goode licks, The Clash had simply reached the critical juncture that all successful bands inevitably reach where they were going through the motions. 'We all knew that we were just doing it for the money,' Mick admitted in 1985. 'We couldn't face each other. In rehearsals we'd all look at the floor. It was the worst.'[8]

It certainly was, because CBS were chomping at the bit to get The Clash back into the studio to capitalise on the success of *Combat Rock*. When reflecting on the events leading up to his dismissal in 2004, Mick revealed how Bernard had taken him to a nearby pub to sound out what sort of records he wanted to make. When Mick said he wanted to make 'rock 'n' roll records, Bernard suggested The Clash 'play like New Orleans guys.'[9]

Mick thought the notion as crazy as it was constricting, but while the idea of The Clash trying to play like New Orleans bluesmen may seem strange, it's worth remembering that Joe was desperate for The Clash to return to basics and Bernard had been schooled in the story of the blues by the American servicemen calling on the Soho street prostitutes that looked after him while his mother worked eighteen-hour days on Savile Row. 'They (the lovelorn G.I.s) introduced me to the music of Muddy Waters, Lead Belly, Bukka White, Howlin' Wolf, and all the other blues greats,' he explained. 'There isn't a note or riff out there that I can't identify.'

Joe might have shared Mick's scepticism about The Clash playing Bourbon Street blues, but only because with Topper gone Mick was the only one in the group capable of laying down a Louisiana groove. With the benefit of hindsight, it's easy to see Joe was stuck in what might be euphemistically termed 'two-man's land'. On the one hand he desperately wanted The Clash to be successful, yet at the same time he was a squat-house rocker at heart who was happy staying a dollar ahead.

But The Clash, of course, were no longer a garageband, and while they still rehearsed in garageland-esque Camden Town, they'd reached the rarefied air where they could command six-figure sums for a show. For some time now The Clash's critics had accused them of being 'professional rebels', but while such snipings wounded Joe deeply it was so much expended ammo to Mick, as he'd always been more chaise lounge than Che Guevara.

What Am I Gonna Do Now?

The musical impasse had been reached simply because *Combat Rock* had raised the bar far beyond anyone's expectation. Yet while Mick was championing new technology – such as the Roland guitar synthesiser – he didn't necessarily want to make a New York dance album. Joe and Paul probably didn't want a rehash of *The Clash*, but their reluctance to follow Mick's lead, coupled with Mick's abhorrence at the thought of The Clash returning to their punk rock roots, left little or no room for manoeuvring.

♪♪♪

No one would have been surprised had Mick retreated from public view in the wake of his sacking, but rather than mope about licking his wounds he kept himself active by manning the mixing desk at several Sigue Sigue Sputnik shows in a show of public support for Tony James' outlandish new cyberpunk outfit. He also accepted an invitation from ex-Beat duo, Dave Wakelin and Ranking Roger, to play guitar with their new project, General Public.

It's always been something of contentious bone amongst Clash fans as to whether Mick was a bona fide member of General Public. Although he's listed in the credits on their 1984 debut album, *Tenderness*, and did indeed play guitar on other tracks such as 'Where's the Line,' 'Never You Done That', and 'Hot You're Cool', he was busying himself formulating ideas for a new musical venture of his own long before the album was released.

'Well, we did a bit of a barter deal,' Wakelin said of Mick's contribution in a 2009 interview. 'He had left The Clash and was starting Big Audio Dynamite, and he said to me that he had a load of lyrics, but he liked the way I played with the vocal melodies, and if he gave me a cassette of instrumentals, would I do some la-la-la and humming and ideas for melodies? And he would fit his lyrics around those, if they fit.'

It was whilst the two were working on melodies to suit Mick's lyrics that Dave mentioned where he and Roger were at with General Public, and asked if Mick would be willing to play on some of the songs they'd written. 'So we gave him the songs as they were demos and let him get a feel for them,' Dave explained in the same interview.

'We asked about rehearsals and that, but he was a very intuitive player, and he said, "No, I've got an idea of the songs now. Wait 'till you've got a finished song that's begging for a lead guitar part, and I'll just come down. I'm not precious about it. I'll just play loads of things and you tell me what fits and throw away the rest."'

However, things weren't quite so harmonious once they went into the studio, owing to Roger's fondness for hearing his own voice, as Dave revealed. 'I wouldn't say he (Roger) was a control freak, but he had a very particular opinion about everything. So Mick Jones would be starting to play something, and Roger would be on the intercom straight away, "Uh, Mick, could you try something like…" And I could see Mick start to get frustrated, y'know? I let it go on about two or three times, and then I thought, "Oh, no, this could spoil stuff." So, eventually, Roger went to push the intercom button, and I grabbed his hand, and I said, "Here's an idea, Roger: why don't you let the best guitarist in the world play what he wants? And if, at the end of the night, you still don't think you've got what you need, then come up with a suggestion. But as you can't actually play the guitar, why not shut up?" And there was a tense little moment, but he let Mick Jones do his thing, thank God!'

Someone who was privy to Mick's immediate post-Clash activities was Kris Needs. Knowing how much The Clash had meant to Mick, Kris had called expecting to find himself offering a supporting shoulder, but was relieved to find his friend bursting with optimism for the future. Though thrilled to discover that Mick was busy sounding out musicians such as ex-Basement 5 bassist and former Roxy barman, Leo 'E-Zee Kill' Williams, and one time Theatre Of Hate saxophonist John 'Boy' Lennard, for his new venture – tentatively called 'Total Risk Action Company' – Kriss felt near compelled to ask why Mick wasn't looking to have his name in lights by taking the solo career option?

'The best way to travel, without a doubt, is with a group of you because you have each other to share the experience,' Mick explained. 'It's much more fun. I don't know what it's like but a solo artist can't have as much fun as a band. You don't get to reach that point that you do with a band, or get to that point that we [The Clash] got to with the bands that we were inspired by. The Clash catered to the imagination and made people think, "Wow," what you can possibly do.'[10]

The 'wow' factor in regard to Mick's new musical venture was that when TRAC headed into a Notting Hill studio in November to record a clutch of new songs such as Hiroshima', 'Interaction', 'Napoleon Of Notting Hill', and 'The Bottom Line' (a reworking of 'Trans Cash Free Pay One', with lyrics provided by Robin Crocker), they did so with Topper Headon in the line-up.

It could be argued that Mick's extending a helping hand to Topper was a way of assuaging himself of the guilt he felt for not being more voluble in his support for Topper at the time of his dismissal from The Clash, but from a musical perspective, it made perfect sense seeing as Topper had been wholly in tune with what Mick had envisioned for *Combat Rock* regardless of his near-permanent drug fug.

Mick was so keen to have Topper at his side again that he paid for his friend to undergo the electro-acupuncture cure that had helped Keith Richards to get himself clean. And this was certainly no flamboyant gesture on Mick's part as money was in short supply owing to his having instructed his lawyer Elliot Hoffman to initiate proceedings whereby all Clash earnings up to the date of his dismissal were frozen, pending mediation.

The news of Topper and Mick working together again certainly caused a stir over in Camden Town where Joe and Paul were busy putting new Clash recruits Nick Sheppard and Vince White through their paces. When responding to The Clash Communiqué announcing his sacking Mick had refuted the claim that he'd 'drifted apart from the original idea of The Clash', and now that he'd been reunited with Topper he was in a position to challenge Joe and Paul's right to the group name. So much so, that when the post-Jones Clash flew out to California in the January, Mick reportedly telephoned Bill Graham to say he was promoting the wrong outfit and that he would be bringing the real Clash to America.

Alas, the prospect of Mick and Topper working together again was consigned to the 'what-might-have-been' pile owing to the latter's failure to give up needles after the acupuncture treatment.

It's unlikely that Mick had been serious about putting an alternate version of The Clash together, but Topper's self-perpetuating slide into oblivion certainly put paid to the idea. In hindsight, Topper's departure proved something of a godsend because it allowed Mick to focus on recruiting open-minded musicians who shared his vision for fusing elements of hip-hop with some Jones-esque jangly guitar to formulate his idea of what The Clash could have been, rather than put together a group obsessed with doing a better version of 'Rock The Casbah' on stage.

To do this, however, was going to require a sizeable influx of cash because the equipment he had in mind for his new venture wasn't to be found in Tin Pan Alley. With this in mind, he instructed Elliot Hoffman to shelve his claim to the Clash name to free up the royalties.

♪♪♪

Mick hit on the idea to bring Don Letts on board with his new musical venture whilst standing between Don and Leo Williams, and his being intrigued at the visual impact of a skinny white dude standing between two burly dreads on stage. In *Culture Clash*, Don described how the incident took place: 'Mick looked to his left and there was Leo, to his right was me, and he thought we looked like a band. There and then Mick asked me to join.'

There was, of course, one slight drawback to Mick's black-and-white design for although Don had once stood guitar in hand on the Hammersmith Odeon stage with Patti Smith at the latter's sell-out show, he'd never so much as strung two musical notes together in his life.

Don was the first to point this out, but Mick simply shrugged his shoulders, told Don to 'just remember Paul Simonon' before handing him a Harmonix sampler. 'When Mick first asked me to join the band I had to point out, "Hey, I can't play anything,"' Don explained in 2008. 'He said, "Well look. Remember how Paul started. We had to put stickers on the fret of his bass." And that's exactly what I did. I put stickers on my keyboard to show me what to do. The difference between me and Paul is I never took my stickers off.'[11]

Even without Don's involvement with Mick in BAD his name has become synonymous with The Clash, be it from his having directed many of the group's promo videos such as 'London Calling', and 'Bankrobber', the 2000 Grammy Award-winning *Clash: Westway To The World* documentary, the 2008 *Clash Live: Revolution Rock* film, and not forgetting the iconic image of him seemingly 'fronting the cops off' at the 1976 Notting Hill Carnival that adorns the front cover of *Black Market Clash*.

Somewhat inevitably, given their mutual love of reggae, Paul was the first from The Clash to befriend Don, and the two quickly cemented their friendship by swapping mix tapes. At the time of their meeting, Don was working at the now-legendary Acme Attractions stall set within the basement of the Antiquarius indoor antique market on the King's Road; from where Bernard was also operating.

As with SEX a short walk further up King's Road, Acme Attractions quickly became a hangout of sorts for the main players on the nascent UK punk scene, and his penchant for playing dub reggae at full volume, coupled with his willingness to share a spliff, saw the perennially-beshaded Don prove the perfect host. Indeed, it was through his culture clash kinship with the Sex Pistols, The Clash, The Slits (whom he also briefly managed), and the other bands intent on making a noise for themselves throughout the latter half of 1976 that led to his being invited to serve as the resident DJ at the Roxy during its fabled one-hundred-day existence.

Aside from wiling away the time between the group's sets playing his favourite dub reggae interspersed with some MC5, Stooges and New York Dolls, with the Pistols' debut single 'Anarchy In The UK' thrown in for good measure, he decided to adopt punk's DIY ethic for his own purposes by picking up a Super-8 camera to capture the zip and safety-pined zeitgeist that was gripping London and would forever change Britain's musical landscape*.

With John 'Boy' Lennard having been long discarded, Mick had also decided to shelve the A Team-esque TRAC moniker, and having found Topper's replacement, the self-taught Greg Roberts, via the *Melody Maker* classifieds, he and Don began pooling alternative names.

---

* Don's footage would be released the following year as *The Punk Rock Movie*.

An early front-runner was Real Westway in homage to the Spanish footballing giants Real Madrid, but Mick was desperate to use the acronym 'BAD' (in keeping with the jargon of the times that anything considered to be 'Bad' was good) but couldn't come up with a meaningful name that incorporated the acronym.

Help, however, was close at hand, and Mick got his wish when Sigue Sigue Sputnik's resident FX lady, Yana YaYa (a.k.a Jane Farrimond), suggested '**B**ig **A**udio **D**ynamite'.

– CHAPTER FOURTEEN –

THE HORSES ARE ON THE TRACK

'I didn't want to do the same thing, because I knew I wouldn't have a chance. So I tried to do something as far away from The Clash as possible... Over a period of time, I sort of forgot what I was good at – guitar chords and melodies.'

– Mick Jones

MICK WAS TAKING A HUGE risk in allowing Don time to learn the Paul Simonon 'finger-to-sticker' approach to making music, because while Paul's learning the bass by rote as The Clash coalesced into a cohesive unit was all part of punk's aesthetic charm, Mick was now a musician of some renown and the music media might not be quite so forgiving of BAD having a novice in the line-up. When reflecting on this period in Culture Clash, Don admits to finding his being the sole non-musician in the group 'quite daunting' and that to find his own space in the group he threw himself into writing lyrics.

Aside from collaborating with Mick on song ideas, Don started collating sounds and snippets of dialogue from various films to give the new songs a visual dynamic. 'BAD philosophy was to utilise all the elements of the media to create a fuller sound,' Don explained. 'It was not just about making music, it was about ideas. None of us had any interest in making mega-budget rock 'n' roll. Big Audio Dynamite had a wide-screen approach to making music.'[1]

As with Paul, Don proved something of a quick learner. So much so, that by October 1984, BAD set out to road test their wide-screen approach to music on several low-key dates supporting Clash-inspired Welsh rockers, The Alarm. Though future debut single 'The Bottom Line' was given it's first public airing, the majority of the songs played on the Alarm dates would be jettisoned by the time BAD went into Sarm West* to record their debut album the following summer. However, with provocative titles such as 'Keep Off The Grass', 'The Nation has A Nervous Breakdown', and 'Strike', it was clear Mick hadn't lost his talent for tuning into current events – most notably the ongoing battle of wills between NUM leader Arthur Scargill and Maggie Thatcher.

Support acts are usually forced to endure the indignity of playing to near-empty halls, and Big Audio Dynamite may well have suffered a similar fate had Mick Jones not been in the line-up. Of course, this didn't necessarily mean BAD were in for an easy passage because the vast majority of Alarm fans had been reared on The Clash, and were no doubt hoping to hear 'Should I Stay Or Should I Go', 'Train In Vain', and possibly even 'Stay Free'. Instead they were treated to an experimental yet exciting hybrid of hip-hop and rock, infused with snippets of dialogue from spaghetti westerns. A further eye-opener came with seeing Mick sporting a baseball cap, and strumming a guitar that wouldn't have looked out of place on *Star Wars*.

The Alarm support slot may have been a means of road-testing the new songs, but according to Don, Mick 'was adamant it should work live – not an approximation, but the shebang, dialogue, samples and all,' he revealed in May 2010 while speaking about the impending release of the Legacy Edition of *This Is Big Audio Dynamite*. 'Now today, that's a button away, but back then we're talking serious Heath Robinson!† I'd be flying in dialogue stuff on cassette from a boom-box and sound effects with an Ensonic keyboard.'

By and large the live reviews of BAD's inaugural outings were positive in the main, but one of two dissenting voices couldn't resist pointing

---

* Sarm West was the former Basing Street studio where The Clash recorded *Give 'Em Enough Rope*.

† William Heath Robinson (1872 – 1944) was an English artist who drew strange, complicated machines that could do simple jobs.

an accusatory finger at Mick for his perceived plagiarising of Sigue Sigue Sputnik's idea to include movie dialogue in their songs. Don, however, dismisses the inference out-of hand: 'We weren't worried 'bout a thing, nor did we consider what anyone else was doing,' he said. 'We were in a space of our own making. Besides, there was a crucial difference to how BAD used sampled dialogue as compared to how S.S.S or anybody else that came after used 'em.

'None of our songs depended on samples – movie or otherwise,' he continued. 'They were only ever salt and pepper to the main meal. In other words, if you removed them you'd still be left with a song. Every word and sound was thoughtfully considered and had to justify its space.'

Tony clearly didn't share the critics' comments as he was more than happy to return the favour, from when Mick had manned the mixing desk at several early Sigue Sigue Sputnik shows the previous year, by volunteering his services to add dub effects to BAD's onstage sound and cinematic synergy.

'Tony's role is to take the group and rip it apart and make something different every night. It's like producing a new twelve-inch single every time,' Mick enthused to *Rolling Stone* early the following year while BAD were stateside supporting U2.

By the time of the *Rolling Stone* interview Tony had gone back to his day job as chief Sputnik and Mick had hired ex-Theatre Of Hate roadie, Adam 'Flea' Newman, to serve a duel purpose as his guitar tech as well as BAD's resident soundman. (According to Don, he also made a mean cup of tea.)

♪♪♪

Big Audio Dynamite were making a positive noise on both sides of the Atlantic, and Mick was naturally keen to get the group into the studio. Such was his enthusiasm that from the moment BAD began penning songs together he forwarded the tapes to Jerry Green at Wessex studio; not so much to get the engineer's feedback on each song's merits, but rather to allow Jerry ample time to familiarise himself with the compositions for when BAD were ready to commit their endeavours to vinyl.

With Jerry having worked on *London Calling*, *Sandinista!*, and *Combat Rock*, there was perhaps no one better suited for the task of harnessing BAD's sound, as he was familiar with Mick's work ethic both in the recording booth and behind the mixing desk. Jerry, however, would literally find himself caught between two stools owing to Mick's choosing to take exception to his working with Topper on the latter's solo album.

According to Jerry, Mick churlishly asked him if he wanted to 'work with Tolstoy or Harold Robbins?'[2] As Jerry had sole control of the mixing console on Topper's solo project he chose to stick with the Harold Robbins paperback; a mistake he would subsequently come to rue.

Just as he had done with The Clash, when BAD headed into Sarm West during the summer of 1985, Mick was armed with a mental blueprint of what he wanted and how best to go about it. To assist him in his quest he brought in Island Records' in-house engineer Paul 'Groucho' Smykle, who'd learnt his craft working with Linton Kwesi Johnson and Black Uhuru amongst others.

Unlike his time with The Clash, however, Mick was able to get on with the job free from record company interference. Maurice Oberstein was naturally anxious to know how his money was being spent, but he was willing to trust Mick's competence.

The Clash had been renowned for tackling social and political issues, and while 'The Bottom Line' can be construed as Mick's personal phoenix-like rise from despondency after his dismissal from The Clash, he and Don didn't seek to shy away from the major issues of the day on *This Is Big Audio Dynamite* as the album was to be called. 'A Party' was a take on the ongoing Apartheid reforms in South Africa, while 'Stone Thames' highlighted the brouhaha surrounding AIDS; the punning title being a play on the US actor Rock Hudson (Rock/Stone – Hudson River/River Thames), who'd been diagnosed as HIV Positive the previous June, and would die from AIDS-related complications the same month the album was released. 'E=MC2' is a tribute to the maverick cinematographer and film director Nicolas Roeg, while 'Sony' was a tongue-in-cheek dig at corporate and cultural hegemony. Fortunately for Mick and Don, however, Sony's board of directors didn't take offence and were happy to fund future BAD projects after acquiring CBS in January 1988.

Given Mick's penchant for aesthetics, there was to be no cost-cutting corners taken with the album's artwork. Photographer Dan Donovan was brought in to take some group photos, one of which would take pride of place on the album's front cover. Dan's introduction to the group came courtesy of Paul Simonon's girlfriend (and later wife) Tricia Ronane. BAD were technically being managed by Mick's New York-based manager Gary Kurfirst, but with Gary's offices being some three thousand miles away from Ladbroke Grove as the crow flies, Tricia had stepped in to provide more tangible, hands-on support.

Being the son of famed Sixties celebrity snapper, Terence Donavon, coupled with his having served his apprenticeship as David Bailey's assistant, Dan was certainly no slouch with a camera. Nor was he bashful when it came to broaching his other talents, and when Mick casually let slip that he was looking for keyboard player to augment BAD's sound whilst out on the shoot in nearby Portobello Road, Dan let it be known he'd spent his formative years learning the piano. However, while Dan was subsequently invited to hang out with the group and kick ideas around about the artwork for the album, nothing more was said about the vacant keyboards position.

Several weeks went by and just when Dan was beginning to think Mick had changed his mind, he was summoned to Sarm West to see if he had the walk to back up the talk.

'The album had been written almost a year before Dan got there, so the music was quite locked down,' Don reflected. '[But] as a kid Dan had studied classical piano for ten years so he came down to play on the record and basically winged it.'[3]

Even then, however, Dan didn't know if he had the gig, and it wasn't until he arrived at Sarm West with a mock-up of the artwork for 'The Bottom Line' that Mick pointed to the group photo and said there was room for him in the frame.

Dan duly made his BAD public bow in the promo video for 'The Bottom Line', shot in Trafalgar Square amid a political protest rally. 'The organisers came over to tell us that we were messing up their protest and I told them, "Fuck off, we are making a video!"' Don explained. 'Which looking back on it was not a very right-on thing to say – especially since it was an anti-Apartheid rally!'[4]

One has to wonder whether the organisers would have objected had they known BAD had penned a song about Apartheid, but with extras dressed in a variety of costumes such as Roman soldiers, Amazonians, astronauts, Puritan preachers, and Chilean huasos all running amok while the group were set up at the base of Nelson's Column (upon which Big Audio Dynamite was superimposed in gold lettering) miming along to the track, it's hardly surprising they took umbrage.

Having said that, of course, the subsequent airings of the video on *The Tube*, and various other TV shows over the ensuing weeks, gave the rally far more exposure than it could have possibly hoped for.

Stateside exposure for both BAD and 'The Bottom Line' came courtesy of Rick Rubin, who, having wanted to work with Mick for some time, released an extended remix of the song on his recently-incorporated Def Jam Records.

Aside from allowing an advance hearing for those who were contemplating buying the single, the promo video also revealed Mick's post-Clash image. In keeping with his calling Notting Hill the 'Wild West End', Mick had adopted a Spaghetti Western-esque guise, replete with cowboy hat, kerchief and fringed-buckskin jacket – Clint Eastwood meets the Westway. Another reason for Mick's 'the man-with-no-name' attire, of course, could have been an obvious attempt to play down his ex-Clash celebrity status, and allow BAD to be judged on merit.

When reflecting on BAD's image in 2008, Don said that no one in the group consciously thought about it: 'It's just the way we were; we walked around looking like that. It's not like we got on stage, or got in the video and dressed up to be in the video. That's how we rocked it, man!

'There was a certain amount of coordination, but it was an unspoken thing,' he conceded. 'If somebody turned up and we all thought it was stupid, we'd be very vocal about it. But for the most part we were all on the same page. There were no stylists back then. You just wore what you thought was cool.'[5]

Somebody at CBS clearly had a sense of the dramatic as September saw the release of both 'The Bottom Line' b/w 'BAD', and The Clash's 'This Is England' b/w 'Do It Now'; the latter, of course, being the lead single from the long-awaiting follow-up to *Combat Rock*, the unimaginatively-titled *Cut The Crap**.

Perhaps not surprisingly, given the paper's anti-Clash stance of late, both records received something of a mauling at the hands of the *NME*, albeit via different poisoned pens. Charles Shaar Murray was at least willing to acknowledge Mick's ambition with BAD, but his damning assessment that 'The Bottom Line' would have made a decent enough Clash record must have been particularly wounding; the salt-rubbing sting subsequently coming with 'The Bottom Line's failure to chart, and The Clash's first post-Jones effort reaching a rather respectable number 24.

The same CBS wag had also slated *This Is Big Audio Dynamite* and *Cut The Crap* for November release. Yet although The Clash again took the chart honours, with *Cut The Crap* peaking at number 16, some eleven places higher than *This Is Big Audio Dynamite*, that it made the Top 20 was attributable to the group's die-hard following believing 'This Is England' was representative of the new material.

Those fans that had caught The Clash on their back-to-basics busking tour of the provinces earlier in the year, might have recognised track titles such as 'Cool Under Heat', and 'Movers And Shakers', but they would have been hard pressed to recognise the songs themselves owing to Bernard – in his Jose Unidos guise – having chosen to bury the songs beneath cacophonous layers of post-industrial guitar grunge, electric percussion, synthesizer, and inane terrace-style football chants in a mix that Moulinex would have indeed been ashamed of, to paraphrase the *Melody Maker*'s Adam Sweeting's memorable line.

Cut The Crap was rubbish by anyone's standards, let along a group whose previous album had graced the Billboard Top 10, and the critics gave it the savaging it so rightfully deserved. Although some of those same critics would lay into *This Is Big Audio Dynamite* with equal

---

* The album was originally to be called *Out Of Control*.

gusto, it was generally accepted elsewhere that in the twelve months since his departure from The Clash, Mick had taken a bold leap of faith into the future, whereas Joe and Paul were viewed as having spent the correlating period in a three-chord time warp.

Of course, by the time *Cut The Crap* was being lambasted from pillar-to-post in the media, Joe had finally seen the error of his ways in choosing Bernard over Mick and called the last post on The Clash.

Arthur Conan Doyle once observed that 'Mediocrity knows nothing higher than itself; but talent instantly recognizes genius.' No one would argue against the classic Strummer/Jones/Simonon/Headon Clash line-up having created flashes of genius, but it's equally undeniable that following Mick's departure mediocrity took root.

'When I got chucked out [of] The Clash they couldn't get it right anymore, and Bernard would say, "No, no, do it like Mick!"' Mick joked in December 2011. 'When I'd left they were shouting at the new guys and Bernard would turn to Joe and say, "See, immigrant blood!" because Bernard had a similar background to me, and he believed it was all in the blood.'[6]

With the blood coursing through his own veins being of diverse stock, Joe may well have shared Bernard's logic, because having given Pete Howard, Nick Sheppard, and Vince White their thousand-pound pay-offs, his next port of call was Colville Gardens.

Having run himself near ragged putting the finishing touches to *This Is Big Audio Dynamite*, Mick had booked a busman's holiday of sorts staying at Chris Blackwell's holiday home in the Bahamas while working with Talking Heads duo Tina Weymouth and Chris Franz on the duo's new sideline venture, the Tom Tom Club. Mick was at home awaiting the taxi to take him, Daisy, their daughter Lauren, and Tricia Ronane to Heathrow when Joe turned up on the doorstep armed with a conciliatory spliff and an apology.

Though taken aback, Mick invited Joe inside and the two retreated into the kitchen. Their peace pow-wow was soon interrupted when the taxi pulled up at the kerb. Rather than leave things in the air, however, Joe booked a seat on the next available flight to Nassau, where – according to Joe's reflections while penning 'The End Of The Clash' for *Uncut* in September 1994 – 'over the course of a long weekend, they got burgled, witnessed a near-fatal car smash and ended up in a crack house looking to score weed.'

'Joe came over and rode around the island on a bicycle for two days looking for me,' Mick revealed. 'Finally he found me, and he said, "C'mon, let's get it back together again." I'd just done the first BAD album, and I said, "No, I've just done this record, come and have a listen to it." So we went over to Compass Point Studio's special listening room. I came in really excited about it. I said, "What did you think?" Joe just said, "I've never heard such a load of old shit in my life!" He didn't mean it. He just wanted me to get [The Clash] back together again.'[7]

Cut The Crap had left The Clash open to ridicule, but their name alone ensured they would be allowed the opportunity to make amends. After all, there was also no shortage of offers for live appearances, and according to Vince White The Clash had tours of Japan and the Far East set for the coming year. Alas for Joe, however, his play came way too late in the day as Mick was now totally committed to BAD.

The suits at CBS must have been praying for Mick to rethink Joe's offer, but Mick's dedication to BAD was vindicated the following April when 'E=MC²' b/w 'This Is Big Audio Dynamite', the second single to be culled from *This Is Big Audio Dynamite*, reached number 11 on the UK Singles chart and thereby equalling the highest UK chart placing ever afforded The Clash.

The primary reason for this achievement, of course, was undoubtedly Mick's decision to finally set aside his objection to appearing on *Top Of The Pops*, and allowing mainstream music lovers to sample BAD's wares. Judging from his beaming smile throughout the performance he was clearly enjoying his inaugural appearance on the TOTP stage, and one is left to wonder what success The Clash might have enjoyed had they bitten the BBC bullet.

The single's unexpected success certainly put an added spring in Don's step as he'd co-written the song with Mick. Speaking with *Uncut* magazine in August 2009, he revealed his anxiety at having to step into Joe Strummer's shoes as Mick's principle songwriting partner. 'I didn't want to let Mick – or Joe – down. It was very hard working in his

(Joe's) shadow,' he explained. 'I approached lyrics like film treatments, which is why they had that cinematic quality. Probably two-thirds of [E=MC2 is] mine, with Mick's guidance. I wrote it after me and Mick went to see Nick Roeg's film, *Insignificance*. I was so moved by the concept of it, and I'd loved Roeg since *Walkabout*. The song lists all his films in a cryptic way. I called it an homage to Roeg.'

Don's preferred method may have been to consider lyrics like film treatments, but his and Mick's songwriting process was pretty much the same formula as the one Mick and Joe had used in The Clash, with Mick messing around on either the guitar or keyboards, while he was huddled in a corner scribbling away. 'It gets your juices flowing when you hear this stuff going around in your head; scribbling notes on paper, sometimes complete verses, sometimes couplets, sometimes nonsense,' he explained. Mick'd go, "Right, put that there, do a little cut and paste" and knock 'em into shape. I have to say, on reflection, it's a great hindsight to have got to be able to do that with Mick, because Mick is pretty good at that. If you look at the hit tunes from The Clash – particularly in America – they're all Mick, except for "Rock the Casbah". Joe used to call 'em "Radio 2 tendencies," which was a slight dig, but hey, we all dig a cool melody.'[8]

Another of Mick's 'Radio 2 tendency' melodies was put to good use in 'Medicine Show b/w 'A Party', the third and final single lifted from *This Is Big Audio Dynamite*. The song, meant as a sideways swipe at mid-Eighties media manipulation, with sampled dialogue from *A Fistful of Dollars*, *A Fistful Of Dynamite*, and *The Good, The Bad, And The Ugly*, may have failed to capitalise on the success of 'E=MC2' (peaking at number 27) but the promo video proved receptive to Clash fans everywhere as it featured cameo appearances from both Joe and Paul. 'We had Joe and Paul playing [Southern] cops,' Don explained. 'There is that poignant shot at the end of the video where Mick is in prison and Joe and Paul are looking at him.'[9]

Mick and Joe, of course, had already smoked a spliff of peace at Mick's flat prior to the Bahamas trip, but Paul's presence in the video was evidence that the hatchet had been truly buried. 'We had loads of fun after we split up,' Mick revealed in November 2007. 'After a short while, we became close and strong friends again. Which I think is quite different from most groups that split up. We were always close, in a kind of... I always felt [we were like] a family.. I read now I might have misread the signs, but that's how I saw it anyway.'[10]

– CHAPTER FIFTEEN –

THEY PLAY KNOCK ON WOOD

'I always felt great about [10 Upping Street], *right from the start. I can't remember a time when I felt so over-awed, or was so happy with what I was doing.'*
— Mick Jones

B Y THE SUMMER OF 1986, CBS were as yet still unsure how to best market BAD, but with This Is Big Audio Dynamite having attained gold disc status in the UK, the label was more than happy to let the group back into the recording studio to begin work on the follow-up album. Rather than return to Sarm West, however, the group moved into Trident Studios in St Anne's Court in Soho, where some three weeks into the sessions – coincidentally, the day of Mick's 31st birthday – Don was making his way along Wardour Street when he happened upon a familiar figure – Joe.

As luck would have it, there was a BAD promo poster on a nearby wall and instead of greeting his friend, Joe grabbed the nearest passer-by and jabbed a finger at Don, 'Look! It's the man in the poster!' Don was mortified and fled into a nearby tobacconist's, but Joe was in a mischievous mood and followed Don inside the shop to continue his playful harangue. Realising he wasn't going to be able to shake Joe off, Don invited him to Trident to no doubt wish Mick a happy birthday, as well as see how the new album was progressing.

Mick and Joe hadn't exactly been strangers since the 'Medicine Show' video shoot, as Joe – having been sweet-talked by American director, Alex Cox, into penning a theme song for his second feature film, *Love Kills**; the tragic telling of Sid and Nancy's doomed love affair – had graciously invited Mick along to Regent Park Recordings in Primrose Hill, north London, to add guitar to both 'Love Kills' and 'Dum Dum Club', which Joe had also written for the film. However, by the time the tracks had been mixed in readiness for release as a single, the majority of Mick's playing had been eradicated.

Given that Joe's already prodigious alcohol intake had taken on epic proportions of late, Mick probably assumed Joe would hang around the studio until knocking-off time before taking Mick for a celebratory drink. But Joe, of course, had other ideas, and aside from assigning himself the co-producer's role, he also helped out with the lyrics on five new songs: 'Beyond The Pale', 'Limbo The Law', 'V Thirteen' and 'Sightsee MC!'

With his creative juices flowing once more, Joe – as was his want in The Clash – erected a spliff bunker out of various flight cases beneath the studio's grand piano, which also served as an ad hoc sleeping quarters. Joe would tell Chris Salewitz that on realising he gave maximum effort to anything he got involved with Don and the rest of BAD were okay with his constant presence in the studio.

When reflecting on the Trident sessions, Don readily admitted that he and the others had been worried about 'Joe's shadow' hovering over the group in the early days. However, he now knew that Mick was now totally committed to BAD, and so welcomed Joe's contribution. 'It was a beautiful thing to see those guys creatively fall in love,' he explained. 'It was beautiful to be a part of and to watch happen; [to] see them bury the hatchet. I didn't feel threatened at all. I got to sing some songs written by Strummer and Jones, and work with them in the studio. That's great.'[1]

Mick was equally appreciative of Joe's input, and clearly still valued his opinion 'What Joe did with me on that record is what he did with me in the Clash. He gave it the once-over, so to speak, with the lyrics and everything. It all went through him.'[2]

Joe would also be credited with coming up with *No. 10, Upping Street* as the album's title; meant as a hip, alternative take on 10

---

* Owing to Cox's eleventh-hour decision to rename the film *Sid And Nancy*, the 'Love Kills' single stalled at number 67 on the UK chart.

Downing Street, the prime minister's official residence. However, not all of Joe's proposals proved beneficial for BAD, most notably the one where he suggested they mix the album at the Hit Factory in New York. Mick would subsequently say this had been Joe's means of gaining revenge for his insistence that *Combat Rock* be recorded at Electric Lady. Yet while decamping to New York would put a serious dent in BAD's recording budget, the final decision about where to mix the new record had rested with him.

However, while it was no secret that Joe was desperate to get The Clash back together around this time, it's unlikely he had an ulterior motive. Indeed, he would subsequently tell Chris Salewitz that he'd suggested mixing the album in New York because he 'wanted it to be like good vegetables – fresh.' Nor would Mick have required much arm twisting, as he'd been enamoured with all things Big Apple ever since playing the Palladium on the Pearl Harbor '79 Tour. And with the city having taken BAD to its heart as it had The Clash, what better place to mix the album?

With BAD in town, the Hit Factory on West 54th Street became a celebrity hangout with the likes of Iggy Pop, the Red Hot Chili Peppers, maverick film director Jim Jarmusch (who would shot the promo video for 'Sightsee MC!'), and actors Matt Dillon and Lawrence Fishburne all dropping by to say hello. Indeed, Matt and Lawrence would end up on the album owing to Joe cajoling them to act out the imaginary scene about an assassin inadvertently killing the wrong person, which appears on 'Dial A Hitman'.

Mixing the album would take three months, and with the majority of the budget being used up in studio time the group were forced to subsist on very little money. Don, however, says it was never about the money with BAD, but rather the chance to travel the world and immerse themselves in different cultures. It was, of course, whilst in New York mixing the album that he met his future wife, Grace.

As Mick, Don, and the rest of BAD were all listening to the Beastie Boys and Public Enemy around this time, it was perhaps inevitable that the Def Jam sound would filter into their own style – most notably 'Sightsee MC!' That they were also enamoured by Brian de

Palma's *Scarface* is evidenced not only with the album cover showing the group posing in front of a Tim Jones painting based on a still taken from the film, but also with the dialogue samples featuring in 'Limbo The Law'.

These days anyone sampling dialogue from films without first attaining permission would find themselves in breach of copyright, but at the time no one thought to question what BAD were doing, as Don explained: 'That was all so early in the history of music that no one knew what to do. We didn't ask anybody's permission. The record companies didn't ask us to clear the samples. They weren't even called samples then, because we really were the first band to have hits with those kind of things. It was all so new that no one really knew what hit 'em. You could never do that now.'[3]

'Sambadrome' featured samples from legendary Brazilian commentator Osmar Santos, who actually joined the group on stage when they played Brazil. The song, about a Robin Hood-esque drug dealer living in the Favalas of Rio de Janeiro proved a surprise hit with the locals, but the city's police chief was less enthused about an English pop act highlighting Rio's escalating drug problems and was pictured in the local newspapers flushing the twelve-inch single down the toilet.

By his own admission, Mick had expected it to take time for those who knew him from The Clash – not to mention the mainstream music-loving public – to appreciate what he was trying to do with BAD, and while he had to put up with the occasional idiot shouting for 'London Calling', the gamble appeared to be paying dividends in terms of ticket sales. BAD's first major UK headline tour had run over from April into May owing to popular demand, and prior to entering Trident to begin work on the new album, they'd appeared on the bill at the free Artists Against Apartheid UK Freedom Festival alongside Peter Gabriel, Billy Bragg, the Style Council, and Elvis Costello.

The festival, staged on Clapham Common on Saturday, 28 June, was the biggest UK outdoor festival since the Isle Of Wight Festival sixteen years earlier, and drew a crowd in excess of 250,000. As the organisers had been worried about the local council's strict 10 p.m.

curfew, headliners Peter Gabriel and Sting had gone on earlier in the day leaving BAD the honour of bringing the curtain down – albeit with a truncated set.

The music critics, however, were proving more difficult to please, and the ensuing reviews following the release of *No. 10, Upping Street* that October were lukewarm at best, with the majority lamenting the album's failure to live up to the promise of the group's debut long-player. It initially seemed the critics had erred in their damning appraisals as the album climbed to number 11 on the UK chart. However, unlike *This Is Big Audio Dynamite*, which remained on the chart for six months, it quickly faded thereafter.

What was even more disheartening was the chart performances of the three singles lifted from the album. 'C'mon Every Beatbox b/w Badrock City', and 'V. Thirteen (Remix)' b/w 'Hollywood Boulevard (Remix)', both failed to break into the Top 50, while 'Sightsee M.C!' b/w 'Another One Rides The Bus' failed to make the chart at all.

Unsurprisingly, Joe's involvement on *No. 10, Upping Street* was at the forefront of the media's interest in the album, and Mick was forced to spend much of his time in the immediate wake of the album's release stressing that there were no plans for Joe to join BAD on a permanent basis. However, his admitting that he and Joe would be working together again in the near future on Joe's proposed solo album – tentatively titled *Throwdown* – only served to stoke the embers on a potential Clash reunion.

The mooted collaboration didn't of course come to pass, largely on account of Mick and Joe being on polar opposite career paths, but 'Beyond The Pale' and 'V Thirteen' – the two Strummer-Jones compositions on *No. 10, Upping Street* – serve as a lasting testament to what might have been.

♪♪♪

In April 1987, prior to heading over to New York where BAD were set to play eleven consecutive nights at the Irving Plaza on East 15th Street to promote the US release of *No. 10, Upping Street*, Mick and Don flew out to Oracabessa in Jamaica for a little rest and recreation. In *Culture Clash*, Don says that he was chilling on the private beach at Goldeneye (James Bond author Ian Fleming's private estate, which was – and still is – owned by Chris Blackwell, and of course lent its name to the seventeenth Bond film), when he saw a dishevelled figure ambling towards him sporting a huge Bowie knife. It wasn't until the figure was almost upon him that Don realised it was actually Keith Richards, who was also holidaying on the island.

Having gotten acquainted over a spliff or three, Keith invited Don and Mick over to his holiday home where the ice was further broken over a bottle of Jack Daniels. Over the ensuing weeks, Mick and Don spent many a debauched evening chez Richards, with Mick realising a fantasy he'd probably nurtured ever since seeing the Stones play Hyde Park some twenty years earlier by jamming with his ultimate guitar hero.

Mick and Don would get to meet Keith's Glimmer Twin, Mick Jagger, when the Stones' frontman dropped by the Irving Plaza with David Bowie to check out BAD. Nor was the New York residency a one-off occurrence, as BAD also enjoyed a seven-night stint at the Roxy in Los Angeles. It would appear that having realised the benefits to be enjoyed from playing residencies compared to the drudgery of criss-crossing America playing scores of shows whilst with The Clash, Mick now preferred to book a show at a low-key venue in a major city and keep the next few nights free should the need arise. And the group's growing popularity on the US college radio circuit ensured word quickly got around town.

Later that summer, BAD served as support to U2 on the European leg of the latter's world tour to promote *The Joshua Tree*. Playing to sell-out stadium crowds was awe-inspiring for Don and the others, but Mick, of course, had seen and done it all before – albeit playing in support of The Who.

Although the tour gave BAD massive exposure in previously untested countries such as Italy, Sweden, and Switzerland, there were undoubtedly times when Mick must have heaved a wistful sigh for what might have been. Don certainly makes mention of his sharing a knowing look with Mick whilst U2 were on stage, and rumour has it that at one show, Bono – on seeing Mick watching from the wings – jabbed a finger at the crowd and hollered, 'This should be you!'

While BAD were out traversing Europe with U2, they garnered unwarranted exposure via US media following the arrest of two high school students in Hudsonville, Michigan, on terrorist charges. Believing the youths had been influenced by watching films and listening to rock music, the Hudsonville police conducted raids on their homes and impounded various items as evidence – including a copy of *This Is Big Audio Dynamite*, which, of course, showed Mick clutching a stick of dynamite.

Following Sony's appropriation of CBS at the beginning of the year, March 1988 saw The Clash back in vogue – not to mention the album charts on both sides of the Atlantic – with the release of the retrospective 28-track compilation album, *The Story Of The Clash, Volume 1*.

'I Fought The Law' had also crept into the UK Top 30 following its re-release the previous month. Perhaps not surprisingly, given that it was a 'best of', the compilation is biased towards those songs released as singles during The Clash's career. Even less surprisingly, given that Mick (with assistance from Tricia Ronane) had been permitted to compile the track-listing as a conciliatory gesture from Joe and Paul, *Cut The Crap* wasn't represented.

While reviewing the album, *Rolling Stone*'s Elliott Murphy punningly-opined that '*The Story Of The Clash* is a story that ended too soon...,' but although the title hinted at a volume 2 being released at some point in the future, there were no thoughts of The Clash reforming to record new material.

The royalties accrued from sales of *The Story Of The Clash, Volume 1*, would come in handy, but the irony wouldn't have been lost on Mick that while the compilation album was riding high in the charts BAD were having to watch the pennies while recording their third album. Having initially toyed with the idea of calling the new album *Dread Astaire*, they finally decided on *Tighten Up, Vol. 88* in homage to Trojan Records' *Tighten Up* reggae compilation album series from the 1960s. Indeed, such was the plight of the group's finances at that time that Mick and Don were forced to hole up in Mick's home studio to work on song ideas before the group as a whole entered Beethoven St. Studio in west London to begin recording the album for real.

Another cost-cutting exercise came with the artwork featuring a Paul Simonon painting of a blues party held within the shadow of Trellick Tower, a monolithic high-rise on Harrow Road. These days, of course, Paul's work is in high demand but at the time of the album's release he'd only just returned to painting.

The hope that BAD had carried through from the previous year was dented somewhat when 'Just Play Music' b/w 'Much Worse' – the lead single from *Tighten Up Vol, 88* – failed to even the breech the UK Top 50 following its release in May. However, the title of the B-side was to prove lamentably apt when the parent album stalled at number 33, some twenty-two places lower than *No. 10, Upping Street*, and five lower than the group's debut.

In hindsight, the single's falling by the wayside could be put down to its being inferior to other tracks such as 'Mr Walker Said', or The Battle Of All Saints Road', but the underlying reason for the album's relative poor showing was due to Mick being rushed into hospital midway through the all-important promotional UK tour after inadvertently contracting chickenpox from four-year-old Lauren.

'We were three-quarters through [the] tour when I noticed these spots on my throat,' he explained in September 1989. 'By the time I collapsed and was taken to the hospital it had turned into pneumonia. I was in intensive care, totally out of it for seventeen days. The doctors said later it was touch-and-go for a while.'[4]

Mick was completely unaware of it at the time, but the hospital he was rushed to following his collapse was St. Mary's in Paddington; a familiar landmark back when he was struggling to put a group together in the basement of the café opposite.

While BAD had been out on the road promoting *Tighten Up, Vol. 88*, Joe was traversing the country on the Rock Against the Rich Tour with his ad hoc outfit, Latino Rockabilly War. Unlike Mick, Joe had suffered no anxiety over dipping into The Clash back catalogue to bolster his set-list – albeit predominantly Clash covers such as 'Police On My Back', Brand New Cadillac', and 'Police And Thieves' – but at various stop-offs he'd also play either 'V Thirteen', or 'Sightsee MC!' – Sometimes playing both numbers on occasion.

During the early stages of the tour an upbeat Joe would shout out the opening line to the song before offering a dedication to 'the guys in Big Audio Dynamite' in obvious celebration of his having worked with Mick on *No. 10, Upping Street*, but following Mick's hospitalisation the dedication took on a more solemn tone.

The Rock Against the Rich Tour had gotten underway with a benefit show for Green Wedge (a Green Party fund-raising venture) at the Tabernacle in Powis Square on Friday, 17 June. Ironically, or serendipitously, depending on one's point of view, the following day saw Latino Rockabilly War and BAD appear on the same bill at an Amnesty International benefit at the 50,000-capacity Milton Keynes National Bowl.

According to LRW guitarist Zander Schloss, when they hit the stage and launched into 'Police On My Back' he saw a befuddled Mick come running onto the back of the stage thinking he's missed his cue. It's a colourful anecdote, but with it being five years since Mick had last played the Equals song, Schloss is obviously over-egging the pudding at seeing Mick come out to catch the performance.

Mick would of course pull through, but it was a classic case of out of the frying pan into the fire as he contracted an undetermined bug – possibly MRSA – and had to be moved to the hospital's AIDS ward. 'When I came to, I was very Gandhi-like, very pale and weak, a bit delirious, feeling love for everyone around me,' he continued. 'I had lung damage, couldn't speak and there was so much nerve damage I couldn't move my hands or walk.'[5]

After his too-close-for-comfort brush with death Mick would undergo something akin to a rebirth as he would spend the next nine months of rehabilitation with physiotherapists and speech coaches. 'I'd been paralysed and I never thought that could happen to me, no one ever thinks they could get that sick,' he said in another American interview three months later. 'When I finally was able to pick up a guitar again and play, I cried. I realised that not only was I nearly dead, but the band was nearly dead after the last album,' he continued. 'When I finally got out of the hospital, I didn't want to make a record that was full of misery. The main point was that we wanted to make a celebration of life.'[6]

♪♪♪

The 'celebration of life' Mick is referring to was encapsulated in BAD's fourth studio album, *Megatop Phoenix*, released in September 1989. Mick was out of action for months on end, but Don and the rest of the group hadn't exactly sat idle and had got together to demo song ideas ready for when Mick was finally able to (in Don's words) 'come in and sprinkle his magic over the tracks.'[7]

With Joe co-producing *No. 10, Upping Street*, and Paul having contributed to the cover artwork on *Tighten Up, Vol. 88*, *Megatop Phoenix* brought another Clash link of sorts with Mick inviting Bill Price to Ray Davis' Konk Studios in Tottenham Lane, north London to help with the production on the album. The Kinks, of course, had featured heavily on the soundtrack of Mick's adolescence, and he'd been a proud card-carrying member of the group's fan club. Such was Mick's admiration for Davis that Don remembers it being the only time he ever saw Mick slightly star-struck.

While Mick had been struggling along the allegorical road to recovery, kids up and down the country were traversing Britain's highways and byways for real in search of secret location, round-the-clock parties – or 'raves', as the new acid house dance craze that was sweeping the nation was known. Whereas punk bands such as The Clash had stripped music back to its rock 'n' roll its roots, acid house had taken punk's DIY ethic to the extreme by largely doing away with musicianship altogether. Instead, the organisers would hire a disused barn or a field from a farmer and have a DJ blasting out hypnotic dance tunes from dusk till dawn.

Just as he had done with punk rock a decade of so earlier, Mick readily embraced acid house. 'The kids want better value for their money,' he explained in 1989, whilst out on the road promoting *Megatop Phoenix*. 'They don't want to be crowded into some stadium, roughed up by the security, with overpriced T-shirts and cold hot dogs, and then kicked out at 11 p.m. They want a place where they can party all night.

'The secret nature of the acid parties makes 'em exciting,' he continued. 'When you buy a ticket, there's no location printed on it, just a phone number you call to find out the location. Most are held in big fields out near the airport... As for the musical mix at acid parties, it's liberal and diverse.'

Regarding the album itself, Mick said the tracks were perhaps more positive and personal than previous BAD albums. 'We used to talk in headlines, recounting news stories,' he explained. This time we mostly looked inside ourselves for the information. We tried to simplify the music, make it more clear so that everyone could hear every word. It's still dense in terms of having a lot of content, but it has clarity of vision.'[9]

In keeping with *Megatop Phoenix*'s dance orientated theme, BAD invited the up-and-coming acid house DJ, Adamski*, a.k.a Paul Adam Tinsley, (who was promoting his debut album, *Liveanddirect*), onto their Autumn UK tour. There was, however, a rather more familiar face within the line-up of the tour's main support act, Havana 3AM.

Whilst tearing around the Texas border on a couple of rented Harley Davidson motorcycles, Paul and his best friend, ex-Whirlwind frontman Nigel Dixon, had fallen in with a rough-and-ready biker gang, which included ex-Sex Pistol Steve Jones amongst its number. And on recruiting Dallas-born guitarist Gary Myrick, they became something of the gang's in-house, roadhouse group.

With several record companies expressing interest in Havana 3AM, the trio returned to London where Paul kindly invited Topper to renew their killer rhythm section partnership. Topper, however, was still incapable of thinking beyond his next fix, so the vacant drum stool had gone to Travis Williams.

New groups such as 808 State, KLF, and The Shamen were all pioneering the acid house rave wave, but *Megatop Phoenix* proved Mick was still capable of keeping apace with the modern pulse beat. The *NME* went so far as to declare the album his closest to capturing the mood of the times since *The Clash*, while *Pulse* magazine's

---

* In May 1990, Adamski would score a UK number one with 'Killer', which he co-wrote with the then unknown Seal, who also sang on the record. Coincidentally, Seal had worked in an unofficial capacity at Beethoven St. Studio where BAD recorded *Tighten Up, Vol. 88*.

Andrew Goodwin declared *Megatop Phoenix* to be the group's finest work so far, commending the combination of acid-house beats and reggae basslines.

The lead single 'James Brown' b/w 'If I Were John Carpenter', which featured sampled dialogue from Mr. Sex Machine himself, surprisingly failed to chart, but the album not only improved on its predecessor's placing on the UK chart, but also reached a very creditable number 85 on the *Billboard* chart, which must have made it all the more perplexing for Mick when Don, Leo, and Greg tendered their resignations to form Screaming Target.

It could be argued that the seed of Screaming Target first took root while Mick was laid up in hospital as Don and the others had too much time on their hands, but away from the onstage camaraderie, BAD were going through all the usual clichés and dramas, and creative and financial arguments that seem to afflict every group at some point.

'We ended up at one point talking to each other through lawyers, and all this stuff,' Don explained in 2008. 'But if you know anything about rock 'n' roll you'll understand that's almost part of the process. And the very fact that lawyers get involved means, "Hey, there must have been something good to fight about in the first place." I got to write some great songs with Mick. I got to be in a lawsuit with Mick. Brilliant!'[10]

Dan Donovan would initially remain loyal to the BAD cause, but would also defect to Screaming Target shortly into the New Year leaving Mick the dubious honour of having been kicked out of one group he'd formed, and abandoned by the other. Further estrangement then followed with Daisy calling time on their six-year relationship.

The Eighties were drawing to a close and within those ten years Mick had endured enough highs and lows to last several lifetimes. The last eighteen months had been particularly tumultuous, as he'd lost his group, his girlfriend, and had very nearly lost his life. So as the chimes of Big Ben rang out to usher in the new decade, the only question Mick had to ask himself as he toasted the future was whether his glass was half full, or half empty...

– CHAPTER SIXTEEN –

SWITCHIN' ON THE STROBE

'["Should I Stay Or Should I Go"] *wasn't about anybody specific, and it wasn't pre-empting my leaving The Clash. It was just a good rockin' song; our attempt at writing a classic. When we were just playing, that was the kind of thing we used to like to play.'*
— Mick Jones

Mick MAY HAVE BEEN downhearted over the BAD exodus, but with *Megatop Phoenix* being the first Big Audio Dynamite record to make an impression on the Billboard chart he was far from down and out. If anything, he was in a stronger position than the one he found himself in after being kicked out of The Clash because with BAD he'd proved he'd been on the right track with his vision for The Clash whereas Joe's had crashed and burned.

Taking friends who couldn't play but looked cool out of the equation, just as he had after picking himself up off the floor first time around, he opted for three relative unknowns from the Notting Hill music scene rather than bringing in named musicians whose egos might bring problems further down the line. The new guns for hire were guitarist Nick Hawkins (who sadly suffered a fatal heart attack in October 2005, aged just 40), Gary Stonadge on bass, and drummer Chris Kavanagh, who was perhaps the best-known of the trio having enjoyed a taste of fame with Sigue Sigue Sputnik. Mick initially intended to keep trading as BAD, but when this surprisingly brought the threat of legal action from Don and the other founder members he was forced into a rethink. Viewing the new line-up as a sequel to what had gone before; he opted for Big Audio Dynamite II.

BAD II received an unexpected boost when the very much underrated 'Free' – the last song the original BAD line-up had worked on together – was commissioned for the soundtrack to a new action-comedy caper called *Flashback**, starring Dennis Hopper and Kiefer Sutherland. On the back of this, 'Free' was issued as a US-only promo single in the hope that the resulting exposure among cinema audiences would see the track take off in the clubs. When this sadly didn't come to pass, 'Free' was given a Mick Jones makeover and subsequently reappeared as the track 'Kickin' In' on the new group's debut album, *Kool-Aid*.

Taking a break from recording the album, BAD II made their live debut at the Alexandra Palace in north London on 10 August 1990, as part of the Town & Country Club's fifth anniversary celebrations.

The following month saw Mick return to the *Top Of The Pops* stage providing his inimitable guitar style and backing vocals on Aztec Camera's 'Good Morning Britain', which reached number 19 on the UK chart. (Mick would also put in guest appearances at certain venues on Aztec Camera's subsequent tour to perform the song)

Kool-Aid, which Mick co-produced with his cousin Andre Shapps, and Olimax (a.k.a Oliver Maxwell), hit the record shops at the beginning of November, and continuing the acid house party theme of *Megatop Phoenix*, the track-listing featured song titles with obvious drug-inferences such as the aforementioned 'Kickin' In', and 'On One'. The vivid album cover was also in keeping with the acid house craze, while the group members are credited as 'Some bloke' (Mick), 'Some other bloke' (Hawkins), 'Some other other bloke' (Stonadge), and 'Some other other other bloke' (Kavanagh). Though an obvious attempt at levity, it nevertheless goes to show that some blokes are created more equal than others.

When reviewing the album, *Q* magazine's Ian McMillan said that *Kool-Aid* was 'a refreshing auditory experience', before going on to add that the common denominator between the tracks was oddly

---

* A remixed version of 'The Bottom Line' was used as the title track for *Flashback*, but wasn't included on the soundtrack.

enough The Clash with 'echoes of, in particular, *London Calling* all over this album.'

What McMillan failed to pick up on wasn't so much that the songs were mindful of The Clash, but rather Mick's way of exorcising the ghosts surrounding his sacking from The Clash, as well as documenting the break-up of BAD. *Kool-Aid* is the closest Mick has ever come to penning an autobiography, which makes it all the more strange that his new paymasters at Sony/Columbia would choose to release the album as a limited-pressing confined to the UK market.

Thankfully, however, the majority of the songs would reappear in different guises on the group's follow-up album, *The Globe*.

♪♪♪

Mick was in the process of putting BAD II together when the ex-Housemartin, and self-confessed Clash fan, Norman Cook, scored a massive UK number one hit with 'Dub Be Good To Me', under his dance music collective umbrella, Beats International. The track melded the SOS Band's 'Just Be Good To Me' (featuring revised lyrics sung by the SOS Band's Lindy Layton), over the instantly-recognisable bass line from The Clash's 'Guns Of Brixton'.

When blowing his own trumpet in the media, the bassist turned bedroom DJ readily admitted to having sampled the bass line as an 'affectionate tribute' to The Clash for their having been a 'huge influence on my growing up, both musically and politically. However, when Paul Simonon went a kicking at Norman's front door for what he believed to be a rightful share of the royalties, the latter shamefacedly backtracked by saying he'd actually lifted the bass line from an obscure ska track. But the future Fatboy Slim was fooling nobody, least of all Paul, and the dispute was eventually settled out of court.

In the meantime, Paul had approached Norman's fellow dance DJ Jeremy Healy to remix 'Guns Of Brixton', but with 'Dub Be Good To Me' having been danced to death, the resulting single 'Return To Brixton' (which also featured the original Clash track on certain formats) stalled at number 57 following its June release.

The entrepreneurial Norman had lifted the bass line to 'Guns Of Brixton' to line his own pockets, but 'Dub Be Good To Me', coupled with the publicity arising over Paul's plagiarism claim, served to bring The Clash back into the public consciousness.

This, however, was merely a tempting hors d'œuvre to the entrée that came the following February owing to jeans giants Levi Strauss & Co. selecting 'Should I Stay Or Should I Go' to serve as a backdrop to the latest TV commercial in the American company's long-running advertising campaign to promote the perennially-popular shrink-to-fit 501s.

The first commercial, featuring Sam Cooke's original 1960 hit 'Wonderful World', was aired back in 1986, and proved an instant hit with the public. So much so, that by February 1991, the 'Levi 501 ads' as they were known, had become almost as popular as the product they were promoting with people playfully second-guessing which rock 'n' roll hit of yesteryear might feature next. The record companies were equally anxious to discover which artists Levi's were considering as with the exception of Eddie Cochran's 'C'Mon Everybody' (1988), every other song used in the ads had scored a Top 10 hit upon re-release, with Ben E. King's 'Stand By Me' (1987), and the Steve Miller Band's 'The Joker' (1990), claiming the coveted number one slot.

The news that 'Should I Stay Or Should I Go' would feature in the latest Levi's ad was greeted with a certain amount of consternation amongst Clash fans; the surprise stemming from the group's hitherto reticence to having their music used as a marketing tool. As with previous approaches from Dr Pepper and British Telecom, Levi's initial approach had been to The Clash, but as the song was Mick's, Joe, Paul, and Topper allowed him the final say.

Mick was painfully aware that their detractors of old would be sharpening their knives in anticipation of The Clash setting aside their principles in return for a fast buck, but he reasoned that Levi's were considered as much a bona fide rock 'n' roll accoutrement as Brylcream and beetle-crushers. A rather less altruistic reason for Mick giving Levi's the green light, of course, was that the cash influx would enable him to keep Big Audio Dynamite II in the black.

With all the attention focused on 'Should I Stay Or Should I Go', no one within the Clash camp stopped to consider which track Mick might select for the single's B-side. Joe, Paul, and Topper probably expected Mick to knock up a remix of the A-side. What they didn't anticipate was Mick – having recognised a gilt-edged opportunity to promote BAD II's forthcoming album – to co-opt 'Rush'*, the lead track on *The Globe*. Paul, who'd been the least receptive to Levi's overtures in the first instance, was said to be particularly incensed at what he saw a flagrant opportunistic tactic on Mick's part, and the ensuing arguments resulted in the opening of old wounds. Of course, one cannot help but wonder why Paul hadn't voiced similar concerns back in June 1982 when 'Should I Stay Or Should I Go' was released with three alternate B-sides?

Mick's opportunism would end up paying dividends as 'Should I Stay Or Should I Go' – accompanied by Don Letts' video of The Clash playing the song at Shea Stadium – climbed to the top of the UK singles chart and held the position for three weeks. Sad though it was that it took a jeans commercial to put The Clash at the top of the charts, the resulting exposure did at least bring the group to the attention of a new audience, as well as serve as a wistful reminder to their fans of old.

Sony/Columbia was eager to see how much cash might be extracted from The Clash cow and re-released *The Story of The Clash, Volume 1*. The album had made the Top 10 back in 1988, and although it stalled at number 13 at the second time of asking, it remained on the charts for two months; plenty enough time to allow further executive exploitation. 'Should I Stay Or Should I Go' was still in the chart when Sony/Columbia released 'Rock The Casbah'. On the back of the single reaching number 15, the label not only reissued the parent album *Combat Rock* in May, but also put out 'London Calling' and 'I Fought The Law', just as it had done at the time of *The Story Of The Clash, Volume 1*'s original release.

That the latter track failed to trouble the chart compilers should have served as ample warning that the rotting carcass had been sufficiently flogged, and it was only when 'Train In Vain' also withered on the vine that the whip was returned to its hook.

Sony's shameless raids on The Clash cookie jar had prompted fresh reunion rumours, and according to said rumours serious money

---

* 'Rush' was a reworking of 'Change Of Atmosphere', which had appeared on *Kool-Aid*.

was being tabled to tempt The Clash back onto the stage. What the promoters failed to take into consideration when tabling their offers, however, was that it was Sony/Columbia doing the cashing in and not the group members themselves. As far as they were concerned, The Clash most definitely weren't for sale. 'I don't think any of us would do it for the money,' Mick told *Vox* magazine's Mal Peachey that April. 'I don't think we'd do *anything* just for the money.'

♪♪♪

Having already used Clash product to promote *The Globe*, Mick borrowed an idea from the ghost of Clash past to mark the album's release by teaming up with the *NME*. As with *The Clash* back in April 1977, a sticker was enclosed within the first pressing of *The Globe*, in conjunction with the *NME* printing a coupon in its 10 August issue. The first 2,000 fans to send sticker and coupon to the paper would receive a copy of *Ally Pally Paradiso*, a nine-track live album taken from BAD II's appearance at the Alexandra Palace the previous August.

With buoyant toe-tappers such as 'Can't Wait/Live', and the title track, 'The Globe' (which featured a sneaky-cheeky sampling of 'Should I Stay Or Should I Go', coupled with more poignant tracks such as the Mott The Hoople-esque 'Innocent Child', the new album appeared to have something for everyone. When reviewing the album *Pulse*'s self-confessed BADophile, Andrew Goodwin, noted how the group's new incarnation had 'shifted its invocations of blackness from dancehall toasting to straight-out rap,' while *All Music*'s Tom Demalon – having praised Mick's songwriting as 'some of his strongest in some time' – went on to say how the album was possibly the strongest effort of Big Audio Dynamite (in any incarnation) and certainly their best work since their debut.'

Mick had good reason to be pleased with himself as BAD II embarked on a UK tour that August. Yet despite all the hard work and critique kudos, *The Globe* stalled on its axis at a desultory number 63 on the UK chart.

Thanks to the unswerving loyalty towards BAD on the US college radio circuit, the album would fair much better in America. Not only did it hit the top spot on the college radio chart, it also climbed twelve places higher than *Megatop Phoenix* on the Billboard chart shifting in excess of 250,000 copies in the process. Meanwhile, 'Rush' reached number 32 on the singles chart, and was also voted Billboard's 'Best Modern Rock Track' of the year. The single also performed well in Australasia, hitting the number one spot in both Australia and New Zealand.

The Globe also featured 'When The Time Comes', and Mick's time almost came again during the group's US September tour when the car he was travelling in was forced off the highway and rolled over several times. Thankfully, however, both he and the driver walked away from the smash. If anything, Mick was left more shaken and stirred by a report in the *NME* claiming that he'd been approached by an American promoter who was supposedly offering The Clash £10 million for a one-off US tour.

Although it was true he'd told *Rolling Stone* that he wouldn't necessarily rule out a Clash reunion at some point in the future, Mick was as yet still fully committed to BAD II. That The Clash were still held in the highest regard in America was beyond dispute, but the idea that someone was willing to table £10 million for a one-off tour was ludicrous. Tricia Ronane was so incensed by the *NME*'s claim that she called their offices and said that if the American promoter did indeed exist then the paper should have him call her. Unsurprisingly, Tricia never heard another word about the mooted deal.

What the latest 'will-they-or-won't they' reformation rumours did do, however, was alert Mick to what he perceived to be Sony/Columbia's apathetic attitude towards BAD II compared to the label's ongoing endeavours regarding The Clash.

Hoping to cash in on The Clash's enduring popularity on the Christmas market, Sony were shamefacedly set to rush-release an A-side compilation CD, the unimaginatively entitled *Singles* (with 'This Is England' having seemingly been airbrushed from the group's history again). Over in New York Kosmo Vinyl was busy collating a bumper consortium – including obscure demos, live recordings, and several previously unreleased songs – for the 64-track, 3xCD boxed set, *Clash On Broadway** (which also chose to ignore anything from

---

* *Clash On Broadway* wouldn't receive a UK release until June 1994.

Cut The Crap) principally for the US market. 'I think they (Sony) want BAD II to fail so maybe I'll have to do The Clash again,' a disillusioned Mick grumbled to the *NME* that same autumn.

In December, 'The Globe' (in a variety of edits and guest remixes by Danny Rampling, and The Orb) was released as a single in the US. Though they would have to settle for number 72 on the mainstream chart, BAD II once again proved their worth on the Billboard Modern Rock Tracks chart by scoring a number three hit.

After several months of relative inactivity, BAD II appeared on the bill at U2's 'Stop Sellafield' show at Manchester's GMEX Centre to protest the operation of a second reactor at the nuclear reprocessing plant. The show was the last date on the European indoor leg of the Irish rockers' mammoth Zoo TV Tour to primarily promote *Achtung Baby*, and in September, the BAD II U2 connection was renewed when Mick and the boys accompanied Bono and co across America on the North American leg of the tour, with further Zoo TV appearances coming in Mexico City in November.

According to the tour programme, the concept for the Zoo TV Tour was inspired by the desensitising effect of mass media, and the stage featured dozens of large video screens showing a range of visual effects, video cut-ups, and flashing text phrases; yet it's worth remembering that BAD were doing something similar – albeit on a reduced 'Flintstones' scale – long before Bono got on his information overload soapbox. So while BAD II's being invited onto the tour could be construed as merely a continuance of U2 paying their dues to The Clash, it could also that be they were acknowledging a more recent Mick Jones influence.

BAD II were out and about around America with U2 when Columbia issued a five-track extended play US-only release CD entitled *On The Road Live '92*. However, although the opening track 'Kool-Aid' was recorded at BAD II's show at The Ritz in New York in April, the others were in fact lifted from a WXRT radio broadcast from a show at Chicago's Riviera Theatre the previous October.

Following their final Zoo TV support slot at the Palacio de los Deportes in Mexico City on 25 November, BAD II slipped into an extended siesta, and nothing more would be seen of the group until the following August when they once again served as main support at U2's two Wembley Stadium dates.

In the interim an even more fanciful yarn than that of two years earlier suggesting The Clash were to reform for £10 million was spun by the *Daily Mirror*'s pop columnist Rick Sky, who announced that 'Punk kings The Clash are getting back together for a massive £50 million world tour after a ten year break.'

The article also claimed that the group's classic line-up – Strummer/Jones/Simonon/Headon – had signed up with a 'top American manager' (Gary Kurfirst), and that they were in the process of 'lining up a string of dates: starting with a huge stadium tour of the US.' Somewhat surprisingly for the *Mirror* there was at least a kernel of truth in the tale, as one-time Clash security guy Ray Jordan (who was now occupying a similar role with BAD II) said the tabled figure was actually £1.5 million.

Ray would subsequently tell *DISCoveries*' Ralph Heibutski that while The Clash had got together at the table to discuss the offer, only three of the four were actually keen to proceed. As to whom poo-pooed the proposal, the tactful Ray declined to say, but Joe would later admit to dragging his heels as he couldn't contemplate The Clash reforming with Kurfirst calling the shots.

BAD II seemed to be in suspended animation, but Mick had kept himself busy lending a hand to the musical score for Rob Weiss' new mobster movie, *Amongst Friends*. Aside from BAD II's 'Innocent Child', he also contributed three instrumentals – 'Long Island', 'No Ennio', and 'I Don't Know' – to the accompanying soundtrack, all of which were credited under his own name. It was the first occasion in a sixteen-year-and-counting career that Mick had been credited as a solo artist, but there were no plans to strike out on his own and in November BAD II flew out to Australia and once again clambered aboard the U2 bandwagon for the last leg of the Zoo TV Tour.

In an attempt to cash in on BAD II's Down Under dates, Sony rush-released *The Lost Treasure Of Big Audio Dynamite 1 & II*, an Australasia-only 2xdisc compilation featuring various remixes of songs from both incarnations of the group. The final track on

CD 2 was a brand new composition called 'Looking For A Song', which Mick had penned with Italian trio Sergio Portaluri, David Sion, and Fulvio Zafret.

– CHAPTER SEVENTEEN –

ENTERING A NEW RIDE

'The thing about guitar playing is that you have to do it all the time. That's how you get good at something – by doing it every day. I do music every day. There's a work ethic to it, and also it is very mathematical. You just keep going at it, and going at it, and then suddenly it'll all fall into place and it's wonderful. Like a puzzle you solve.'

– Mick Jones

WHEN SPEAKING ON THE *www.gibson.com* website in 2006, Mick said that of all the great late-Sixties and early-Seventies guitarists he'd come to appreciate whilst practising daily in his room, Mick Ronson had been his particular favourite. Ronson sadly lost his battle against liver cancer on 29 April 1993, but twelve months on BAD II were among the acts invited to honour the man who'd given the Spiders From Mars their distinctive bite at the Hammersmith Apollo. A week or so after the Mick Ronson Memorial Concert, MTV News reported that Mick would be requiring a memorial concert of his own after supposedly succumbing to a bout of pneumonia.

What had given rise to the spurious rumour of Mick's demise was never established, but to paraphrase Mark Twain, the report of his death had been greatly exaggerated. Indeed, at the time of the report Mick was in the recording studio putting the finishing touches to the group's new album, *Higher Power*, which they'd been working on sporadically for several months. Although *The Lost Treasure Of Big Audio Dynamite I & II* had probably served as notification of his intentions, when the album was released it was under the snappier-sounding 'Big Audio'.

To augment Big Audio's sound, Mick's cousin Andre Shapps joined on keyboards, while Mickey 'DJ Zonka' Custance was brought in to provide Deejay-style toasting and backing vocals. As he had done on *The Globe*, Mick shared the production chair with Andre, while their pal, Boston-born producer Arthur Baker served as co-producer on the track 'Modern Stoneage Blues'.

The previous December, *Q* magazine had polled a cross-section of celebrities, music industry types, DJs, and musicians as to whether The Clash should reform in the coming year. Mick's old mucker Tony James thought they should 'because attitude lasts forever', yet that summer he found himself working with Mick on what would eventually become future project Carbon/Silicon.

Deciding that 'maybe experience could be edgy too' after watching the Bruce Willis movie *Die Hard*, Tony had invited Mick round to his place and the two began bouncing ideas off of each other as they had done at the Paddington Kitchen during their London SS days. According to Tony's recollections on *www.carbonsilicon.com*, the ideas got more left-field as the evening wore on, with the two signing off on the madcap notion that Jack Nicholson was still cool enough to pull off fronting a rock 'n' roll group.

Mick was still committed Big Audio, but he and Tony would convene in the latter's garage-cum-studio in Maida Vale to work on a set of Tony's lyrics with nothing more than an acoustic guitar and a Linn 9000 drum machine. It was the first time they'd written songs together in nearly twenty years, and just as he had back in the day Tony found himself marvelling at Mick's seemingly effortless ability to conjure up so perfect a melody for the lyric that anyone hearing the finished song would believe the melody must have come first.

'That was and is Mick's gift – to look at lyrics and hear the song finished already, finished inside his head with the tune playing along in time to the rhythm of the words,' Tony enthused. 'He always says that the lyric defines the song; that it's already written out there in the ether. You just have to find it and you'll hear it, just like seeing a sculptured head inside a block of stone.'

Their first composition – perhaps not surprisingly – was called 'Rock and Roll with Jack', while other titles worked up during these ad hoc Garageland get-togethers included 'Expensive Habits', 'Age Up' and 'Experience'. 'We didn't really think about what we would do with the songs,' Tony revealed. 'The fun was just in the writing. One day Mick said he knew Val Kilmer and I should ask him to sing because after all he looked great in *The Doors* movie!'

They decided against calling Val, but Mick and Tony continued with their one-song-a-week quota until they had around eight songs in the can – or captured on Tony's Sony V-O-R mono tape recorder.

With Mick still signed to Sony, the next logical step would have been to submit the 'Rock and Roll with Jack' cassette tape to Muff Winwood – if only to get some critical feedback from the label's long-serving A&R chief. Instead, they did nothing, because in Tony's words the moment had passed. 'One day we just stopped,' he explained. 'The idea wasn't fully formed, and more importantly looking back I wasn't ready either because the idea was not yet from the heart, it was from the head because it was just a film and a cartoon, made up. Something I would learn to understand in the future.'

♪♪♪

On the back of a twelve-inch promo of 'Looking For A Song', *Higher Power* was given a worldwide release in early November. The critics were less than kind in their appraisals, and rightly so, because while certain tracks such as 'Light Up My Life' (penned in honour of his ten-year-old daughter, Lauren), and 'Harrow Road' (Featuring Ranking Roger on backing vocals), were decent enough, the album as a whole was bordering on monotonous. So much so, that only divine intervention was likely to save it from ignominious failure.

To those on the outside looking in, it might have appeared that the album's substandard fare was due to too many chefs spoiling the broth, but it later transpired that Mick was merely fulfilling his contractual obligations to Sony. The label had been questioning Mick's creativity levels for some time now, and so when the album failed to chart they agreed to drop BAD from their roster.

One of the tracks on *Higher Power* was called 'Lucan', and Mick was probably wishing he could perform a similar disappearing act to that of the disgraced Earl. Indeed, aside from rare sightings such as at the Notting Hill Carnival, Mick spent the early part of 1995 closeted away from public gaze. Of course, with Mick now being a free agent as it were, it was inevitable that his severance from CBS/Sony would set The Clash reformation rumour mill's rusting wheels turning once more.

The latest reports had us believe The Clash had been offered somewhere in the region of $6 million to headline that year's Lollapalooza Tour, and according to those in the know, the other acts on the package tour had been informed of this fact.

Needless to say, The Clash didn't dig out their pop star army fatigues, but had the decision been Mick's alone to make then things might have turned out differently. Speaking with the *News Of The World* in September, Tricia Ronane confirmed the amount tabled, but said that while Mick, albeit via his manager, Gary Kurfirst, had 'thought it a good idea', Paul had sided with Joe in steadfastly refusing to enter negotiations.

With Mick having publicly stated he wasn't ruling out a Clash reunion at some unspecified point in the future, Tricia's comments didn't cause much of a stir. However, it was a different story when Heidi Robinson, one of Lollapalooza's organisers, gave her version of events to the media. According to Heidi, Joe's reasons for vetoing the proposal had stemmed from Topper's having only just completed yet another rehab course at the time the offer was tabled, and that there'd been insufficient time between the offer and the opening date of the tour for The Clash to get back to their fighting best.

It was then that Heidi dropped her bombshell. Having cited The Clash not having a new album to promote as another of Joe's reservations, she then claimed that Joe had told her he, Mick, Paul, and Topper would be recording a new album together before the year was out, and that The Clash might therefore be in a position to headline the following year's Lollapalooza.

The only Clash-related albums to hit the shops that year were Big Audio Dynamite's *F-Punk*, which the group – having reverted back to its original name – released in August through Kurfirst's independent label, Radioactive, and the BAD compilation album, *Planet B.A.D*, which Columbia issued in September.

With its front cover unashamedly copying the green and pink typeface from *London Calling* (which The Clash had of course borrowed from Elvis Presley), a lead single titled 'I Turned Out A Punk', and a supplementary Sniffin' Glue-esque 'how to tune your guitar' guide, *F-Punk* can perhaps best be described as a semi-autobiographical opus in terms of Mick exploring his punk roots. 'The words were first this time,' Mick revealed to *Pulse* magazine's Michael Jarrett. 'I had a tape machine. I worked on the rhythm of the words by reading them. Then, I put them down. I put the chords later. I've never done that before.'

Further nods to his Clash past come with 'Psycho Wing' evoking memories of the 'Can't Explain' riff from 'Clash City Rockers', the gutsy guitar vamp of 'Singapore' being reminiscent of 'Somebody Got Murdered', his dueting with daughter Lauren (who also penned the lyric) on 'I Can't Go On Like This' bringing shades of 'Shepherd's Delight', while the unlisted track 'Suffragette City' (in tribute to Mick Ronson) tagged onto the end of the album was a repeat of 'Train In Vain's clandestine inclusion on *London Calling*.

When asked if his approach to making music had changed with the new album, Mick said that they tended to learn a new song in the morning and then record it in the afternoon. 'We record it very basically, with the group all playing together, then we take it to another place; we remix parts of it,' he explained. 'That's how you come to hear the band really playing and, the next minute, it's completely different. It's not like funny time signatures or anything.'[1]

F-Punk was the eighth studio album to bear the BAD brand and Mick was well versed in having to explain the dichotomy of playing to the mutually exclusive audiences of pop and rock. 'There are two crowds,' he said. 'One's a dance crowd. They need to be shown that guitars can be cool. Then, there's the rock crowd. They need to know not to be afraid of the dance scene. We like to go and play at dance places, and we like to bring some of that to our gigs. It's important to take stuff that's going on around you and add it to your arsenal.'[2]

Mick believed *F-Punk* proved Big Audio Dynamite still packed an explosive punch, and while *Guitar World* hailed the album BAD's 'most cohesive work since their debut,' 'bridging the gap between rock and underground dance music—this time acid house, ambient and the ultra-fast beats of jungle,' *BAM*'s Tom Lanham offered something of a backhanded compliment by describing the album as 'leaner, meaner, and more ill-tempered than anything this often-forgettable group has done since its sharply inventive '85 debut.'

The mixed reception, coupled with Radioactive's less-than-searing presence within the music industry, which made the album virtually impossible to get hold of, consigned it to the same fate that befell *Higher Power*. And of course, with Columbia immune to such distribution problems, any hopes Kurfirst had in rectifying the situation were swept asunder when *Planet B.A.D* went on sale the following month.

♪♪♪

Nothing, as they say, sells quite like nostalgia, and with 1996 marking the twentieth anniversary of UK punk, the marketing men who were already set to make a killing received an unexpected bonus in March when the Sex Pistols' founding line-up of John Lydon, Steve Jones, Paul Cook, and Glen Matlock announced they were reforming for a world tour. With the warring Pistols having set aside their petty grievances to get their hands on some filthy lucre (a reported £1 million each), there were many who expected The Clash to finally follow suit – possibly even get together with the Sex Pistols on one of the latter's yet unconfirmed UK dates?

Owing to his friendship with Glen, Mick would have probably been privy to the cloak-and-dagger negotiations prior to the Sex Pistols taking to the stage at the 100 Club on 18 March to face the world's media.

In hindsight, every one who'd ever bought *Never Mind The Bollocks here's the* Sex Pistols should have perhaps agreed to make a donation to stop them from reforming because while the Filthy Lucre tour enabled those who'd either missed the Pistols first time around, or had come of age hearing their own musical heroes citing them as a major influence to see them in the flesh, the sight of four middle-aged men trying to recapture the chaos of yesteryear was ultimately a sad spectacle.

During the aforementioned *Pulse* interview Mick had revealed that he 'still [thought] it better to look good and play terrible, than to play good and look terrible.'

Yet although The Clash having more than one album in their canon meant they could compile a killer set-list without straying beyond *London Calling* should they reform, with seventeen years having passed since they'd last took to the stage together they still ran the risk of tarnishing their reputation.

Whether there was any truth in Heidi Robinson's claims about Joe saying The Clash would be ready to headline the '96 Lollapalooza on the back of a brand new album, with the punk's original bad boys set to hog the sepia-tinged limelight for the remainder of the year it's doubtful whether Mick or Joe would have been interested in stepping back into the Sex Pistols' shadow.

And Mick, of course, had rather more pressing matters to attend to at the time owing to Gary Stonadge and Chris Kavanagh bailing out on BAD after *F-Punk*'s failure to bring about a reversal in the group's recent fortunes.

A new rhythm section was found in Darryl Fulstow and former Under Two Flags drummer Bob Wond, and Mick also recruited Ranking Roger as a full-time member to add another dynamic. Having broken in the new recruits with a clutch of enthusiastically-received BAD Soundsystem club nights in and around London through the autumn, the group entered the studio in the new year to begin work on what would become *Entering A New Ride*. The last couple of years had been something of a roller-coaster ride for BAD, but Mick was hoping they'd finally turned a corner.

As the new album neared completion, *Rolling Stone*'s September issue proclaimed it was time for 'old Clash fans and younger BAD fans [to] join hands' as – according to Radioactive's spokesperson

Jimmy Auth – *Entering a New Ride* promised a return to 'the really early BAD sound,' and that the lead white-label (promo-only) single 'Sunday Best' was already getting airplay in London's hippest nightspots,' before signing off by informing its readership they could check out all the latest BAD info, on the 'band's ultra-cool website, maintained by Mick himself.'

It must have come as a surprise to *Rolling Stone* and every other major music magazine, therefore, when Mick handed the finished master tapes to Radioactive and the label refused to release it! Having to kowtow to a corporate giant such as Sony was one thing, but having the independent label owned by your manager questioning your creative talents proved too much to bear and BAD left Radioactive soon thereafter.

Just because Radioactive had rejected the album out of hand didn't necessarily mean the master tapes would be left to gather dust on the shelf and throughout 1998 Mick drip-fed the album track by track via the aforementioned BAD website. Once again, Mick appeared at the forefront of technology by releasing *Entering a New Ride* into cyberspace, but finding himself without a label for the second time in three years was still a major cause for concern.

Mick's worries over what to do about BAD's plight were temporarily sidelined, however, following Sony's announcement that they intended to release a live Clash compilation album. Having also released The Clash's back catalogue on CD, the label commissioned Don Letts to make a Clash documentary using footage from the group's personal archives, coupled with up-to-date interviews.

As Joe had finally come in out of the cold with the Mescaleros, and was fully occupied with recording his new outfit's debut album, *Rock Art And The X-Ray Style*, he was happy to allow Mick and Paul to oversee *On The Road With The Clash*, as the project was initially called before being re-titled *From Here To Eternity*.

Instead of releasing a complete show that would capture The Clash in full uninterrupted onstage glory, replete with Joe's inter-song asides and banter with the audience, Mick and Paul surprisingly opted to select nineteen tracks from various shows throughout the group's career; the earliest being 'London's Burning' from the Rock Against Racism festival at Victoria Park in April 1978, to 'Career Opportunities' at Shea Stadium in New York in October 1982. Less surprising, of course, was the blatant absence of any recordings from shows following Mick's departure.

To coincide with album's release in October 1999, a fifty-minute cut of *Westway To The World*, was aired on BBC2 that same month. Perhaps because the interviews were conducted separately, Mick, Joe, Paul, and Topper were far more forthright with their recollections and viewpoints than they might have been had they all been in the same room.

Topper had the grace to apologise for letting the side down whilst admitting he'd probably go off the rails again if given the chance to relive his time in The Clash because that was his nature. Paul also said he wouldn't change anything if given the chance, while Joe reasoned there being something good about coming on, saying your bit, and then taking your leave. Mick was introspective insofar as admitting to the lack of self-control that had brought about his dismissal, and yet his forthrightness didn't extend to acknowledging that The Clash had carried on in his absence by saying how the coda to '1977' had proved prophetic by ending on 1984 as 'it was probably always meant to.'

♫♫♫

The royalties from the recent spate of Clash products may have eased any financial worries Mick may have had of late, but career wise things were literally going from bad to worse as the dawn of a new millennium dawned. Whilst he'd had been busy collating tracks for *From Here To Eternity*, Columbia released a second BAD compilation album, the insipidly-titled *Super Hits*. With nothing to do but sit around twiddling their thumbs Ranking Roger, Darryl Fulstow, and Bob Wond all drifted away without actually serving notice, and this latest mass desertion, coupled with Sony releasing yet another BAD compilation album – the equally tritely titled *Big Audio Dynamite I & II* (which featured several tracks that had appeared on *Super Hits*) – appeared to serve as the group's death knell.

Aside from directing a promo video for 'Oscar', the latest single by the Liverpool-based outfit, Shack, and contributing guitar on *Open Mind*, the latest album from Glen Matlock's ongoing side project, the Philistines, little was heard from Mick until the following May when he took his place beside Joe, Paul, and Topper (who was on crutches having recently suffered a broken leg), at the Grosvenor Hotel on Park Lane where The Clash were honoured with an Ivor Novello Award for their 'Outstanding Contribution to British Music'.

'I know the Ivors is a bit Establishment,' Mick told the BBC, 'but the reason we came is that it's [in] recognition of our craft – and for the laugh.'

The award was as long-overdue as The Clash's classic line-up coming together; as it was the first time Mick, Joe, Paul, and Topper had been in the same room together in eighteen years. When subsequently reflecting on the evening with Kris Needs, Topper said how they'd spent the first ten minutes apologising to each other before bursting out laughing.

With the hatchets having been well and truly buried, a similar get-together was expected at the launch party for Bob Gruen's Clash photo book exhibition at the Proud Gallery in Camden Town in September. Yet although Mick and Joe were in attendance (along with half of London, or so it seemed), there was no sign of either Topper or Paul.

Aside from Barry 'Scratchy' Myers serving as DJ for the evening, other attendees from The Clash's inner-circle of old included Johnny Green, Jock Scott, and Pennie Smith. To everyone's astonishment, the hermetic Bernard Rhodes shuffled in clutching a sheaf of papers to his chest.

Bernard had apparently intended on making a speech to the gathering, but on realising he wasn't going to be allowed a platform he instead settled for giving Mick and Joe a personal reading and dragged them both off into a corner. His one-time charges, however, were no longer interested in what he had to say.

While telling Chris Salewitz (who had contributed to the Bob Gruen book) that he and Joe had told Bernard to 'go away', Mick mentioned being asked to sign a fan's book and spotting the inscription 'I started it all'*, after which Bernard had appended his signature.

Mick also chose the occasion to enquire what had become of the new songs he'd co-written with Joe for the Mescaleros' recently released follow-up album, *Global A Go-Go*. 'No, they weren't for that,' Joe had playfully corrected him. 'They are [for] the next Clash album.'

It wasn't until he appeared on BBC 6 Music alongside Paul and Topper in October 2013 that Mick finally expanded on the story surrounding the songs he and Joe had collaborated on for The Mescaleros. 'We did write some more songs together and he was going to do them with the Mescaleros,' he revealed. 'We wrote a batch – we didn't used to write one, we used to write a batch at a time – like gumbo. The idea was he was going to go into the studio with the Mescaleros during the day and then send them all home. I'd come in all night and we'd all work all night.'

In reference to Joe's comment about keeping the songs for a new Clash album, Mick said that the idea came to nothing because both he and Joe knew it wasn't going to work. 'Later on, a few months later we were at some opening or something (the Bob Gruen exhibition) and I said, "What happened to those songs?" If you didn't do them straight away and get them back straight away, it was like, "What's wrong with them?" So, I went, "What happened to the songs?" He went, "Oh man, they're the next Clash album."'

---

* I was the fan in question. The book wasn't Bob Gruen's hefty tome, but rather Pennie Smith's *The Clash: Before and After*, and the full quotation (which I had to scribble before handing the book to Bernard to sign) read: 'From the guy who started it all... but hasn't started yet.'

– CHAPTER EIGHTEEN –

SOUND OF THE JOE

'There were a few moments at the time [when] I was up for the Hall of Fame reunion. Joe was up for it, Paul wasn't. And neither, probably, was Topper. It didn't look like a performance was going to happen anyway. I mean, you usually play at that ceremony when you get in. Joe had passed by that point, so we didn't.'

– Mick Jones

ALTHOUGH A NEW CLASH ALBUM was never likely to materialise, the possibility of a Clash reunion was back on the agenda in October 2002 following the announcement they were to be inducted into the Rock and Roll Hall of Fame the following March along with AC/DC, Elvis Costello and the Attractions, the Police, and the Righteous Brothers.

At the time of the announcement Mick was enjoying the plaudits for his production work on the Libertines' debut album, *Up The Bracket*, while Joe was gearing up for a Mescaleros' UK tour, which as to be followed by a two-week booking at Rockfield Studios in Monmouthshire where they were set to record their third album. However, as it was customary for those acts accepting the award to perform one of their best-known hits at the gala ceremony (held at the Waldorf-Astoria Hotel in New York), prior to going out on the road he and Mick got together over a liquid lunch to mull over the pros and cons of playing the ceremony.

This, of course, was far from the first time that the two had convened to chew the fat over getting The Clash back together, but it was the first occasion they'd done so without a cash incentive sullying the air. While they both recognised the annual Rock and Roll Hall of Fame ceremonies were little more than back-slapping corporate affairs, they knew it was still a great honour to be inducted because – as with the Ivor Novello Award the previous year – it was their peers that had voted them in. And if they didn't play, they faced the unpalatable prospect of having other people playing their songs whilst they sat and watched.

Topper's condition was undoubtedly a concern, but while Terry Chimes was also being inducted, Joe provided Topper with a twenty-four carat incentive by saying he wouldn't get up on stage unless it was with the classic Clash line-up.

Having said that, however, Paul was refusing to even consider the idea of playing the ceremony on account of the tickets costing a colossal $1,000 a head. In an attempt to cajole him into strapping on his Fender bass again, Joe – only half-jokingly – threatened to give the gig to Primal Scream's bassist, Mani. Paul's telling response was 'go ahead.'[1]

With the opening date of The Mescaleros' Bringing It All back Home Tour – a star-studded benefit for Diane Fossey's Gorillas' charity at the Royal Opera House on 10 November – occupying his thoughts, it's unlikely that Joe would have wanted to make any serious decision about The Clash playing the Hall of Fame date until he'd at least emerged from Rockfield Studios.

♫♫♫

Following on from the Royal Opera House bash The Mescaleros' tour took in dates in Edinburgh, Newcastle, and Blackpool, before returning to London for another benefit show – this one for striking workers of the Fire Brigades Union at the Acton Town Hall on Friday, 15 November.

Technically, the firemen were no longer on strike as the two-day action that had begun two days earlier had officially ended at 6 p.m., but with the FBU having failed to broker a new pay deal further strike action was inevitable. Joe had agreed to play the benefit back in September whilst The Mescaleros were in Japan, and although it was a noble gesture on his part, the show was set to be no different than any other date on the tour.

With the news of The Clash's impending induction into the Rock and Roll Hall of Fame doing the rounds, the main topic of conversation in the bar leading up to showtime was whether The Clash would reform to play the ceremony. And rumours that Mick was coming along to see the show served to gave the proceedings an added air of excitement. It didn't take long for the five-hundred-or-so punters to discover that Mick was indeed in the house as Joe announced as much from the stage early into the set. Mick would subsequently admit that he'd almost been forced to cancel owing to a friend letting him down at the eleventh-hour, and that it was only because he was already suited and booted that he'd hailed a cab to the town hall.

Once the cheering had subsided Joe toasted Mick for his recently becoming a father again (Mick had named the new arrival Stella in honour of his beloved Nan). Having shouted out 'this one is going out to Stella,' Joe hit the opening chord to 'Rudie Can't Fail.'

As was Joe's custom, the Mescaleros' set was peppered with other notable Clash standards such as '(White Man) In Hammersmith Palais', 'Police And Thieves', 'Police On My Back', and 'I Fought The Law'. Those standing closest to Mick were no doubt amused to see him singing along to the songs he'd last played some nineteen years earlier at the Us Festival in San Bernardino, California. But no one expected to see him emerge from stage right clutching a guitar when The Mescaleros returned to the stage for the encore and Joe began strumming the opening chords to 'Bankrobber'.

A momentary hush filled the air as the audience tried to fathom whether what they were witnessing on stage had been pre-planned, but the reaction of Tymon Dogg and the rest of The Mescaleros as Mick – somewhat apprehensively, it has to be said – came across and plugged into Joe's amp told its own story. 'Alright, baby, play that guitar now – for the baby,' Joe teased; his voice brimming with undisguised merriment.

In that instant the years rolled away and at the song's finale a beaming Mick stepped up to the mic and dedicated the song to the Harlesden and Willesden Fire Companies. As Mick had had no preconceived idea of getting up on stage, he was in the dark as to what song was coming next. He didn't have to wait long, however, as Joe – having mischievously slotted 'White Riot' into the running order at the Royal Opera House – bellowed out 'In the key of A' before ploughing into the one song Mick had thought to never again play.

What had already proved an extraordinary evening was brought to a highly apt conclusion with 'London's Burning'.

When reflecting on the events of that momentous night with Kris Needs in September 2004, Mick said: 'I just felt compelled to go up there. It was halfway or a third of the way through "Bankrobber". He [Joe] was just there playing and I ended up on stage with him, which I felt totally compelled to do. It wasn't planned in any way.'[2]

When Kris asked Mick what Joe's reaction had been on seeing him come out on stage, Mick responded: 'Joe was happily surprised. He shouted out when he saw me, "play guitar now!" just like that, and then the next number was… he wouldn't say what it was. He just said, "You know it". And he went into the A position, [but] he didn't let me know that we were playing ["White Riot"].

'It was great. He was being driven home and the guy who was driving him said, "Well, what did you think when Mick got up on stage?" and Joe went, "Bloody cheek!" But he was only joking.'[3]

Needless to say, Mick's joining Joe on stage and playing Clash songs together went viral on the internet, and not only did it further fuel the likelihood of The Clash reuniting for the Rock and Roll Hall of Fame ceremony, but possibly also beyond that date?

Sadly, however, The Clash reunion would never come to pass owing to Joe suffering a (supposed) fatal heart attack at his home in Broomfield, Somerset, on Sunday, 22 December.

The subsequent autopsy would reveal that Joe had in fact died as a result of his being born with a congenital heart defect – a main artery that should have gone around his heart passed through it instead – which meant he could have been struck down at any time.

It seems Joe had collapsed whilst reading *The Observer* shortly after returning home from walking the dogs. Although the unfinished Mescaleros album* would have been at the forefront of his mind, Sony were rush-releasing a new compilation album† to coincide with The Clash's induction into the Rock and Roll Hall of Fame event and Joe – as indeed, had Mick, Paul, and Topper – had been asked to choose which tracks he wanted on the album.

Performing at the ceremony was also occupying his thoughts it seems because prior to going out on his walk, he'd faxed his song suggestions to Tricia Ronane, coupled with a postscript asking Paul to reconsider his stance.

By his own admission, Joe spent some considerable time wandering aimlessly within 'the wilderness' as he described his ailing career between his calling time on The Clash and his return to form with the Mescaleros, but judging from the media's response – with many newspapers running two-page obituaries – it was obvious that he was still held in great esteem.

Fans the world over were left to reflect on their own personal memories of Joe either with The Clash, The Mescaleros, or one of his solo shows in-between, and raised a glass to the man who had been the voice of a generation. First and foremost, however, Joe was a family man, and his wife, Lucinda, daughters, Jazz Domino and Lola Maybelline, (and step-daughter, Eliza), were left mourning a husband and father.

Mick was one of the first to hear of Joe's death, and found it all the more bewildering as he'd spent an enjoyable evening with Joe at the Groucho Club in Soho just two days earlier. 'A friend of Lucinda's called in the afternoon,' he told Kris Needs. 'I didn't know this person at the time. I didn't know if it was completely true, but then I found out it was. It was quite soon after... It must have been a couple of hours or so. It was a terrible shock.'[4]

Managing to regain some of his composure Mick called Paul and Topper to give them the tragic news. As it so happened, Topper was playing his first gig in years with a Dover-based blues outfit at a local

---

* *Streetcore* was released in December 2003.
† *The Essential Clash* was released in March 2003.

pub, and though he'd seen the messages from Mick saying to phone him urgently he was understandably nervous about performing in public again and decided to leave off finding what the problem was until after the gig.

Johnny Green, who was with Topper that night in a show of moral support, said that Topper hurled his phone across the room before crumpling to the floor when Mick told him Joe was dead.[5]

It's unlikely that Mick got much sleep that night, but the following morning he dutifully drove down to Ivy Cottage to do whatever he could to help Lucinda. 'I went down there the next day in the morning, because all the people would be calling,' he explained. 'I would know all the people from the Clash part of Joe's life so I went to help with all the calls, which was massive.'[6]

As the public tributes began pouring in from across the globe Mick issued a simple, yet heartfelt statement: 'Our friend and compadre is gone. God bless you, Joe.' He also paid tribute to Joe in song by releasing an already written tune online called 'Sound Of The Joe'.

Christmas was just two days away and although Mick had a family of his own he would be a near-constant presence at Ivy Cottage dealing with the press and helping out with the funeral arrangements. He and Joe had long since settled their differences, but had Joe died during their estrangement Mick would surely have acted no differently. Though it was probably of little consolation at the time, he could at least be thankful that they got to share a stage together one last time.

♪♪♪

Tony James revealed on *www.carbonsilicon.com* that it was Mick's producing the hedonistic, indie-rocking Libertines' debut album *Up The Bracket* during the summer of 2002 that proved the inspiration behind Carbon/Silicon. Having chosen to embrace the internet as the 'saviour of creativity, rather than its downfall', he and Mick had got together in the March to pick up where they'd left off in 1994 to see if they could 'find the drive and inspiration to create something new again.'

They'd penned a couple of new songs – 'M.P. Free' and 'Why Men Fight' – in the 'home' studio (built into Mick's lock-up on an industrial estate in Acton, west London) but were still 'enjoying the magic [of] writing and recording together,' rather than thinking about putting a group together. However, after seeing how Carl Barât and Pete Doherty had bounced off each other in the studio they'd started to write and record with a set game plan in mind.

Despite the glaring similarity to what Mick had already achieved with Big Audio Dynamite in combining rock samples and dance beats, Tony says the fruits of their latest labours sounded like 'nothing else around', and gave them 'a new musical palette to work from.'

Speaking on www.teletext.co.uk in 2007 at the time of the release of their first 'physical' album, *The Last Post*, Mick explained that his approach to songwriting hadn't changed all that much since he and Tony first collaborated together.

'One of the first lessons I learnt was to write about what affects you. We write about what it's like to be us now, our lives as fifty-year-olds. We make no apologies for that. It's what we did in the Clash. It's about trying to be good people. It's a very up, positive attitude. Music should rejuvenate the soul.'

As for the songs themselves, Mick admitted that if he was having trouble fitting a lyric to a melody he'd simply put it aside and go home and watch television. 'Songs come to me on the bus or walking; I walk all the time,' he said. 'As long as I don't hear anything else before I get home, this will be great. It's all a culmination. I know how to do this, and I feel better than ever.'[7]

By the following July, Mick and Tony had conjured up two six-track albums' worth of material from their musical palette – *Sample This – Peace*, and *Dope Factory Boogie*. While this might not appear all that noteworthy considering Mick's songwriting capabilities, it's worth remembering that he had to contend with the aftershocks from Joe's death during this time. Tony described new material as 'excitable, but unreleasable'; the latter (improvised) adjective no doubt alluding to the risk of certain copyright infringement laws that had come into force since BAD had first begun sampling for fun.

Undeterred, the duo continued through the winter months, the twin-guitar-attack getting heavier as the project slowly took shape. After reading a magazine article by Susan Greenfield about how the future of human intelligence would be enhanced by use of silicon computer implants, they decided upon the name 'Carbon/Silicon as 'it represents the sound of the band – Mick's "Soul" – Carbon combined with Tony's "Computers" – Silicon.'

They may not have set out to form a group, but it was the next logical step if they were to progress. 'It was Mick's idea,' Tony revealed on *carbonsilicon.info*. 'He said, "I think we should get a bass player and drummer… and get a band. I thought, "Shit I'm sacked already!" And he said, "I'll teach you to play, you can have the [Les Paul] Junior again; learn some chords this time."

Having brought in their Mancunian pals Danny 'The Red' on drums and William Blake on bass to augment the Carbon/Silicon sound, March 2004 saw them take the all-important litmus test by performing a selection of songs in front of an eager assortment of friends and fellow musicians*.

Speaking about these 'illegal gigs' with *The Guardian*'s Anna Chapman in December 2008, Mick said that with the studio being so small they'd had to put sofas in the corridor for their guests. 'The VIP lounge was upstairs, accessible to anyone who dared go up the ladder,' he chuckled. 'Jonathan Ross turned up and was impressed by my comic collection. Pete Doherty's been here, too, to watch us rehearse.'

As with The Clash's 'behind-closed-doors' showcase at Rehearsal Rehearsals back in August '76, Carbon/Silicon's low-key unveiling within the compact surroundings of their Acton lock-up proved a resounding success, and thus inspired, Mick and Tony decided it was time to take their show out onto the road. They were both accustomed to breaking down musical barriers, first of all with London SS, and later individually with BAD and Sigue Sigue Sputnik, but going out on tour with Carbon/Silicon was nevertheless a daunting prospect because at that juncture the group existed nowhere other than in cyberspace.

Demos were freely available for download on their recently-incorporated *www.carbonsilicon.com* website, but there was no new

---

* Those invited to attend the showcase were given a six-track promo CD, *The Grand Delusion*, as a memento.

album to promote (or indeed record label support to call on), and with the media paying scant regard to what they were doing, their only hope of avoiding potential embarrassment was in attracting Clash/BAD fans through the door. The paradox there, of course, was that those same fans would know not to expect to hear anything from Mick's (or indeed, Tony's) back catalogue.

Such was Mick and Tony's determination to further break down the barriers – not to mention thwart any bootleggers in the audience – Carbon/Silicon openly encouraged those coming to the shows to bring along their MP3 players and DVD cameras to record or film the proceedings and then upload their efforts onto the website so that anyone else with an interest in the group could log on and share the experience, as well as hopefully spread the word.

Perhaps not surprisingly, given Mick's relationship with the British music media in recent years, Carbon/Silicon was dismissed as 'two ageing punks throwing a retirement party'.[8] Yet those with a more discerning eye were quick to recognise that unlike the Rolling Stones or The Who, Mick and Tony were striving to give rock 'n' roll a modern age twist rather than simply go through the motions. Indeed, it was their use of pre-programmed rhythms that prompted Creation Records founder Alan McGee – who was managing The Libertines at the time – to liken a Carbon/Silicon show to watching 'the Stones jamming with laptops.'[9]

Seeing as they were being heralded as elder statesmen of punk, Mick and Tony were happy to poke fun at themselves. 'Our fans were all slap-heads,' Mick joked. 'We'd go down into the front rows, slapping their bald heads, da-da-da, like The Benny Hill Show.'[10]

He also revealed that when he and Tony first hooked up as teenagers they used to amuse themselves by pondering what they'd be like in later years. 'We saw ourselves looking like Winston Churchill,' he chuckled. 'We thought we'd be artists, guys sitting in big straw hats, painting by a riverbank. I started as a painter; Tony did computer science, back when you punched cards into computers. He should be Bill Gates and I should be Picasso.'[11]

After appearing in the Strummerville/Leftfield tent at Glastonbury, Mick was forced to put his Carbon/Silicon period on temporary hold whilst producing the Libertines' follow-up eponymous album (which topped the UK album chart in the first week of release), but he and Tony were soon holed up again in their tiny west London studio writing new material.

Possibly as a result of Mick's working with Messrs Borât, Doherty, Hassall, and Powell again, Carbon/Silicon began moving away from sequel-sampling to a more conventional rock 'n' roll sound; the first sign of which came with their abandoning programmed drum beats in favour of real drums.

After compiling a fourth six-track demo album available for download, *The Homecoming*, Carbon Silicon once again went into hibernation for the winter due toe the studio lacking any form of heating.

♪♪♪

On 25 April 2005, Carbon/Silicon headed into the BBC's legendary Maida Vale Studios – where The Clash and Generation X had both recorded sessions – to record a session for Andy Kershaw's Radio 3 Sunday evening show.

In keeping with the group's 'free music for all' policy, the BBC agreed to stream three of the four songs recorded during the session – 'The Gangs of England, 'Soylent Green' and 'Tell it Like It Is', and the accompanying video from the session. The songs would also be made available on the internet via the Carbon/Silicon website.

Carbon/Silicon's 'word of mouth' following was such that within an hour of the show being broadcast on Sunday, 15 May, the songs and video had been downloaded an incredible 2000 times in the first twelve hours alone. The remaining track, a cover-version of Mott The Hoople's 'Original Mixed-Up Kid' was broadcast on the following week's show.

Since making their home studio debut the previous March, Carbon/Silicon had played around fifty shows to date, and that same month Mojo Club offered them a mini-tour of Barfly UK dates in Glasgow, York, Liverpool, London, and Cardiff. Despite the burgeoning interest in Carbon/Silicon, however, they had yet to ping a publicist or record label's radar.

They followed up the Barfly dates with an appearance at the open-air Evolution Festival in Gateshead on the late May Bank Holiday weekend, and further exposure came in June when Patti Smith was invited to curate that year's Meltdown festival at the Festival Hall on the South Bank. Patti not only invited Carbon/Silicon as one of her guest acts, she joined them on stage midway through their encore rendition of Jimi Hendrix's 'Hey Joe'.

The fans came away from the Festival Hall happy enough, but *The Independent* proved less than kind in its review. After dismissing Carbon/Silicon as 'a guitar-driven quartet dressed in the mandatory middle-aged rockers' dark suits and open-necked shirts, it proceeded to attack the sound system as being 'so awful [that] not a single sung word was decipherable.'

Though a sensitive soul at heart, Mick had been around the block enough times to know he couldn't please everybody, but getting bad reviews in the broadsheets was nothing compared to the *Daily Mirror*'s exposé of Kate Moss' cocaine shenanigans with her bad-boy lover Pete Doherty – replete with photographs showing the supermodel hunched over the console at the Metropolis Studios in Chiswick, west London where Babyshambles were recording their debut album, *Down In Albion* – with a rolled-up £20 shoved up her nostril. Kate had been dating Doherty since the turn of the year, and although the *Mirror*'s undercover agent was solely interested in capturing La Belle et la Bête* *en flagrante*, the photo accompanying the front-page story revealed a silhouetted Mick Jones hovering in the background. According to the *Daily Mail*'s account, the *Mirror* had other photos catching him in the act, he was also facing the possibility of being charged with being in possession of a Class A drug. Fortunately for Mick, however, he was let off the hook when the Crown Prosecution Service decided there was insufficient evidence to bring charges against Kate.

'I thought it was going to be the last record I ever made', Mick chuckled when recounting what was undoubtedly one of the more

---

* 'La Belle et la Bête (The Beauty and the Beast), on which Kate provides backing vocals, is the opening track on *Down In Albion*.

awkward moments of his career. 'I don't completely think that anymore.'[12]

With the Babyshambles album in the can, Mick returned to Carbon/ Silicon duty to begin work on the group's first sample-free album, *A.T.O.M* (A Twist Of Modern).

Being creatures of habit, Mick and Tony retired to their west London studio and spent the winter months writing, recording and producing. Rather than wait until they'd finished the album as a whole, however, they opted to release it piecemeal by making each of the twelve tracks – complete with hi-res artwork – available as free downloadable MP3s from the website to allow the fans to compile their own version of the album.

– CHAPTER NINETEEN –

A TWIST OF MODERN

'I'm always thinking that tomorrow is going to be the day. I want to be in the moment... always cautiously optimistic about the future but with no expectations. It's only chasing an illusion. I try to be fresh by ignoring everything I've done up 'til now. I don't find it hard to be original; I just do what I do instinctively and don't even think about it.'

– Mick Jones

NO SOONER HAD THE FINAL A.T.O.M track, 'Grow Up', been despatched into cyberspace than Carbon/Silicon set to work on a new album, which they called Western Front, and consisted of re-recorded versions of the best of their early material such as 'Why Do Men Fight', 'National Anthem', and 'I Loved You'. Once again, the songs were made available for free download from the website. Figuring their fans had more than enough new tunes to savour, as well as deliberate over on the group's forum page, Carbon/Silicon retreated into their Acton enclave and spent the remainder of the year either rehearsing or writing and recording new material in preparation for a spring offensive.

Aside from recording a couple of songs with former Spandau Ballet boy turned actor, Gary Kemp*, Carbon/Silicon emerged into daylight

---

* The special two-track EP: 'Maybe That's The Meaning Of Life'/'The Inconvenience Of Truth' was made available for download on the carbon/Silicon website in July 2008.

with six brand-new compositions earmarked for a new mini album. To keep things fresh and exciting, prior to releasing *The Crack-up Suite* as the new download album was called, Mick and Tony took the decision to remove all previously free MP3 tracks from the website – giving those fans who hadn't yet availed themselves of the downloads a thirty-hour window in which to do so.

Fans were still debating the Carbon/Silicon spring-clean clear out when it was announced that Danny the Red and William Blake were leaving the group to be replaced by Mick's old BAD compadre, Leo Williams and former Reef drummer Dominic Greensmith.

Mick's first return to the live arena since the previous year came not with Carbon/Silicon, however, but rather with a guest appearance with Primal Scream (who were being honoured with the 'Godlike Genius Award') at the *NME* Shockwave Awards ceremony at the Hammersmith Palais performing (appropriately enough) '(White Man) In Hammersmith Palais'. And of course, with *Rolling Stone* having recently hailed the Strummer/Jones songwriting partnership to be the third greatest behind Lennon/McCartney and Jagger/Richards, it was perhaps only fitting that he marked his first public appearance of the year with a Clash track.

Since their coming together five years earlier Mick and Tony had given away some twenty-odd songs with nary a thought for recompense, yet June 2007 saw them make their first 'hardware' release, a four-track CD EP called *The News*, on their own Carbon Silicon Records label. That same month, having played a warm-up show of sorts at the Bush Hall in west London on 31 May, the new Carbon/Silicon line-up played the second day of the Isle of Wight Festival, alongside Amy Winehouse, Muse, and Kasabian.

Speaking with the *NME* after their six-song set Mick made light of their lowly afternoon billing. 'We're really happy with the performance,' he said. 'To use a footballing analogy, we used the space well, packed the box, and everyone did what they had to do. It was all about keeping your composure and standing tall. It was the biggest gig we've played and it was great. I think this band can play on any stage.'

Despite their featuring way down on the festival's pecking order, however, Mick was in element as the following night's bill saw the headlining Rolling Stones giving their first British festival appearance since Knebworth back in 1976.

September brought the release of a second commercial CD EP, *The Magic Suitcase*, which served as a lead single for Carbon/Silicon's debut conventional album, *The Last Post* the following month. With the exception of 'Acton Zulus', the remaining eleven tracks were Bill Price remixes of tracks from *A.T.O.M* and *Western Front*. It was the first time Mick had worked with Bill since *Megatop Phoenix*.

To promote the album Carbon/Silicon embarked on a UK tour, and in December they embarked on their first US venture with two sell-out shows in New York and Los Angeles. 'I want to go everywhere, obviously, if we can manage it,' Mick said at the time.[1] 'But it's just a couple of dates; then hopefully we'll come back and do some more in the new year. It's just a first taste. We're looking forward to it. I haven't been in the States for over twelve years.'

Mick may have been excited about the prospect of returning to the states, but when speaking with *CNN*'s Peter Wilkinson prior to going over to America he and Tony offered a caveat to those ticket holders expecting to hear some Clash, BAD, or Generation X songs in the set. 'If we played the old stuff, people just wouldn't be interested in anything new,' Mick shrugged, while Tony added that if all they'd wanted to do was get played on the radio they could have simply called themselves 'Clash X'.

Wilkinson would liken Carbon/Silicon's sound on *The Last Post* to 'a garage sound tinged with electronica and glam.' When he'd asked why they'd done away with sampled sequencing on the album, Mick said: 'We used samples at the start of Carbon/Silicon so we had a full canvas but our music ain't about that. It's about an emotional connection so we've taken most of that stuff out 'cos it's not us.

'We found that the samples became a constraint 'cos you always knew where you were going to go, so you were never free. It somehow took the heart away. The important thing is to have a contemporary rhythm section that informs the music but without slavishly using other people's stuff. Now we've seen the light.'

Throughout January and February 2008, the Inn On The Green was the place to be, as Carbon/Silicon served as hosts for seven dates over consecutive Fridays at the tiny Ladbroke Grove venue (built into the concrete piles propping up the Westway) under the 'Carbon Casino' banner. Tony had hit upon the idea for the residency after watching the Martin Scorsese film *Casino* on DVD, while Mick chose the venue.

'Our rough plan [was that] there wouldn't be a set list,' Tony explained on the Carbon/Silicon website. 'We'd just make it up on the night with no pressure, have a chance to try out songs we rarely played rather on big shows where you felt you must play the professional set. Then we'd have support groups getting to play a couple of numbers and then maybe in the encore we'd have a friend or two to play with us.'

The bijou venue, which was a cross betwixt a student union bar and a youth club, could hold around two hundred at a push, but with said 'friends' including Glen Matlock and Paul Cook, Pete Wylie, and James Dean Bradfield there were so many punters crammed inside that condensation dripped down from the ceiling like rain.

While the plethora of support groups – The Dirty Curtains, British Voodoo, Usual Suspects, Hello Kitty, Taurus Trakker, and Rotten Hill Gang – were worthy of the £10 admission price alone, the highlight of each show was undoubtedly the 'special guests' encore segment.

The first night proved an emotional affair for Mick in particular as Topper joined Carbon/Silicon on stage to provide the beat on 'Train In Vain', and 'Should I Stay Or Should I Go', while the following weeks saw the Sex Pistols' rhythm section, Glen and Paul; Tymon Dogg; James Dean Bradfield; the Fun Lovin' Criminals, and Alabama 3 all joining in the fun.

Another 'special guest' was Hard-Fi's Richard Archer whom Mick had befriended the previous year when his name was mooted as a possible producer for their next album. 'I guess I can have a lot of fun at this stage in my career and I like working with young people such as Rich because they're full of new ideas,' Mick said of his relationship with Archer. 'I wouldn't say I'm a mentor to him, though. I just like to try to have some fun and play a few tunes.'[2]

One of the tunes Mick and Rich played together came during Hard-Fi's performance at the *NME* Awards show at Koko in Camden Town at the beginning of February, when Mick joined the group on stage for a brilliant rendition of 'Should I Stay Or Should I Go.'

Carbon/Silicon would go on stage each week without a preferred set-list, but for the final show they had twenty songs painted on a huge multicoloured wheel and invited celebrity guests such as Sienna Miller and Rhys Ifans to come up on stage and give the wheel a spin for the next song played. The final night's performance would be released as a limited-edition CD the following year.

The Carbon Casino dates have not only gone down in West London folklore, they have proved the only occasion to date where Carbon/Silicon have dipped into the Clash goody bag. Aside from playing 'Train In Vain' and 'Should I Stay or Should I Go' with Topper on the opening night, the latter song received a second airing when Rhys Ifans gave the Wheel of Fortune a spin, while Lauren Jones had also joined the group on stage earlier in the residency to duet 'Hitsville UK' with her old man.

To commemorate the Carbon Casino shenanigans, photographer Pete Stevens put together a limited edition book – with each of the 200 copies personally signed by Mick and Tony – featuring 280 photos from the seven shows.

Following the final residency date on 29 February, Carbon/Silicon bid a fond farewell to the claustrophobic confines of the Inn On The Green and embarked on a full US tour, taking in major cities on both seaboards. They also made three appearances at the SXSW (South by Southwest) in Austin, Texas, as well as the Coachella Valley Music and Arts Festival in Indio, southern California on 26 April.

Mick, of course, had visited the Sunshine State many times in the past, both with The Clash and BAD, but this was the first time he'd experienced the harshness of the Colorado Desert. 'We've heard it's very hot in the desert,' he dead-panned during a pre-festival interview.

'I'm going to have one of those hats on that has a fan in the middle of it.'

Three days prior to the festival Carbon/Silicon performed at the inaugural NME Awards USA at the El Rey Theatre in Los Angeles where Mick was also honoured with the Inspiration Award. Presenting the award was the delectable Sienna Miller, who had, of course, been in attendance at the final Carbon Casino date. 'He's helped all of you lot make the music you're making,' she declared after presenting Mick with the award. 'He is my most inspiring friend.'

One has to wonder what Mick made of his being honoured by the magazine that had wilfully lambasted The Clash at every turn from *Sandinista!* onwards, but when explaining how the decision had been reached, the *NME*'s Conor McNicholas – having declared Mick to be 'an innovator, a visionary, a class songwriter, a great singer and a demon guitarist' – said that although the Inspiration Award is usually hotly debated amongst the *NME* editors, the decision had been unanimous as 'Mick Jones is a true hero to *NME*.'

Upon their return to London, Carbon/Silicon headed into Channel 4's Riverside Studios for an appearance on the station's new weekend music show, *The Nokia Green Room*. Aside from performing 'Why Do Men Fight' live in the studio, Mick and Tony were filmed larking about with the show's host Chris Needham in the backstage Green Room.

July and August were taken up playing festivals such as Guilfest, the V Festival, and the Neapolis Festival in Naples, and in September Mick and Tony headed over to Paris for three days of TV, Radio and Press interviews – making the front cover of *XRoads* magazine's October issue. Although they were in the French capital primarily to promote the impending French 2xCD release of *The Last Post* and *Carbon Casino*, Mick was called on to field questions on the soon-to-be-released Clash live album: *Live At Shea Stadium*.

Joe had supposedly happened upon the original masters whilst moving house, but the question remains why Sony didn't simply opt for releasing the Shea Stadium date instead of having Mick and Paul trawl through hours of tapes while compiling the set-list for *From Here To Eternity*?

Carbon/Silicon brought their live commitments for the year to a rambunctious finale with two sell-out Carbon Casino shows at the Hammersmith Club in Rutland Grove on Monday 15 and Tuesday 16 December. Apart from giving several new tracks their first public airings, the second night saw them joined on stage by Fun Lovin' Criminal frontman Huey Morgan for a rendition of FLC's 1996 hit 'Scooby Snacks', and a cover of the seminal Stones' classic, 'Honky Tonk Woman'.

♪♪♪

No sooner had the festive fug receded than Mick and Tony reconvened at their home studio to work on song ideas for a new Carbon/Silicon album. Such was the buzz surrounding the two ageing punks who were seemingly happy to give their music away for free, that Reuters sent along one of its field operatives to their Acton hideaway.

'We grew like an Internet community; a worldwide community, sharing stuff and not charging people,' Mick revealed on being asked their long-term plan for Carbon/Silicon. '[We're] working in an immediate media, getting immediate feedback from people.'

'We're in the middle of a revolution,' Tony added. 'People are not buying CDs. How are we going to get paid? Nobody knows, but creativity will flourish. It's a very exciting time, but it's also chaos.'

Amidst the ongoing chaos Mick not only found time to collaborate with Lily Allen in re-recording 'Straight To Hell' for the *War Child: Heroes* charity album, but he and Tony also penned 'Mr Extraordinary', which was intended for the soundtrack to the forthcoming film *Mr Nice* based on the extraordinary adventures of Howard Marks, the author and former drug smuggler who achieved notoriety as an international cannabis smuggler through high-profile court cases.

For those in the know, the Acton lock-up didn't only serve as Mick's home studio, it also housed the cornucopia of pop culture history that he'd been collecting since childhood: a jaw-dropping, shelf-buckling archive comprised of reams of pop magazines, stacks of rare comics, and piles of dog-eared paperbacks, newspaper supplements, vinyl albums, and kitsch slot machines – not to mention a plethora of memorabilia from his time with The Clash and Big Audio Dynamite.

As part of his treasure trove was about to go on public display as 'The Rock & Roll Public Library' at the Chelsea College of Art And Design, Mick spoke with *The Quietus*' Jude Rogers. Perhaps not surprisingly, Rogers' opening gambit was to ask what had first set Mick off on his collecting compulsion? 'People say it's because I had a bit of a difficult childhood, and perhaps that's true. But I got so much pleasure out of it, I just kept going,' Mick revealed. 'Maybe it's in the genes because my mum did the same, too. When I first was in the Clash, she'd make scrapbooks of our tours, cut out pictures, hoard, hoard, hoard.' On being asked what he envisioned for the collection beyond the Chelsea exhibition Mick said that ideally he wanted to make it available as an educational resource. 'I imagine school parties coming to see this. That's what I dream of, really,' he explained; 'for them to learn something really exciting, as they see all this dirty, lovely stuff from the past. It hit me a while back when people coming in here would say, you know what? This is great. Cos when people come in, they go wow. Nah, they go WOW!

'When I used to go to the States with the Clash and BAD I'd get excited looking through all these thrift shops that had all this cool stuff. Because, at our age, you see, we'd grown up on American culture but had never really seen it. And that feeling was fantastic. That's why I want kids to feel the same excitement with what we're trying to do here. Get the same kind of "WOW!"'[3]

During the interview Mick had said how he wanted to find a permanent home for the collection in its entirety. His dream location would have been the Commonwealth Institute in Holland Park as the once beautiful building was now in a state of disrepair, but that 'any old house would do' just so long as it was in West London.

In July, Mick got his wish of sorts when the Rock & Roll Public Library – set within a 3,000 sq ft office space at 2 Acklam Road, Portobello Green – opened to the public for a five-week run. A delighted Mick described his 'civic endeavour' as a 'direct artistic challenge' to the corporate blandness of other music museums such as the O2's British Music Experience.

The exhibition was certain to attract Clash fans, but Mick hoped that it would also have a wider appeal. 'These are relics of the last century; a part of British music history,' he said. 'It's a very personal collection, but I don't want the library to be only for Clash addicts. I hope it can be a resource and spark people's imaginations, create an idea of continual creativity.'[4]

It was at the library that Mick got together with his old BAD muckers Dan Donovan and Gary Stonadge, Gaz Mayall, sculptor and occasional Alabama 3 harmonica man Nick Reynolds, actor Dudley Sutton, and a supporting cast too numerous to mention, to record the track 'Ronnie Biggs', which he'd co-written with Mayall. The idea was to release the song as a single to add support to the ongoing petition to get the ailing Great Train Robber released from prison on compassionate grounds. Biggs, who'd been on the run since his escape from Wandsworth Prison in July 1965, had returned to Britain under his own volition in May 2001. He'd promptly been rearrested and sent to HMP Belmarsh to serve the remainder of the 30-year sentence he received for his part in the robbery.

Simon, who is perhaps best-known for penning *The Wire*, is also something of a mean guitar player, and according to Gary Stonadge, played better than anyone else on the day. The engineer, however, forgot to record his guitar part, and by the time the mistake was realised Simon had left and was en route to Heathrow. Thinking on his feet, the scriptwriter got out his guitar in the back of the cab and replayed his part down the phone.

Somewhat ironically, Biggs was finally granted a pardon on 'compassionate grounds' on 7 August (his eightieth birthday) by the then Home Secretary, Jack Straw, just as the single was going to press.

Carbon/Silicon's continual creativity saw the release two albums in the space of four months. In November 2009, they released *The Carbon Bubble*, with all twelve tracks being made available for free download from the group's website, and the following February they released an updated version of *The Crack-Up Suite*. But even then there was no respite as having come up for air to appear at the Steve New benefit at the 100 Club, Mick and Tony threw themselves into kicking out the jams on a new studio album.

However, the frenetic pace would ultimately prove too much for Leo, and he was replaced on bass by Ronnie Wood's son, Jesse.

♫♫♫

Mick and Paul had stood shoulder-to-shoulder at the Waldorf-Astoria while accepting The Clash's induction into the Rock and Roll Hall of Fame in March 2003, but no one within The Clash cognoscenti ever thought they'd live to see the day where the two would be performing on stage together – despite Paul having dusted off his bass again to play with Damon Albarn's The Good, The Bad & The Queen. TGTB&TQ only released one eponymous-titled album (in January 2007), but Paul's relationship with Damon led to his being invited to make a guest appearance on 'Plastic Beach', the title track from the third album by the latter's 'virtual band', Gorillaz, which was released in March 2010.

Hearing of Paul's involvement with the Gorillaz didn't come as much of a surprise, but Clash fans everywhere were astonished to learn that Mick had not only made a guest appearance on the album, but had contributed additional guitar to the same track as Paul.

Mick and Paul wouldn't necessarily have been required in the studio at the same time during the recording process, but when Gorillaz were invited to perform two songs from the album – 'On Melancholy Hill' and 'Clint Eastwood' – on *Friday Night With Jonathan Ross*, they both accepted Damon's offer to accompany him into the BBC studio. Somewhat surprisingly, given Wossy's supposed love of punk rock, despite this being the first time in seventeen years that Mick and Paul had shared a stage, he made no mention of it during his introduction.

Why Mick and Paul chose to dress like a couple of First World War U-boat commanders is anyone's guess, but those watching the Gorillaz' performance that were not aware of Mick and Paul's previous history could have been forgiven for thinking the two had never set eyes on each other before that night.

The immediate thought that sprung to mind watching them ambling about the stage maintaining a steady distance while looking anywhere rather than at each other was that they'd had another of their occasional fallouts in recent months.

This didn't appear to make sense, for whilst Mick and Paul had been forced to share a stage during The Clash's endgame, neither had any obligation to being on the studio stage that night. What made it all the more surprising was when they not only subsequently appeared with Gorillaz at Glastonbury, but also signed up for the Escape To Plastic Beach Tour later in the year.

Mick and Paul would also make a contribution to the follow-up Gorillaz album, *The Fall*, which was recorded at various stop-off points whilst the group were traversing the globe on what was effectively their first world tour.

Despite being part of history in the making, as the tour reached its climax in New Zealand on 21 December Paul was happy to get back to his painting, whereas having played arena dates for the first time in twenty years had left Mick with a taste for more.

Of course, as yet, arena dates were way beyond Carbon/Silicon's play grade, but with the Legacy Edition of *This Is Big Audio Dynamite* having received favourable reviews following its release back in May, the door was open to a BAD reunion.

Mick had already sounded out Don Letts with the idea of getting the original BAD line-up back together once his Gorillaz commitments were at an end at the time of the *BAD Legacy* release, and Damon Albarn and Jamie Howlett's constant bigging up of Big Audio Dynamite throughout the tour proved sufficient for him to make the idea a reality. Confirmation of this came on 25 January 2011 with the announcement of a nine-date UK tour commencing at the Liverpool O2 Academy on 29 March.

'The great thing about doing Gorillaz was that all the responsibility was on Damon, not me. But that definitely gave me the appetite for doing bigger gigs again,' Mick explained in March 2011, whilst rehearsing in preparation for the BAD tour. '[It] helped me come out of myself. 'They (Damon and Jamie) were always saying, "We love BAD!" Through the second half of the year, everyone was saying, "You've got to do BAD." It feels timely.

'People will ask: why is it okay to reform BAD, when it wasn't okay to reform The Clash?' he continued. 'Everybody knew the story of The Clash, so it always had that limitation to it, and, in the end, it's just like a beautiful memory to everybody. With BAD, we weren't overplayed back then, so we've got more of a chance as a present thing. It's about doing something that fits me as I am now. I don't want to be chasing some illusion continually into old age. That's not a good look.

'The best reunion gig I've seen was Mott the Hoople (October 2009), because two of those guys hadn't played at all for thirty-five years. One (Overend Watts) had been an antiques dealer, so they came back with fire; with meaning!' [5]

Midway through the opening date at the Liverpool O2 Academy date Mick playfully said that Big Audio Dynamite were sounding better than the last time they'd been on Merseyside as they'd brought 'age and wisdom' to the proceedings. *The Guardian*'s Dave Simpson was in agreement, and after saying how age had indeed 'withered a few group members,' he qualified it by adding how Mick still looked 'impossibly cool in his undertaker suit and gangster shades.'

Having complemented Mick's voice and guitar, he lauded the 'exuberant pop thrill of [BAD's] sing-a-long hits, "Medicine Show", "E = MC2", a roof-removing "C'Mon Every Beatbox", and "The Bottom Line", before pondering why it was that – 'Gorillaz moonlighting notwithstanding' – Mick didn't 'occupy a stage more often.'

The Independent's Simon Price felt compelled to make mention of the BAD boys having 'dated very badly', while also poking fun at Mick's 'Leonard Rossiter/Campari ad comb-over,' and one cannot help but wonder what barbs a reconstituted Clash might have had to endure had they reformed on the back of their induction into the Rock and Roll Hall of Fame.

As with his opposite number at *The Guardian*, Price had the grace to admit that 'for all the clunky shortcomings of their Eighties recordings, the (modern) live versions achieve some sort of alchemy.'

With BAD set to play a few dates stateside in the coming weeks, *CNN*'s Peter Wilkinson, was in attendance at the first of their two sell-out shows at the Shepherd's Bush Empire on Sunday, 2 April.

Unlike his British counterparts, however, Wilkinson made no mention of wrinkled skin, or receding hairlines, but this was hardly surprising as Americans tend to appreciate a musician's talents regardless of their age. As with anyone else who had even a passing interest in Mick's post-Clash career, he knew there was no Dorian Gray-esque portrait lurking in Mick's attic.

Although much of Wilkinson's prose were dedicated to Mick – such as his being 'greeted like a conquering hero as BAD take to the stage' – he was careful to praise Greg and Leo for playing their respective parts in the 'exceptionally tight set', while complimenting Don's energy as he 'bound[ed] around the stage energetically, occasionally rapping alongside Jones.'

After the final UK date at the Bristol O2 Academy on 9 April, BAD took a welcome break before heading out to Indio, California, for the Coachella Festival.

The Empire Polo Club had become something of a home from home for Mick in recent years as this was his third festival appearance in as many years. Indeed, it was Gorillaz' headlining the previous year's festival that had served as the catalyst in his decision to reform BAD, with the final nudge seemingly coming from the event's co-founder, Paul Tollett, as Mick revealed in a pre-festival interview: 'He [Tollett] said, "Mick, tell me when you want to come back and play. We will always have you."'

The Coachella organisers may have been happy to have Mick on the bill under any pretext, but his returning with the reconstituted BAD left him open to accusations of trying to cash in on former glories. When one reporter asked whether BAD might be tempted to squeeze the odd Clash song into their set, Mick retorted: 'If I were you, I wouldn't expect that to happen, no.'

In a further attempt to clarify his reasoning for reforming BAD Mick gave an interview to the *LA Times*. 'What we've done is try to carry on with the original spirit with which we did it,' he explained. 'I like things to jump out. The way they sample these days, it's all the same things put through a process. It's pushed down. That's what you hear on the radio now. Samples don't jump out and challenge you and hit you over the head. So we're trying to carry on from what we did then, as if that whole period hadn't happened.'

Three days later the BAD medicine show breezed into New York for a show at the Roseland Theatre, but if Mick was hoping for the

Big Apple bonhomie that he'd enjoyed in days gone by he was in for a rude awakening.

The *New York Times*' Jon Pareles started off his critique by saying that although BAD's coming to town had 'inspired some nostalgia for the days of cassette boomboxes and rare 12-inch vinyl,' before dismissing the once-pioneering hipsters as sounding 'like a standard rock band,' whilst the songs – 'without their once-futuristic metamorphoses, stood revealed as singsong mid-tempo rockers, far less ambitious than their lyrics or production.'

But Pareles' desultory chiding didn't end there as he went on to cite Mick's 'milquetoasty voice' as being BAD's 'main shortcoming' on the night. 'On the albums, it's genial and good-humoured,' he derided, '[while] onstage, it's just weak and inexpressive; even with other band members singing along.'

♫♫♫

BAD were booked to appear at many of 2011's major musical festivals, starting with an appearance on Glastonbury's Park Stage on Friday, 24 June. America's media may have been sluggish in its appreciation of the group, but with the UK tour having been deemed an unqualified success by reviewers and audiences alike, Mick, Don, Leo and Greg could look forward to a summer of festival fun and frolics.

Following on from Glastonbury they flew out to Japan for the Fuji Rock Festival at the end of July. The visit would prove an emotional one as Mick revealed whilst speaking with the *Sabotage Times* later in the year.

'At the Festival they have a "Strummerville" type thing going on. Joe once found an off-season ski resort and he found this disused old cable car that he'd sit in. Over time people had written lyrics of Joe and paintings of him all over it and it's amazing. We were in there in the pouring rain and I was just sitting there in the presence of Joe.'

Another highlight came in headlining the Beautiful Days festival at Escot Park, Devon, in August. Invigorated from their appearance at Lollapalooza a couple of weeks earlier they put in a performance that left John Robb purring.

The festival (organised by folk rockers, The Levellers) had been fostered in the spirit of The Clash, and although John starts off his *Louder Than War* review by saying BAD would have been guaranteed a rapturous reception regardless, he is quick to point out that the group were fully deserving of the crowd's devotion. 'There is a fantastic groove to what they do; the mixture of the break-beats and Greg Roberts fantastic drumming makes each track a lesson in hypnotic grooves. They build and build and pull you in and you are lost in their rhythmic world.'

Even Mick's American detractors had to admit they couldn't help being swept along with his infectious *joie de vivre*, coupled with a sheer joy of being on stage. He is clearly in his element, telling jokes between songs, while cutting guitar shapes from what John describes as his 'neo-camp Chuck Berry shuffle, to the bent-arm-guitar-in-the-air-thing that is reminiscent of prime-time Clash.'

– CHAPTER TWENTY –

GREAT TOMORROWS LIE IN WAIT

'I think what's gonna happen [in London] *is that all the* [music] *scenes are gonna come together into one massive scene. I really do think that is gonna happen. Because they're massively diverse… so they can't help but come together. Because with unity, comes a great future. I think we are where it mixes best. I don't see many places where it's multi-cultural like this.'*

– Mick Jones

IF IT COULD BE ARGUED THAT Mick's jamming a couple of Clash numbers with Topper during the Carbon Casino residency at the Inn On The Green in January 2008 was part of the healing process he'd initiated by joining Joe on stage at the Acton Town Hall back in November 2002, then his Clash catharsis was made absolute when Paul joined him on stage at The Scala in King's Cross on 8 December 2011.

The two had of course played together on the Gorillaz tour the previous year, but this was the night they played Clash chords together in front of an audience in nigh on three decades. However, whereas they'd taken to the Us Festival stage for money, this time they were doing it in support of a cause as noble as any The Clash had championed: to promote awareness of the 'Justice for the 96' campaign, and its ongoing struggle to bring justice for those ninety-six souls who went to a football match in April 1989 and never came home.

'I know the truth of what happened all those years ago at Hillsborough and [the way] all those fans conducted themselves and the rescue operation,' Mick said. 'All of them, they acted impeccably you know, and they were slandered.

'I think Joe would be with us completely,' he added in reference to his and Paul's dusting off The Clash songbook. 'I feel he is with us all the time. He would be pleased we are doing this for sure, and that it's not a waste of time doing the numbers for some pointless nostalgia tour.'[1]

Although a quarter of a century has passed since that fateful April Saturday afternoon, to those of a certain age the word 'Hillsborough'* evokes harrowing images of fans being crushed to death at the FA Cup semi-final between Liverpool and Nottingham Forest. At the time of the disaster, the vast majority of football grounds in the UK had high steel fencing in place to prevent pitch invasions – both friendly and hostile – yet while the fences kept the fans in place, caging them in like animals was a disaster in the making.

Ninety-six people died, and hundreds more were injured in the crush, but the instead of holding their hands up and acknowledging their own culpability, the powers-that-be – wilfully aided and abetted by the *Sun* newspaper – shamefully tried to lay the blame at the door of the Liverpool fans themselves.

The world irrevocably moved on, and the Hillsborough disaster was overshadowed by other tragedies such as the death of Princess Diana, 9/11, and the 7/7 bombings, but the families and friends of the victims refused to accept the official verdict and on 12 September 2012, their struggle was finally vindicated when the Hillsborough Independent Panel concluded that no Liverpool fans were responsible in any way for the disaster; that its main cause was a 'lack of police control', and that crowd safety was 'compromised at every level'.

This, of course, wasn't the first time musicians had come together under the Hillsborough banner. In May 1989, Sir Paul McCartney, Gerry Marsden from the Pacemakers, ex-Frankie Goes To Hollywood frontman Holly Johnson, and the Christians recorded a charity version

---

* Hillsborough is the home of Sheffield Wednesday FC.

of the Pacemakers' 1964 Top Ten hit 'Ferry Cross The Mersey', with all the proceeds going to the disaster appeal fund.

In total, the Hillsborough Disaster Appeal Fund raised some £12 million, but while each and every one of the donations was greatly appreciated, more than anything the people of Liverpool simply wanted those who were at fault that day to admit their guilt.

♪♪♪

Initially put together for a one-off show, the seed that would grow into the Justice Tonight Band had been planted several weeks earlier when Mick accepted Farm frontman Pete Hooton's invitation to join the city's latter-day musical local heroes such as Pete Wylie, former Cast and the Las frontman John Power, Amsterdam's Ian Prouse, and of course, The Farm, for an emotionally-charged evening at the Liverpool Olympia on 24 September 2011.

'The tour started as a one off gig in Liverpool, and when I was asked to do it I was straight in,' Mick explained. 'I have had close ties to Liverpool for years. They are like my brothers these people, and if there is ever any band I want to play with it's these guys in The Farm because they really understand my work. Years ago I did this thing with The Farm at one gig then we went out later and they all sang an acapella version of "White Man In Hammersmith Palais", and it was so moving to see what that song meant to people.' [2]

When speaking backstage after the Olympia show, Mick said how he was privileged and proud to be associated with the people and artists of Liverpool: 'We've [The Clash and BAD] played here many times from the punk days playing Eric's and meeting a lot of these guys like Pete Wylie. I remember giving him a guitar because he was starting his band and I was encouraging them all, you know, but initially it all started with the Beatles and that was my first connection to the city.

'I've been really lucky,' he enthused. 'Because I've been taken in by all these guys so they've welcomed me in even though I'm not a Scouser, which is a special thing to me because to see it through my eyes, being a Cockney, not many people like me get the chance to experience all that on such an emotional level. What's important to me is to carry what we did in The Clash and try and stay true to that original idea. I haven't played a set of Clash songs since I was in The Clash and this seemed like a really meaningful forum for them. We are not chasing any illusions here; I just wanted to put the songs to a good use. That's why I'm doing this. I might as well make myself useful and use the stuff that I have to contribute to the thing.'[3]

When reviewing the Olympia show, John Robb described it as 'a meeting of pop, politics, football, and community', yet while The Farm and the inimitable Pete Wylie had the 1,300-strong crowd swaying in terrace-like tandem with anthemic sing-alongs such as 'All Together Now', and 'Heart As Big As Liverpool', the roar that greeted Mick's arrival on stage was akin to that which greeted any cup final winning goal.

Mick may have performed the odd Clash song in the past but this was the first time he'd purposely composed a Clash set-list, and Joe was surely pumping his electric leg in approval on the celestial stage in the sky as Mick plugged in his Les Paul and strummed the readily-identifiable G/C/Bm/Am intro to 'Stay Free'.

The pomaded hair may have receded somewhat, and the pop star army fatigues had given way to a bespoke shiny grey suit, but the spirit of The Clash was most definitely in the house.

Mick certainly felt a certain spiritual presence. 'Joe is with me all the time,' he said. 'He's here tonight with us right now and he was with me when I went on stage and when I was playing tonight. I can feel him in so many ways; it's something that's with me a lot of the time.'

It's doubtful that Pete Wylie was providing Joe's chops on the guitar Mick had gifted him all those years ago when he was first putting The Mighty Wah! together, but never in his wildest dreams would he have thought to find himself singing The Clash song most associated with Mick. Those fans who were disappointed that Mick hadn't done the honours himself didn't have to wait long to hear those dulcet tones as he took centre stage for 'Should I Stay Or Should I Go'.

There was no question of anyone going anywhere, now, and while Pete Hooton stepped into Joe's shoes for a spine-tingling '(White Man) In Hammersmith Palais', Mick was back at the mic for BAD's 'Rush', and 'Armageddon Time'.

Playing benefit gigs was The Clash's stock-in-trade back in the day, and while the 'Don't Buy The Sun' show was conceived as a one-off to keep the Justice for the 96 campaign in the public consciousness – with all proceeds being donated to the Fazakerley 9 Charity in memory of 18-year-old Jamie McVey, who died as a result of the injuries he sustained in an unprovoked attack five months earlier – now that he was back in the Clash saddle so to speak, Mick was keen to continue lending his voice to the Hillsborough campaign.

'That first gig was so successful that we thought we should try and do some more,' he explained. 'We knew it wasn't just Liverpool that cared about this thing – and there is the bigger picture as well, the primary cause is Liverpool and the Hillsborough 96 and the campaign but it's all connected to things like Occupy Wall Street, St. Paul's, [and the] Arab Spring.

'It's a feeling and we are part of that feeling and we are also reminding people of what gigs could be about rather than what they have become,' he continued. 'It's so disappointing with what they have become. The reason why that happened was that the corporations are not just happy to just sponsor the culture, they want to be the culture and we need to claw that back for our own self respect, our own feeling of self worth, because we are worth a lot. People have been made into morons basically, very subtlety, so this for me gave myself a meaning in my life, and I give all I have to give here. We are not chasing nostalgia, not doing that at all. The songs stand up.'[4]

With indie-rock 'n' rolling luminaries such as James Dean Bradfield, Billy Bragg, Ian Brown, John Squire, Primal Scream, and Starsailor's James Walsh all making guest appearances, the six-date Justice Tonight tour undoubtedly achieved its aim in keeping the Hillsborough and Don't Buy The Sun campaigns in the spotlight.

It also served as a beacon of light to illuminate the bigger picture of the corporate-sponsorship intrusion into counter-culture that Mick had alluded to in the *Louder Than War* interview, but it was Paul's joining him on stage at The Scala that ultimately proved the tour's talking point.

As with the other tour dates The Scala's poster stated that the evening would be brought to a climax by 'Mick Jones & Friends'. But whereas Mick's joining the Mescaleros on stage at the Acton Town Hall had taken the audience by surprise, the famous King's Cross venue was abuzz with the news that one of tonight's 'Friends' was none other than Paul Simonon; the news having been authenticated by a score or more snapshots that appeared on Facebook and other social media networks showing Mick and Paul jamming 'Brand New Cadillac' with Primal Scream's Bobby Gillespie and Barrie Cadogan at the soundcheck.

John Robb was one of those lucky enough to have a ringside seat, and would subsequently describe it as 'quintessential rock 'n' roll.' 'When Paul walks onto the stage during the soundcheck with his bass held like an AK 47 all the other bands to a man grab their iPhones and are snapping pictures,' he enthused. 'The Farm, who have had top five albums and huge selling singles, revert back to being the kids who fell in love with The Clash as teenagers. The chemistry between Mick and Paul is so natural and so electric that everyone in the room is riveted. This isn't a soundcheck, this is a moment... and everyone knows it.'

Several warm-up acts, including the Rotting Hill Gang (featuring Paul Cook's step-daughter Holly on vocals), served to get the crowd in anticipatory mood, but as with the Liverpool Olympia show it was the Farm who got the evening swinging for real. Having been joined on stage by Pete Wylie and Mick, the travelling musical menagerie kicked into the by now familiar run-through of the Farm's 'Altogether Now', Pete's Mighty Wah! classics: 'Come Back', 'Story Of The Blues' and 'Sinful', and a heart-rending version of Johnny Thunders' 'You Can't Put Your Arms Around A Memory'.

For the tour, The Clash medley had been expanded to include 'Train In Vain', 'Bankrobber' (with Holly Cook ad-libbing on vocals), and 'Clampdown' (with Hard-Fi's Richard Archer guesting on vocals), but the main event was, of course, still to come.

Following a brief interlude, instead of the Farm and Pete Wylie, Mick was joined on stage by Primal Scream, but the audience is still taking this in when Paul – looking über cool in his pork-pie hat, black leather jacket and biker boots ensemble, and none the worse for his recent two-week stint of incarceration in Greenland for storming an oil rig platform during a Greenpeace demo – bounded out onto the stage carrying the battered black-and-white Fender with his name carved into the body that had played many a Clash tune back in the day.

After getting the second leg of the proceedings underway with a blistering version of Primal Scream's 'Rocks Off', it was Clash time again and a stomping 'Jail Guitar Doors' was followed by an equally rip-roaring 'Brand New Cadillac', before Paul (surprisingly sans bass) skanks his way to centre stage for 'Guns Of Brixton'.

Paul may have played the song whilst on the road with The Good, the Bad & The Queen, but it's fair to say that a sizeable majority of the 1,000-strong audience probably weren't even born the last time he'd done so with Mick standing stage right and supplying the song's lilting reggae riff.

With Paul having taken a well-deserved bow, Mick was joined on stage once again by the Farm and Pete Wylie for 'Armageddon Time', and 'London Calling', before the curtain was brought down on what was truly a night to remember with a three-song encore of 'Janie Jones' (with a crowd-surfing John Robb guesting on vocals), 'All Together Now' and BAD's 'Rush'.

The Justice Tonight Band would subsequently support the Stone Roses at several dates on the Mancunians' 2012 Reunion Tour, and – billed as the 'Justice Collective' – would also claim that year's Christmas top spot with a cover of the Hollies' 1969 hit 'He Ain't Heavy He's My Brother'.

♪♪♪

Paul was one of the special invitees at the opening of the latest instalment of Mick's Rock & Roll Public Library on Friday, 7 March, 2013. Although smaller than either of its two previous homes, the Subway Gallery – set within a converted key-cutting shop, and owned by a friend of Mick's who would also be serving as curator during the library's month-long run – was the perfect setting as the underpass beneath the Bakerloo line exit of Edgware Road tube station in which the gallery stood had been renamed in honour of Joe in December 2009.

Aside from the predictable Clash and BAD memorabilia, and assorted punk ephemera, the library featured a fully-stocked bookcase of war books, window displays of *Zulu* posters and toys (still Mick's favourite film), as well as sandbags, old military photographs, and a complete collection of Commando Comics

Casting his eye over the exhibits, the *Sabotage Times*' James Brown couldn't help but notice what he described as an 'overwhelming sense of war' within the collection. 'That's because we are at war,' Mick retorted when Brown voiced his musings. 'There's a real war we're in, we're at war with the government; families are at war.'

With libraries closing at a similar rate to pubs of late, Mick once again re-iterated his hope that he could find a permanent home for his entire collection. He still envisaged it serving as a permanent reference library for use by both the local and international community as it 'comprises a personal, cultural and social history of our times, and through that it extends beyond the local to the global.'

Mick isn't the only member of his family to play a mean rock 'n' roll guitar as Taurus Trakker, one of the bands that had supported Carbon/Silicon at the Carbon Residency shows in early 2008, is fronted by his cousin, Martin Muscatt. (The group also features ex-Alternative TV and Raincoats drummer Alison Phillips, and ex-X-Ray Spex sax player Dave Wright in the line-up)

'The name is from Martin reading the Bob Dylan Chronicles in which it's written that Dylan once owned a gun called a "Taurus Tracker", but they added an extra "K" so it doesn't get mixed up with the gun itself,' Mick explained in the December 2012 *Sabotage Times* interview.

Mick goes on to say how he's supported Taurus Trakker 'all the way down the line', as he not only produced the group's 2009 single 'Monks, Punks & Drunks', but also plays additional guitar and bass on the title track on their May 2012 follow-up, *Building Ten*. 'I've played live with them a few times, and if I can make it I'll get on stage with them again,' he enthused. 'Martin is the same as me [about] his music, which is important these days. Both Alison and Martin are great and I love playing with TT.

Martin is several years younger than Mick, but with his having a cousin in The Clash, he was allowed to hang around with the group on occasion. 'The first thing I recall with him back in the Clash days was a football game he organised with the kids from the estate versus The Clash,' Mick revealed. 'He was working on an adventure playground in Camden as a youth worker and put the game together, which was great fun. Joe was in goal with his Elvis T-shirt and worker boots on. Martin still has pictures from that day.'

Taurus Trakker wouldn't be the only ones to benefit from Mick's musical munificence in 2012 as he also provided additional guitar and backing vocals on two tracks – 'Misfits and Lovers' and 'Reboot the Mission' on *Glad All Over*, the latest album from LA rockers, the Wallflowers, which, although a group in name, basically serves as a vehicle for Bob Dylan's son Jakob's talents.

Following its being premièred at the Transmissions festival in Madrid at the end of June, the Catalonia-born filmmaker Danny Garcia's highly-anticipated new Clash opus, *The Rise And Fall Of The Clash*, received its inaugural UK screening in Nottingham at the Broadway cinema on 5 September, before finally being aired on The Clash's home turf at the Portobello Film Festival three days later. Although Garcia was predominantly at the helm during the filming process, he was aided and abetted by celluloid Clash stalwarts Don Letts and Dave Mingay.

As the Wagnerian title suggests, the film charts The Clash from the heady heights of the US Combat Rock stadium tour through to the group's inglorious Gotterdammerung three years later. Too young to have seen The Clash in action, Garcia was nevertheless a huge fan, and got his idea for the film after coming across Vince White's book *Out Of Control* in a local book store in 2008.

Vince, his fellow latter-day Clash sidekicks, Pete Howard and Nick Sheppard, as well as Ray Jordan, Pearl Harbor, Norman Watt-Roy, Viv Albertine, and Jock Scot, all make telling talking-head contributions, yet it's Mick who does the lion's share of the on-screen talking.

'My initial idea was just to focus on those two and a half last years of The Clash, from the minute that Mick gets fired,' Garcia explained to *www.musicfilmweb.com*'s Andy Markowitz on the eve of the Los Angeles screening. 'But looking at it and talking to people like Nick Sheppard, I understood that for people to understand the collapse of the band, you would have to start before, when Bernie rejoins the band.'

Garcia isn't the only one confused as to why Mick, Joe, Paul, and Topper wilfully chose to revise of the group's history in the *Westway* documentary – not to mention the official *Clash* book – when a factual account of The Clash#2's short-lived odyssey had already been documented in Marcus Gray's *Last Gang In Town*? 'That was the official version of events until Joe died,' Garcia continues. I wanted an explanation for me, for the fans, for everybody.'

Speaking with *www.clashblog.com*'s Tim Merrick earlier in the year, Garcia said how he'd run into opposition following his announcement that he intended to make a film focusing solely on The Clash#2 years. 'The idea didn't sit well with some people in high places,' he revealed. 'I received a few calls and emails, but I kept telling these people that I'm a free human being and that they couldn't stop me from telling any story I wanted to tell. I also told them that I bought *Cut The Crap* back in '86 and I wanted my money back.'

Didn't we all…

♫♫♫

London's Berwick Street – which lies within the heart of Soho – is renowned for its traditional outdoor fruit and veg market, but in years gone by it was also regarded as something of a Mecca for music lovers as it boasted a glut of music emporiums; so much so that it enjoyed the sobriquet, the 'vinyl mile'.

Today's teenagers, of course, prefer to download music onto their MP3 players and iPads rather than trek to Berwick Street and seek them out in Sister Ray, or Reckless Records, or indeed, HMV. Yet whilst Mick had been happy to play his part in this seismic shift in music consumerism by making the Carbon/Silicon canon freely available for MP3 download, he reverted to more traditional methods for the release of a Clash box-set bonanza on in September 2013.

It had been five years since the last official Clash product (*Live At Shea Stadium*) hit the shelves, but like the fabled late bus, Monday, 9 September saw three more come along with the simultaneous release of two box sets – the thirteen-disc *Sound System*, the eight-disc *5 Album Studio Set* – and a 2xCD best of called *The Clash Hits Back*. Not only would the box-sets be available via all the usual outlets, but Mick, Paul, and Topper got in on the 'pop-up shop' trend by leasing 73 Berwick Street for a fifteen-day period trading as 'Black Market Clash'.

According to *www.clashmusic.com*, the ground floor would house rare memorabilia from The Clash's own collection including instruments, stage clothes, rare memorabilia, and original manuscripts, while the first floor sold exclusive merchandise. Alongside this, having struck a deal with Fender, fans would be able to take part in plug & play demo stations, as well as exclusive master classes themed on the group's work. And on the eve of the shop's official opening, Mick, Paul, and Topper were all in attendance at a special VIP gathering.

Working on *Sound System* had proved therapeutic for the trio as the project had brought the three of them together under the same roof for the first time since Topper's sacking at Paul's basement flat in Oxford Gardens more than three decades earlier. 'It's for us, more than anybody,' Mick revealed. 'It was just an opportunity to do something now to represent the music. I like the idea of the ideas carrying on somehow – like Che Guevara's. It's also a restoration, because the tapes would've rotted soon, so it's just the recorded works, presented as best possible – no different from the complete series of *Kojak* or *Breaking Bad*. That's how everyone buys things these days, isn't it?'[7]

Needless to say, it was *Sound System* (with eye-catching boom-box style packaging courtesy of Paul) that was perceived to be the jewel in the Triple Crown. Aside from the re-mastered studio albums (sans *Cut the Crap*), the box-set comprised a further three discs featuring demos, non-album singles, rarities, B-sides. There was also a DVD containing a mixture of promo videos and previously unseen live footage, an owner's manual booklet, reprints of both *The Armagideon Times* fanzines (as well as a brand-new issue edited by Paul, and a plethora of merchandise such as dog tags, badges, stickers and the obligatory poster.

'The concept of the whole thing is best box set ever,' Mick, who'd overseen the remastering process, told *Rolling Stone*'s Andy Green at the time of the releases. 'Remastering's a really amazing thing. That was the musical point of it all; because there's so much there that you wouldn't have heard before. It was like discovering stuff, because the advances in mastering are so immense since the last time [The Clash catalogue] was remastered in the Nineties. We had to bake the tapes beforehand – the oxide on them is where the music is, so if you don't put them in the oven and bake them, that all falls off, because they're so old.

'Also, they found that since the last time they were remastered, there's actually a bigger playback head now,' he continued. 'So we might have missed music on the edges of the tape. Now we're getting all of it. If you're familiar with the music, you're getting stuff you didn't get before. To me, that's more enjoyable than listening to a bunch of odds and sods.'

Three retrospective releases in one day could be construed as not so much *Give 'Em Enough Rope*, but rather 'give-us-your-money-for-old-rope', but with hitherto unreleased gems such as '1977' and 'London's Burning' from the group's first-ever recording session at Beaconsfield Film School in 1976, and 'Stay Free' 'Jail Guitar Doors', and 'Cheapskates' from The Clash's Lyceum show on 28 December 1978, together with previously unseen footage from the group's 25 May 1977 outing at Sussex University on the accompanying DVD, Christmas had indeed come early for Clash fans young and old.

'There's some great video footage on this set,' Mick explained. 'I watched it and thought, "Bloody hell, that's some energy level! We had a real moment. They say the best time to make an album is when you come off tour, because you have that momentum. And when the four of us came together, we were more than our parts. The same goes for the audience. We were one of the bands that helped break down that barrier between the audience and the group. We broke though that barrier.'[7]

Even the critics proved surprisingly receptive with *Rolling Stone* declaring: 'It takes a band as myth-saturated as The Clash to live up to a career-summing box as ambitious as this one. But Joe Strummer and his crew of London gutter-punk romantics fit the bill'

In spite of discovering guitar parts he couldn't remember playing during the remastering process, Mick is adamant that *Sound System* would serve as The Clash's epitaph. 'I'm not even thinking about any more Clash releases,' he pointedly told *Rolling Stone*'s Andy Green. 'This is it for me, and I say that with an exclamation mark.'

So what does the future hold in store for the hip-pop pioneering punk icon as he approaches his sixtieth birthday milestone? For whilst he's been careful to heed the pitfalls of his putting too many hours in at The Clash coalface, and spends time with his partner Miranda and the girls, and has several non musical pastimes such as going to Loftus Road on match days to watch his beloved Queens Park Rangers, his having been a founding member of 'the only band that matters', the driving force behind Big Audio Dynamite, and his being a major cog in the free music download revolution with Carbon/Silicon, there's little chance of his deciding it time to rest on his laurels any time soon. And as there's no statute of limitations on talent or creativity there's no reason why he should.

Speaking with *www2.gibson.com* in November 2007, Mick said how he always feels that his best work is yet to come. 'I think it will come tomorrow, or the next day,' he mused. 'And even if it doesn't, I just carry on working. I just go where my heart takes me.'

Mick isn't the first creative soul to allow his heart to rule his head, but perhaps his being a Cancerian means he'll have suffered for his art more than most. Yes, there have been times when he's been lost in the metaphorical supermarket, and people haven't always stood by him as he might have wished, but as an eternal optimist he knows 'great tomorrows lie in wait'…

NOTES

Chapter One:
1. *The Clash*
2. *The Clash*
3. *The Clash*
4. *Time Out*, September 2008.
5. *The Clash*.
6. *The Clash*.
7. *Time Out*, September 2008.
8. *The Clash*.
9. *Joe Strummer and the Legend of The Clash*.

Chapter Two:
1. *www.gibson.com*, 2006.
2. *The Clash*.
3. *The Clash*.
4. *Joe Strummer and the Legend of The Clash*.
5. *The Clash*.
6. *Passion Is A Fashion*.

Chapter Three:
1. *Clothes Clothes Clothes Music Music Music Boys Boys Boys*.
2. *Clothes Clothes Clothes Music Music Music Boys Boys Boys*
3. *Sabotage Times*, December 2011.
4. *www.blogs.citypages.com*, November 2007.

Chapter Four:
1. *Mojo*, March 2003
2. *The Clash*.
3. *The Clash: A Visual Documentary*
4. *The Clash*.
5. *The Clash*.
6. *Last Gang In Town*.
7. *www.gibson.com*, 2006.
8. *www.gibson.com*, 2006.
9. *The Clash*.
10. *www.gibson.com*, 2006.
11. *www.gibson.com*, 2006.

Chapter Five:
1. *Punk: An Oral History*.
2. *Punk: An Oral History*.
3. *The Clash*.
4. *Last gang In Town*.
5. *The Clash*.
6. *Passion Is A Fashion*.
7. *The Clash*.
8. *Passion Is A Fashion*.
9. *The Clash*.

Chapter Six:
1. *The Clash*.
2. *The Clash*.
3. *Sabotage Times*, December 2011.
4. *Melody Maker*.
5. *www.blogs.citypages.com*, November 2007.
6. *Melody Maker*.
7. *Melody Maker*.
8. *NME*.
9. *NME*.

Chapter Seven:
1. *The Clash*.
2. *A Riot Of Our Own*.
3. *Passion Is A Fashion*.
4. *Passion Is A Fashion*.
5. *The Clash*.
6. *Passion Is A Fashion*.
7. *Passion Is A Fashion*.
8. *Sabotage Times*, December 2011.

Chapter Eight:
1. *www.gibson.com*.
2. *A Riot Of Our Own*.
3. *Q* magazine's 2001 retrospective.
4. Joe's *NME* Diary.
5. *Q* magazine's 2001 retrospective.
6. *Q* magazine's 2001 retrospective.
7. *Route 19 Revisited*.
8. *Passion Is A Fashion*.

Chapter Nine:
1. *Passion Is A Fashion*.
2. *A Riot Of Our Own*.
3. *The Clash*.
4. *NME*.
5. *Route 19 Revisited*.
6. *Clothes Clothes Clothes Music Music Music Boys Boys Boys*.
7. *Clothes Clothes Clothes Music Music Music Boys Boys Boys*.

NOTES

Chapter Ten:
1. *Passion Is A Fashion*.
2. *A Riot Of Our Own*.
3. *The Clash*.
4. *Passion Is A Fashion*.
5. *The Clash*.
6. *The Clash*.
7. *Passion Is A Fashion*.
8. *Passion Is A Fashion*.
9. *Passion Is A Fashion*.
10. *NME*.
11. *Joe Strummer and the Legend of The Clash*.
12. *www.blogs.citypages.com*, November 2007.

Chapter Eleven:
1. *NME*.
2. *The Clash*.
3. *Passion Is A Fashion*.
4. *Passion Is A Fashion*.

Chapter Twelve:
1. *The Clash*.
2. *The Clash*.
3. *www.blogs.citypages.com*, November 2007.
4. *www.blogs.citypages.com*, November 2007.
5. *www.gibson.com*, 2006.
6. *The Clash*.
7. *Rolling Stone*.
8. *Rolling Stone*.
9. *Passion Is A Fashion*.
10. *Joe Strummer and the Legend of The Clash*.
11. *www.deangoodman.com*, 2008.

Chapter Fourteen:
1. *www.deangoodman.com*, 2008.
2. *Return Of The Last Gang In Town*.
3. *www.deangoodman.com*, 2008.
4. *Culture Clash*.
5. *www.deangoodman.com*, 2008.
6. *Sabotage Times*. December 2011.
7. *Joe Strummer and the Legend of The Clash*.
8. *www.deangoodman.com*, 2008.
9. *Culture Clash*.
10. *www.blogs.citypages.com*, November 2007.

Chapter Fifteen:
1. *www.deangoodman.com*, 2008.
2. *The Telegraph*. 2013.
3. *www.deangoodman.com*, 2008.
4. *www.philly.news.com*, September 1989.

5. *www.philly.news.com*, September 1989.
6. *Chicago Tribune*. December 1989.
7. *www.deangoodman.com*, 2008.
8. *www.philly.news.com*, September 1989.
9. *www.philly.news.com*, September 1989.
10. *www.deangoodman.com*, 2008.

Chapter Seventeen:
1. *Pulse* magazine.
2. *Pulse* magazine.

Chapter Eighteen:
1. *Passion Is A Fashion*.
2. *Joe Strummer and the Legend of The Clash*.
3. *Joe Strummer and the Legend of The Clash*.
4. *Joe Strummer and the Legend of The Clash*.
5. *Passion Is A Fashion*.
6. *Joe Strummer and the Legend of The Clash*.
7. *www.teletext.co.uk*, 2007.
8. *www.teletext.co.uk*, 2007.
9. *NME*.
10. *www.teletext.co.uk*, 2007.
11. *www.teletext.co.uk*, 2007.
12. *www.blogs.citypages.com*, November 2007.

Chapter Nineteen:
1. *popmatters.com*.
2. *NME*.
3. *The Quietus*.
4. *The Quietus*.
5. *The Telegraph*.

Chapter Twenty:
1. *Sabotage Times*, December 2011.
2. *www.louderthanwar.com*.
3. *Sabotage Times*, December 2011.
4. *Sabotage Times*, December 2011.
5. *Sabotage Times*, December 2011.
6. *The Telegraph*.
7. *The Telegraph*.